Community and
Sustainable Development

Community and Sustainable Development

Participation in the Future

Edited by Diane Warburton

Published in association with WWF-UK

Earthscan Publications Ltd, London

First published in the UK in 1998 by
Earthscan Publications Limited

Cover photo © Larraine Worpole

A catalogue record for this book is available from the British Library

ISBN: 1 85383 531 5 (paperback
       1 85383 530 7 (hardback)

Typesetting and page design by PCS Mapping & DTP,
   Newcastle upon Tyne
Printed and bound by Biddles Ltd, Guildford and King's Lynn
Cover design by Yvonne Booth

For a full list of publications, please contact:

Earthscan Publications Limited
120 Pentonville Road
London N1 9JN
Tel: (0171) 278 0433
Fax: (0171) 278 1142
Email: earthinfo@earthscan.co.uk
http://www.earthscan.co.uk

Earthscan is an editorially independent subsidiary of Kogan Page
Limited and publishes in association with the WWF-UK and the
International Institute for Environment and Development.

This book is printed on elemental chlorine free paper from
sustainably managed forests.

Contents

Contributors

Diane Warburton is a writer and researcher specialising in community participation and sustainable development working with community organisations and national bodies including WWF-UK and The Countryside Commission.

Professor Robert Chambers is Research Fellow at the Institute of Development Studies, University of Sussex.

Sue Clifford is a founder director of Common Ground. Common Ground's role is to inspire people with the courage to express their values about the commonplace nature, ordinary landscapes and everyday culture about their lives and to take some responsibility for their care. Through model projects, collaborations, publications, exhibitions and events, they encourage debate and practical action for the commonplace in both professionals and local people in city and country.

Professor Amitai Etzioni is the director of the George Washington University Center of Communitarian Policy Studies and the founder of the communitarian movement.

Geoff Fagan is a lecturer within the Department of Community Education and Director of the CADISPA research and development project, at the University of Strathclyde, Glasgow. He was made a Fellow of the Royal Society of Arts in 1996 and has been on a number of national and international committees concerned with sustainable development including President Clinton's Task Force on Sustainable Development.

J Gary Lawrence is a Fellow at the Institute for Public Policy and Management, University of Washington, USA.

Alex MacGillivray is co-ordinator of a team working on community indicators at New Economics Foundation (NEF), the research charity working for a just and sustainable economy. NEF has been involved in a wide range of community indicators activities in the UK and elsewhere, and can be contacted at 1st Floor, Vine Court, 112 Whitechapel Road, London E1 1JE, UK.

Professor Timothy O'Riordan is based at the Centre for Social and Economic Research on the Global Environment (CSERGE) at the University of East Anglia.

Murray Stewart is Professor of Urban and Regional Governance at the University of the West of England, Bristol; **Philippa Collett** is Development Worker for the Recycling Consortium, Bristol.

Marilyn Taylor is Reader in Social Policy at the University of Brighton, UK.

Ken G Webster is Senior Education Officer – Community at WWF-UK.

Judy Ling Wong FRSA is Director of the Black Environment Network, an organisation established to promote equality of opportunity within the ethnic community in the UK in the preservation, protection and development of the environment. She has worked extensively in the arts, in psychotherapy and in community involvement.

Ken Worpole is the author of many studies of urban and cultural policy, and has worked extensively with two independent research bodies and think tanks – Comedia and Demos – in recent years.

Acronyms and Abbreviations

ACTAC	Association of Community Technical Aid Centres
BEN	Black Environment Network
CADISPA	Conservation and Development in Sparsely Populated Areas
CDP	Community Development Project
EGO	Extra-Governmental Organisation
GDP	Gross Domestic Product
ILM	Intermediate Labour Market
IMF	International Monetary Fund
INLOGOV	Institute of Local Government Studies, University of Birmingham
IUCN	The World Conservation Union (formerly International Union for Conservation of Nature and Natural Resources)
JRF	Joseph Rowntree Foundation
LA21	Local Agenda 21
LEC	Local Enterprise Company
LGMB	Local Government Management Board
LETS	Local Exchange Trading Systems
PRA	Participatory Rural Appraisal
SEA	Self-Critical Epistemological Awareness
SRB	Single Regeneration Budget
TNC	Transnational Corporation
UN	United Nations
UNCED	United Nations Conference on Environment and Development
WCS	World Conservation Strategy
WWF	World Wide Fund For Nature

Figures, Tables and Boxes

Figures

Tables

Boxes

Foreword

Jonathon Porritt

In a remarkably short period of time, 'sustainable development' has become one of those protean concepts that means a hundred different things to a hundred different people. Books like this, which bubble over with the fruits of many people's experience and insight, add new layers of meaning to that concept, deepening our understanding of what for me is the most important political challenge of our age – by a very long way.

Perhaps the most striking of all these insights is the conclusion that sustainable development and community participation *must* go hand in hand. You can't have the one without the other. You can dress up all sorts of useful things at the local level in the trappings of sustainable development, but unless those useful things are rooted in and permanently nurtured by their host communities, they simply won't deliver the long term environmental or social dividends now available to us.

For many local councillors and government officials, this is proving to be a harder pill to swallow than they ever imagined. Local Agenda 21 (LA21) which, six years on from the Earth Summit in 1992, has become the all-encompassing framework for making sustainable development operational at the local level, specifically requires local authorities to undertake some kind of 'consultative process', and indeed to reach some kind of 'consensus' on what local people want.

As Ken Webster's contribution to this collection makes clear, the results to date are pretty patchy. Whilst there are some stirring examples of truly empowering participative processes, there are many more that are just going through the motions. I am lucky enough to live in Gloucestershire, where the Vision 21 initiative has made considerable headway by steadily involving more and more communities, but there are some that are still old-fashioned, top-down exercises in paternalistic pseudo consultation.

Happily, things are moving in the right direction. I have met many councillors and officers who have come to accept that LA21 not only promises real benefits by way of people's quality of life and the physical environment, but rather more subtle benefits by way of revitalising local democracy itself.

This emerging mutuality of interest is very heartening. Elsewhere in this book, Amitai Etzioni points out that for many years now the environment movement and the communitarian movement have moved forward in parallel, but have rarely converged. Not to put too fine a point upon it, many community activists saw environmentalists self-indulgently exercising their 'privilege of concern' for the natural world, whilst many environmentalists couldn't understand why community activists appeared not to care at all for their all-important environmental causes.

If nothing else, the debate about exactly what sustainable development means has narrowed that gap – it's not just community participation that walks hand in hand with sustainable development, but social justice too. Nowhere has this found more powerful expression than in the Real World Coalition, which brings together organisations like World Wide Fund For Nature (WWF) and Friends of the Earth with the Poverty Alliance, Save the Children, the Quakers and a host of groups working at community level to improve people's lives.

It's slow work. But as Tim O'Riordan argues elsewhere in this book, we'd probably have more cause to be worried if it wasn't slow work! Communities move by degrees, not by quantum leaps, and so great is the level of disaffection with government that winning the genuine participation of communities is nothing like as simple as it may sound.

There's nothing 'virtual' about community in this sense. It means dealing with real people in real places. And though I like Judy Ling Wong's definition of community as 'a web of relationships defined by a significant level of mutual care and commitment', I would be tempted to add the words 'in a defined geographical area'. Those who rhapsodise about the new electronic communities of the internet are for me at least several human beings short of a real community. Common Ground's gentle but telling emphasis on 'local distinctiveness', encouraging people to re-value places by personally re-engaging in their hard-edged physical features as well as their history and spirit, provides one of the most important contributions to this book.

What I particularly like about this collection is its warts-and-all approach. Diane Warburton's scene-setting introduction shows how little room there is for the saccharine advocacy of localism for its own sake, as well as the risks of getting so worked up about the importance of community that we ignore real politics elsewhere, be that at the local, national or international level.

For the emerging profession of environmental coordinators, and the many others employed both by local authorities and non-governmental organisations, this raises some very interesting implications as to the appropriate style of professional account-ability in such a different context. Must they not, to use Murray Stewart's well-chosen words, 'be locally present in the community, responsive to local needs, listening rather than professing, support-ing rather than imposing'?

But if there are important messages in this book for local government, they are all the more important for national govern-ment – for MPs, civil servants, and government ministers. A super ministry now integrates environment, transport and the regions, charged both with setting up new regional development agencies, and with delivering on the government's many commitments to sustainable development. Until now, completely different sets of politicians and civil servants have dealt with these two priority areas, but unless they are comprehensively integrated, in the government offices in the regions as well as in the department itself, expect nothing but muddle and copious amounts of what at Earth Summit II in June 1997 was dubbed SLUDGE (slightly less unsustainable development genuflecting to the environment) over the next few years.

This may seem harsh, but I can't quite persuade myself that our politicians have fully understood this sustainable development business. The UK government focus on jobs, training, economic development and so on: it's all about the macro economy, equipping people with old-fashioned skills to get ever-scarcer full time jobs in the formal economy to enhance our international competitiveness. Fine as far as it goes, but what about the *local* economy? What about the skills that more and more people now need to be self-reliant, social entrepreneurs in their own communities? And what about some genuine and lasting convergence of economic and environmental imperatives?

There is still a very long way to go. For many people, this timely and important book will be a real inspiration as they head on down that sustainability road.

Jonathon Porritt
Gloucestershire
January 1998

Preface

This book is about the future, but its origins go back over almost two decades, when a few people in the UK began to make the connections between environmental action and community-based activities. Since those early days, the debate has developed, and international, national and local initiatives and experiments have come and gone. But that original commitment – to ensuring that there are opportunities and resources to enable local people to participate in the decisions and activities which affect their living environment – has remained. As the concept of sustainable development has begun to be increasingly influential in policy and programmes, internationally and in the UK, these linked ideas are beginning to be more acceptable and established.

Although the achievements of local communities in environmental action have become better known, there remain many underlying issues in the whole field which need to be aired more fully. In particular, there is a need for better links between theory and practice, and it seemed timely to make a contribution to the development of a theoretical underpinning based on practice but also on which practice could continue to be developed by all those involved in sustainable development, including architects, planners, designers, health workers, councillors, educators, community and social workers and many others.

As a result, this publication was conceived to bring in a range of opinions from some of the leading thinkers in the relevant (but not always collaborating) fields which relate to community participation and sustainable development. The idea was not to provide simple polemic ('community action in the environment is a good thing'), but to open up the debate in all its complexity – and to invite a number of eminent authors to make contributions which would provide various shafts of light to illuminate some of the underlying issues.

For the purposes of this book, the definition of sustainable development is the original one proposed by the Brundtland

Commission (more formally known as the World Commission on Environment and Development), which was used throughout the United Nations Conference on Environment and Development (UNCED) in Rio in 1992 (the Earth Summit):

> *Humanity has the ability to make development sustainable – to ensure that it meets the needs of the present without compromising the ability of future generations to meet their own needs.* (WCED 1987, p8)

The brief for contributors was based on the notion that community involvement has been accepted in principle as an essential element in sustainable development, but that many practical and theoretical questions remain, including:

- Can the community produce the goods?
- How realistic is the development of collective action in an era of individualism?
- How can scientific evidence be allied to the knowledge of local people? Whose knowledge counts? Whose reality counts?
- How can experts and professionals be supported and encouraged in working with local communities?
- Is there such a thing as 'the community' any more? Is it an aspiration rather than something to be discovered?
- How does community action relate to democracy and wider accountability?
- What are the specific values and skills needed for community involvement in sustainable development?
- How can community action be stimulated, encouraged, supported and resourced?
- Can we be optimistic about the potential of local people to change the world?

The relevance of these issues was confirmed by the eminence of the authors willing to participate in the project.

This book is aimed at all those who are involved in local community level action, those who are trying to support that action at local, regional, national and international level, and at policy makers and others who may develop policy initiatives (and other support) for community action. This is likely to include those in local and national government, European institutions, NGOs and research institutions; academics; community activists; students; politicians at all levels; journalists; and anyone interested in social, economic, environmental and political change.

We hope it will inspire all readers not only to rethink the assumptions which so often lie under the surface in these debates, but also to risk much more experiment – so that the whole field can move into a new and creative era based on valuing the contributions of all members of society.

Diane Warburton
Brighton
January 1998

References

WCED (World Commission on Environment and Development) (1987) *Our Common Future* Oxford University Press, Oxford

1

A Passionate Dialogue: Community and Sustainable Development

Diane Warburton

The role of community in sustainable development has caused excitement and confusion in almost equal measure amongst practitioners and policy makers over recent years, and particularly since the UN Conference on Environment and Development (UNCED) in Rio in 1992, when world leaders signed up to Agenda 21 as the agenda for the twenty-first century, confirming that sustainable development requires community participation in practice as well as principle.

Sustainable development was defined in the Brundtland Report:

> *'Humanity has the ability to make development sustainable – to ensure that it meets the needs of the present without compromising the ability of future generations to meet their own needs'.* (WCED 1987, p8)

In spite of 'environment' not being mentioned at all in this definition, it has been the environmental implications that have received most attention, not least because of the origins of sustainable development, following on from the 1972 UN Conference on the Human Environment and the World Conservation Strategy in 1980.

The priority given to the environment in sustainable development has always been a matter for debate. Indeed, the Brundtland Commission's report specifically says:

> 'When the terms of reference of our Commission were originally being discussed in 1982, there were those who wanted its considerations to be limited to 'environmental issues' only. This would have been a grave mistake ... the 'environment' is where we all live; and 'development' is what we all do in attempting to improve our lot within that abode. The two are inseparable'. (WCED 1987, pxi)

However, although the environment is only one aspect of sustainable development, it must be recognised that without the involvement of environmentalists, and the environmental movement, in debating and promoting sustainable development, even though it often caused them great difficulty, it is unlikely that the concept would have retained its centrality to policy.

The concept of community is equally contested. Beyond the notion that community is a 'good thing', and imparts a warm glow to policies, there seems little consensus about what it actually means, let alone what it means for sustainable development. This book addresses these problems positively. It is designed to open up the debate; to provide a few shafts of light to illuminate some of the issues; and to examine some of the values and assumptions that lie behind those issues.

The importance, and relevance, of the role of community in sustainable development is reflected in the eminence of the contributors to this volume, but it will be apparent to all that this is far from a universal view. Some environmentalists will still argue that priority should be given to the search for the scientific evidence which will win the technical argument, or the professional solution which will solve the problem. To others, sustainable development is just the next stage in the battle for environmental issues to be taken seriously in public policy and commercial strategies. These approaches can, and must, continue, but something else is now needed.

Challenges are being made to the conventional scientific

discourse with the emergence of the concept of a 'civic science' which recognises that science must become an increasingly inter-active process between lay and expert people, reconnecting science and its cultural context, and argues that science must increasingly be linked to empowerment and activism and involve transfers of respect and power (O'Riordan, Chapter 6 this volume). Alongside these new ways of thinking about science itself, conventional professional approaches are increasingly challenged by arguments for more participatory approaches which devolve power to the poor and explicitly encourage professionals to make changes to their personal, professional and institutional values and practices (Chambers, Chapter 7 this volume).

These pressures for change continue a well-established recogni-tion that sustainable development requires not just new solutions but new methods. The Brundtland Report, which introduced the concept of sustainable development to a world well versed in environmental catastrophe, states:

> 'The time has come to break out of past patterns. Attempts to maintain social and ecological stability through old approaches to development and environmental protection will increase instability. Security must be sought through change'. (WCED 1987, p309)

The concept of sustainable development is itself a critique – not only of earlier forms of development and its social and environ-mental consequences, but also of the way development has been undertaken in the past. The concept of sustainable development brings these ideas together and presents a fundamentally challeng-ing shift in global politics creating, for the first time, an ethic which encompasses a challenge to the inevitability of poverty and inequality, which recognises not only the need for economic devel-opment to meet human need but also the imperative to halt environmental destruction, and which involves maximum community participation, empowerment and local activism.

As old political ideas are being discarded, sustainable develop-ment offers a new political ethic, presented in all the guises of international agreements, national strategies and local plans.

However much critics argue that the agreements in Rio lacked substance, and that achievements since Rio have been less than we hoped, the acceptance of the principle of sustainable development by world leaders succeeded, as the Brundtland Report had originally hoped, in 'elevating sustainable development to a global ethic' (WCED 1987), in theory at least. Then, no one quite knew what it meant or what would happen next. We are only now beginning to understand its profound implications and to take up its challenges.

The formal recognition of the importance of community participation and empowerment, in creating and implementing the changes that are required in a sustainable world, allows us to build on a movement supporting community-driven environmental action that has gained strength and knowledge slowly over the past 20 years. This movement has now reached a level of maturity which allows it to begin to move from the evangelical to the reflexive, and to ask some hard questions. This book is one contribution to that reflexivity.

The aim of this collection is to contribute to a critique of the role of community in sustainable development, but a critique in the sense of a positive, sympathetic analysis on which we can build, not a negative criticism. At its most ambitious, the hope is that this book will support a spirit of radical doubt:

> 'Radical doubt is a process ... of liberation ... a widening of awareness, of imaginative, creative visions of our possibilities and options'. (Fromm in Illich 1973, p10)

Sustainable development requires not just new techniques but new ways of thinking about social, economic and environmental goals and how to achieve them. It is also, clearly, not going to happen overnight. In Chapter 6 O'Riordan describes the process of change as the 'sustainability transition', and shows how economic performance, environmental stewardship and increased localism, empowerment and self-reliance, must be integrated to provide ways forward to sustainable development: an approach which requires not only the clarification of underlying values and principles, but also new ways of developing and articulating those values.

The field represented in this book is not a clearly bounded one. It brings together specialists in participation, in planning, in community education, in development studies, in environmentalism, in politics and political theory as well as in social action. There are differences in approach, in analysis and in the identification of ways forward. Many of the contributors have strong and differing views, and the purpose of this book is to support open debate with provocative and informed contributions, rather than to attempt to present a consensus.

The contributors do, however, share a commitment to investigating the potential for greater grassroots action for sustainable development. This introduction to their contributions will do just three things:

1) look at the current context for an increasing role for community participation in sustainable development;
2) offer a brief overview of the links between community action and the environment; and
3) raise some of the key issues and questions we aimed to address in this collection, particularly the links between poverty, community, capacity building and sustainability.

The Context

To begin to take stock of the current position of community-driven sustainable development requires a recognition that it is still a minority interest. The rhetoric of community participation has been rehearsed many times, but it remains the exception rather than the norm on the ground. Realism about current and past achievements is vital if progress is to be made in ensuring that community approaches are accepted as an essential element of sustainable development, recognised as being as necessary as government action and scientific research. It is especially important to bring together the rhetoric and the reality of community-driven sustainable development now as there seem to be real opportunities for community and grassroots action to become part of the mainstream.

It is worth recalling exactly what was important in Agenda 21, the agenda from Rio for the twenty-first century. The very first paragraph reads:

> *'Humanity stands at a defining moment in history. We are confronted with a perpetuation of disparities between and within nations, a worsening of poverty, hunger, ill health and illiteracy, and the continuing deterioration of the ecosystems on which we depend for our well-being. However, integration of environment and development concerns and greater attention to them will lead to the fulfilment of basic needs, improved living standards for all, better protected and managed ecosystems and a safer more prosperous future. No one nation can achieve this on its own; but together we can – in a global partnership for sustainable development'.* (Agenda 21, paragraph 1.1)

It is hard to remain unmoved by this sort of rhetoric, but its inspirational impact is dampened somewhat by the deeply daunting scale of the action that is needed to tackle global problems of this complexity. However, the Brundtland Commission argued that the first step in the pursuit of sustainable development is 'a political system that secures effective citizen participation in decision making' (WCED 1987, 65). They recognised that:

> *'The law alone cannot enforce the common interest. It principally needs community knowledge and support, which entails greater public participation in the decisions which affect the environment. This is best secured by decentralising the management of resources upon which local communities depend, and giving these communities an effective say over the use of the resources. It will also require promoting citizens' initiatives, empowering people's organisations, and strengthening local democracy'.* (WCED 1987, p63)

Agenda 21 contains many references to community participation in sustainable development, including the following (italics added):

- Successful implementation of sustainable development is 'first and foremost the responsibility of Governments', but it also argues that *'the broadest public participation ... should also be encouraged'* (Agenda 21, 1.3).
- Chapter 3 of Agenda 21 states that 'A specific anti-poverty strategy is ... one of the basic conditions for ensuring sustainable development. An effective strategy for tackling the problems of poverty, development and environment simultaneously should begin by focusing on resources, production and people and should cover demographic issues, enhanced health care and education, the rights of women, the role of youth and of indigenous people and *local communities and a democratic participation process in association with improved governance'* (Agenda 21, 3.2).
- 'Activities that will contribute to the integrated promotion of sustainable livelihoods and environmental protection cover a variety of sectoral interventions involving a range of actors, from local to global, and are essential at every level *especially the community and local levels* ... In general terms, the programme should ... *focus on the empowerment of local and community groups through the principle of delegating authority, accountability and resources'* (Agenda 21, 3.5).
- 'Sustainable development must be achieved at every level of society. People's organisations, women's groups and non-governmental organisations are important sources of innovation and action at the local level and have a strong interest and proven ability to promote sustainable livelihoods. *Governments, in cooperation with appropriate international and non-governmental organisations, should support a community-driven approach to sustainability'* (Agenda 21, 3.7).
- 'National capacity-building for the implementation of the above activities is crucial and should be given high priority. *It is particularly important to focus capacity-building at the local level in order to support a community-driven approach to sustainability* and to establish and strengthen mechanisms to allow sharing of experience and knowledge between community groups at national and international levels' (Agenda 21, 3.12).

Figure 1.1 *Agenda 21 and community participation*

Agenda 21, itself contains extensive reference to community participation and empowerment, including much emphasis on capacity building (see Figure 1.1).

These priorities have since been incorporated into European and UK environmental policy. The European Commission's Fifth Environmental Action Programme, called *Towards Sustainability*, recognised the importance of participation:

> *'The strategy for achieving sustainable development can be really successful only if the general public can be persuaded that there is no alternative to the action proposed. Therefore the public must be informed about the issue and means for protecting the environment and, crucially, involved in the process'.* (CEC 1992, p7)

The UK government's first strategy for sustainable development, developed in response to Rio and Agenda 21, echoed this commitment (HMSO 1994a), and the first UK Biodiversity Action Plan spelt out that 'the conservation of biodiversity requires the care and attention of individuals and communities, as well as Government processes' (HMSO 1994b, p94).

The UK Biodiversity Action Plan goes on to argue that

> *'Biodiversity is ultimately lost or conserved at the local level. Government policies create the incentives that facilitate or constrain local action ... In addition to the role of public bodies and landowners the attitudes and actions of local communities have an important part to play in supporting these strategies [ie to conserve and enhance biodiversity]'.* (HMSO 1994b, p111)

To this end, the Plan recognises that:

> *'To exercise appropriate environmental care local people need motivation, education and training ... In this context it (capacity building) can be defined as the process through*

> *which people and organisations develop the skills neces-*
> *sary to manage their environment and development in a*
> *sustainable manner'.* It stresses that *'the starting point*
> *for promoting biodiversity is the resident community,*
> *calling on others for assistance according to the circum-*
> *stances'.* (HMSO 1994b, p111)

The commitment to community participation in sustainable development is continued through to local government. The first
guidance notes on Local Agenda 21 (LA21), produced by the Local
Government Management Board for local authorities, were on
Community Participation in Local Agenda 21 (Bishop 1994).

The approaches of local government, through LA21s, have
produced some impressive innovation in community participation
including bottom-up neighbourhood-based LA21s (including
several programmes supported by WWF-UK; see Webster, Chapter
10 this volume), working groups, forums, visioning and 'future
search' exercises, community audits and other mapping exercises,
work with schools and young people, state of the environment
reports, environmental networks and round tables (Church 1995).
These, and many other participatory initiatives, build on the experience of a few innovators who have fought to make links between
environmental issues and community action over recent years.

Links between Community and Environmental Action

Some individuals and organisations have been examining the
potential for the community approach to environmental action
for more than 20 years with some success. In the 1970s, the practical links between community participation and environmental
action tended to be either in relation to formal participation in
town and country planning (following the Skeffington Report in
1969), or associated with conservation volunteers.

At the same time, in the late 1960s and early 1970s, community development and community work were being developed

through the establishment of the Community Development
Projects (CDPs), Community Projects Foundation (later to become
the Community Development Foundation), and the growth of
rural community councils and councils for voluntary service
throughout England, and community councils in Scotland. These
developments were based on both an increasingly sophisticated
critique of traditional voluntary service, and a political belief in
the potential for community development at neighbourhood level
to create social change and tackle poverty and inequality. Methods
were participatory and aims included increasing political
consciousness as well as improving living conditions.

By contrast, the environmental movement in the 1960s and
1970s tended to involve two types of activists: those with a scientific and technological training and approach, and those with a
more holistic and spiritual view of nature (O'Riordan 1981).
Environmental action was aimed at conservation as well as change,
and focused on global issues rather than neighbourhood concerns.
Methods were often confrontational and campaigning, rather than
developing dialogue with consumers, policy-makers or public institutions. Poverty, and social and economic development, tended
not to be key concerns.

There began to be greater links between environmentalists and
those involved in community action in the 1980s, when the
environmental movement became increasingly concerned with
two new aspects: firstly, urban wildlife (as valuable in itself and as
a refuge for wildlife retreating from an increasingly threatened
countryside); and secondly, the importance of the commonplace
as well as the special in nature and landscape conservation. Both
these developments required a closer link to the public generally,
and to local residents in particular, and community action and
participation in environmental issues grew in popularity among
environmentalists and conservationists.

At the same time, complementary developments were emerging: participation in planning and urban design grew (Bishop et al
1994), the community architecture movement grew in popularity
and influence (Wates and Knevitt 1987), the interest in growing
food in cities was increasing, development trusts were bringing

public, private and voluntary sectors together with the local community to regenerate run down urban and rural areas, and recycling was becoming a community interest.

The development of the Groundwork Trusts over the decade (from the first in St Helens in 1981 to over 50 in 1997), the development trusts movement (now supported by the Development Trusts Association), the growth of the community technical aid movement (supported by their national body, ACTAC, Association of Community Technical Aid Centres), the city farms movement and allotments groups, the changed emphasis of environmental grants schemes such as the Shell Better Britain Campaign (since 1981), and the Department of the Environment's Environmental Action Fund and Local Projects Fund, with their increasing priority for community participation and community-based environmental projects: all these provided organisational support and advice (and in some cases funding) to community-based environmental action.

In wildlife and countryside conservation, there were specific developments. English Nature (then the Nature Conservancy Council) ran programmes such as the Partnership in Practice initiative which aimed to increase joint working and community-based nature conservation, and the Community Action for Wildlife grants scheme in the 1990s. The Countryside Commission ran a series of highly innovatory community action projects in the 1980s, which promoted a community approach to countryside management and rural development (BDOR 1991). A meeting at Losehill Hall, Derbyshire, in 1988 brought much of this thinking together and consolidated the commitment to a community approach by these and other agencies (Warburton et al 1988).

In 1992, the Countryside Commission and English Nature, together with the Rural Development Commission (bringing an institutional commitment to community development and rural economic regeneration), formed Rural Action for the Environment in partnership with five non-governmental bodies. Rural Action was designed specifically to provide support and funding at local level for community environmental action through their own new county networks and the already well-established county rural community councils.

Developments were rather different in urban areas. One of the early contributions to the promotion of community participation in urban environmental issues was the work on *The Livable City*, published as one of the seven specialist reports which formed the UK response to the World Conservation Strategy (WCS).

The WCS was launched by the International Union for the Conservation of Nature and Natural Resources (IUCN) in the UK and 33 other countries in 1980, and was a forerunner of sustainable development, being concerned with 'matching the superficially conflicting goals of development and conservation: development as a means of meeting human needs and improving the quality of life and conservation as the use of resources, especially living ones, in a sustainable way, safeguarding all their benefits for future generations' (Davidson and MacEwen 1982, p1). The WCS urban report recommended a five-year Livable Cities Programme combining conservation with urban regeneration to provide a focus and support for local initiatives integrating resource saving, job creation, training and environmental improvement; reprogramming and reallocating existing funds; and providing new funds for pump priming projects (Davidson and MacEwen 1982).

Davidson and MacEwen recognised then that:

> 'One of the most significant of recent developments in the environmental movement has been the progression of some groups away from the view that conservation is mainly needed elsewhere (in the Third World, or in the countryside) towards a concern to promote and sustain local action in resource saving and creating better environments for living, especially in the city'. (Davidson and MacEwen 1982, p54)

They also recognised the importance of participation and community action:

> 'Increasing pressure by individuals and community groups for participation in decisions which affect their locality

has been a notable movement of the past decade ... there
is increasing enthusiasm for local action which offers great
scope for building a resource saving society'. (Davidson
and MacEwen 1982, p70)

By 1986, the Department of the Environment had recognised that:

'Overall the projects that have involved the voluntary
sector compared favourably with those that have not.
Indeed, community-based revenue supported environmen-
tal improvement projects have been particularly cost-
effective'. (DOE 1986)

However, in common with their rural equivalents, the funding
programmes which supported these developments were faced with
constant change and financial limits. The Urban Programme was
abolished and replaced by City Challenge, and more recently by
the Single Regeneration Budget (SRB).

In spite of these funding uncertainties, links between community action and environmental issues have increased through these
regeneration programmes, especially since more recent government policy has made community participation and partnership a
condition of funding in many cases (MacFarlane 1993; McConnell
1993; Hastings et al 1996). Unfortunately, real partnership and
participation remain the exception rather than the norm (Clarke
1995) and financial resources for community-based schemes have
become increasingly scarce.

Throughout this time, environmentalists have tended to take
far less interest in programmes such as SRB than in the much
smaller programmes run by the national public agencies with
whom they have traditionally worked – the Countryside
Commission and English Nature, Scottish Natural Heritage and
the Countryside Council for Wales. This reflects the history of the
environmental movement's focus on rural conservation, particularly nature conservation and land (countryside) management.

However, in the context of sustainable development, urban
development programmes are clearly a priority. It is here that

programmes to tackle poverty and deprivation and to support
communities are most often located, and here that the conflicts
between development, environmental impacts and social justice
are most apparent. There are some hopeful signs, but the continuing need and potential for developing more participatory
sustainable development initiatives in urban areas remains
(Worpole, Chapter 8 this volume).

Overall, the links between the environmental action and
community participation have been becoming stronger in both
urban and rural areas. Indeed, 'the recent history of environmental
policy and community policy in Britain shows evidence of a steady
drawing together of these two separate strands' (Roome 1993,
p206). As understanding and experience of joint working grow,
however, some of the complex dilemmas underlying community
participation in sustainable development begin to become more
pressing.

Nature of 'Community'

One of the difficulties in expanding the community approach to
sustainable development has undoubtedly been confusion and
misunderstanding about the notion of community. Unlike sustainable development, everyone thinks they know what community
means. Since the concept of community seems almost always to
come with a warm glow, which can be useful when policy-makers
want to attach it to a questionable new initiative, some analysis
has fought shy of trying to pin it down. To some extent, the
concept of community has been defined so often that the result
ceases to be definition. However, some common understanding of
the term is required in order to establish how it may link to sustainable development: particularly the essential link between
community and place.

Community is usually understood as being to do with 'locality', with 'actual social groups', with 'a particular quality of
relationship' which is 'felt to be more immediate than society',
and when used in conjunction with other activities, such as
'community politics', is 'distinct not only from national politics

but from formal local politics and normally involves various kinds of direct action and direct local organisations, "working directly with people"' (Williams 1988, pp75–6). Community may perhaps be more easily understood not as an isolated concept, but by recognising what it is not: it is not state, society, association, individual, self (Scottish Community Development Centre 1996).

To add to this confusion, concepts such as community always have several meanings, any one or more of which may be dominant but which exist alongside other meanings which are emerging or waning.

Two further descriptions of community contribute additional nuances which link it more firmly to 'place':

> *'Concern for familiar topography, for the places one knows, is not about the loss of a commodity, but about the loss of* identity. *People belong in the world: it gives them a home. The attachment to place – not just natural places, but urban places too – is one of the most fundamental of human needs ... The important thing about places, of course, is that they are shared. Each person's home area is also other people's. The sense of place is therefore tied to the idea of "community"'.* (Jacobs 1995, p20)

> *'"Community" is that web of personal relationships, group networks, traditions and patterns of behaviour that develops against the backdrop of the physical neighbourhood and its socio-economic situation'.* (Flecknoe & McLellan 1994, p8)

These descriptions refer to the 'location' of community. One of the major critiques of community approaches to policy in recent years has been the post-modern emphasis on fragmentation, globalisation and movement (eg Hall 1995). Hall argues that there is no such thing as community because people no longer have long-standing personal local connections which continue over generations, and that people now have much wider, transitory and impersonal connections (including through computer technology). In contrast to some analyses of community which may incorporate the notion of a return to a golden age, Hall's view has been that new relationships are needed, based on the experience of the fractured communities of the South who 'do retain strong links to and identification with the cultures, traditions and places and histories of their origin or places of descent. But (who) are without any illusion of an actual 'return' to the past' (Hall 1995, p55). However, it is possible to see Hall's critique of community more in terms of the impossibility of a return to the past rather than the end of located communities: attachments to locality do not have to be permanent or continuous to be meaningful.

Indeed, although some groups of people have lost traditional settled communities (especially refugees in the South), the mobility of people, at least in the UK, may have been overplayed: 'over half of British adults live within five miles of where they were born' (Gray 1997). Moreover, research by MORI suggests that 'Overall, there is a clear focus of attachment on the most local area ... where strong attachment is found to a significant extent, it only exists at the most local level of the village or neighbourhood' (Gosschalk and Hatter 1996, p14). In this country at least, local connections and local attachments do still exist and remain important to many people.

Locality is also where environmental issues matter most to most people: 'Locality is crucial: it is local landscape, traffic and litter that make "the environment" real for most people as a fundamental political issue' (Christie 1996, p30). The traditional global concerns of the environmental movement remain, but there is also recognition that:

> 'Most people have an environmental horizon which is very local – the end of the street or the top of the next hill. Sustainability has first to make sense at that neighbourhood level, if it is ever to reach global proportions'. (Baines 1995, p14)

The phrase 'Think global, act local' was first widely used in the 1980 World Conservation Strategy, and has since become part of mainstream environmental discourse.

The concept of community is not without its critics, especially where community is used as a moral voice 'in order to shore up the social, moral and political foundations of society' (Walker 1995; and see Etzioni, Chapter 2 this volume). Not everyone is happy about shoring up all these traditional foundations. For example, 'accusations are now flying fast and furious from libertarians and feminists that ... behind these pleasant words about building communities lies the imposition of a traditional social order upon people' (Phillips 1995). Indeed, 'the litany of "community" is becoming a new religion, with its own holy trinity: community, family, individual' (Campbell 1994), bringing with it all its hierarchical and sexist implications. Similarly, Pahl argues that 'Community life in the past was imposed on people, being largely based on involuntary relationships' (Pahl 1995, p21), which may have been oppressive and were certainly rigidly hierarchical.

Hall points out that there have been many communities which have attempted 'to secure identities by adopting closed and exclusivist versions of culture or community ... refusing to live with difference' (Hall 1995, p54). This creation of identity by demonising the 'other' and the 'different' is a nightmare scenario which finds echoes in the 'gated communities' in the US, and parts of the UK, where wealthy people seal themselves off with private security systems from the rest of the city (Worpole and Greenhalgh 1996).

Certainly, the idea of community is easily over-romanticised and, as Taylor points out 'Communities ... can be the scene of conflict and exclusion as well as togetherness, and many of the stresses of modern life work against a community "spirit"' (Taylor 1992, p2). However, it is only by confronting these negative views that a new and positive vision of community can be created: communities which are inclusive, open and creative, and in which difference is welcomed and valued. This concept of community is as radical and challenging as sustainable development itself.

For me, the notion of community has two elements: one to do with relationships between people, and one to do with relationships between people and the place in which they are located. It is to do with a common feeling based on sharing a place which creates a particular type of relationship. Judy Ling Wong has characterised this as a 'caring relationship' (Wong, Chapter 12 this volume): we care about our neighbours in a community – they are no longer strangers. Along similar lines, it has been suggested that

'Community is a morally charged concept because it is about the obligations and expectations one has to those people one lives closest to' (Revill, quoted in Worpole and Greenhalgh 1996, p35).

Some definitions of community relate to the characteristics of the members of the community and common interests which tie members together and give those characteristics a shared significance. This could encompass the 'neighbourhood' focus outlined above, but also suggests that community can be based on shared characteristics such as ethnic origin, religion or sexual orientation (the black community, the Jewish community, the gay community). However, this extension of the term community to other groupings not based around locality starts to create difficulties, particularly as community can become associated with the exclusion of difference. The danger is that 'community' becomes a creed of 'not so much toleration as homogenisation. We should all be the same. That way, we can all get along.' (Stock 1996). While recognising that certain groups are likely to have common needs and aspirations, and would benefit from joint action for equality, the danger in solidifying these characteristics into 'community' is that it may lead to unwanted ghettoisation.

By focusing any future vision of community firmly in relation to locality, and on principles such as openness and inclusiveness, we can learn not just to accept difference but to welcome it as a positive contribution to a radical and creative way of life (see, for example, Wong, Chapter 12 this volume). Using the concept of community in this way offers the potential for new and positive relationships which may begin with, but go beyond, the physical characteristics or social and political history of the people who live in a particular place.

It is a mistake to think we all know what community is, if only we could articulate it, because it is in some senses a myth – with different meanings in different contexts and to different people. My own view is that, for many people, community is an *aspiration* rather than a reality to be discovered or returned to. Community is not a thing, it is a dynamic process in which a shared commitment creates and recreates community through action by people who are aware and committed to the principle of working together for a better life and world.

It is beginning to be recognised that community is neither the 'end' nor the 'means' of a process of development or participation, it is creating something new which is based partly in people's memories, real or imagined, and partly in future visions of society. Community can then be fully understood as an aspiration rather than a definition, based on certain types of (caring) relationships in a shared place. This conjunction of ideas, which are not reducible to specific space or time constraints but are to do with people's relations with each other and to the physical world in which we live (and want to live), is what gives, and has always given, community its power and meaning.

Community remains a 'warmly persuasive word' (Williams 1988, p76), and many (although not all) recent uses of the concept of community stress the visionary, critical and constructive aspects of community (Yeo 1988), linked to notions of social change. Community has begun to regain its link to positive action: 'people are beginning to put things together in pursuit of that elusive concept, community. Self-help groups are burgeoning; the inner cities are spawning grass-roots initiatives to restore the social fabric' (Phillips 1995c). Indeed, 'Despite easy cynicism, "community" is more than an empty rhetoric word ... Community is the recognition that people are not just individuals, that there is such a thing as society to which we belong, which makes us who we are, and without which there can be no true human flourishing' (Jacobs 1995, p21).

The difficulties of definition, and the radical implications of the community approach, have led to a great deal of oversimplification and avoidance of difficult issues. We are now ready for, and capable of, far greater rigour and far more powerful arguments for the community approach to sustainable development. The continuing strength of these arguments, however, depends on finding answers to some of the further underlying questions about the links between community and poverty.

Poverty, Community and Sustainable Development

Sustainable development provides a new focus for tackling poverty and linking the implications of poverty to ecological damage:

> 'Poverty is not only an evil in itself, but sustainable development requires meeting the basic needs of all and extending to all the opportunity to fulfil their aspirations for a better life. A world in which poverty is endemic will always be prone to ecological and other catastrophes'.
> (WCED 1987, p8)

Traditional community development always had two objectives: to tackle poverty and deprivation, and to increase the political participation of excluded groups (particularly those who are poor and disadvantaged). However, not only do poor people, understandably, resent being categorised as such (eg Corden 1996), but there is often also an assumption that community is really only needed for the poor: the poor need communities in which they can look after each other; the rich do not need community because they can buy what they need. This assumption may be because community development began as a method of development applied specifically to disadvantaged people, initially in developing countries and then increasingly in the UK and US.

When top-down approaches to development were seen to have failed to solve the problems of poverty, environmental degradation and urban decline (Hastings et al 1996, Oakley 1991, Rahman 1995), the emphasis shifted from developing imported technical professional solutions to 'community development', based on valuing the skills of the people living in poverty, and making efforts to engage them in new and more participatory programmes. These programmes developed techniques which aimed to enable local residents to find their own solutions, to participate more fully and to take more control of the processes which affect their lives. These new approaches brought professional and personal challenges, but enormous social, environmental and personal rewards began to be achieved (Chambers, Chapter 7 this volume).

However, it is clear that community development alone cannot solve the problem of poverty:

> *'It was once supposed that local community activity could help to reduce poverty. But poverty is mainly a function of low income and of the distribution of wealth, income and opportunities. Community development projects, community action programmes and the like can help individual participants to develop their capacities and perhaps move out of poverty, but the belief that such small-scale schemes could have any fundamental impact on social and economic structures has long been exposed as mistaken'.*
> (Willmott 1989, p34)

Increasing the amount and effectiveness of community participation in sustainable development alone will not solve the problem of poverty because that implies that poverty is only a problem for poor people that only they can solve. In fact, poverty is a problem for all people. Sustainable development requires that poverty is not treated like a disease that some people have and others do not: it must be seen as a result of conscious political decisions which can be challenged and changed over time. This requires a change of attitude to poor people. The Victorian charitable idea that the poor should be helped, like wayward and vulnerable children, has had its day. The poor are no different from the rich – they just have less money, less power and fewer opportunities.

Focusing anti-poverty programmes on the poor may not only shift all the responsibility on to them, but may force poor people into continuing to be victims in order to maintain access to resources. Targeted community empowerment may contribute to the disempowerment of targeted communities. Meekosha argues that:

> *'"Difference", "specificity" or "special needs programmes" can either legitimate inequality or hide inequality from view, as can be demonstrated in housing, health, education and welfare services that become even more selective and 'targeted' as time goes by ... Groups become trapped*

by the need to continue to demonstrate oppression or disad-
vantage or victim status for funding purposes, rather than
continue the project of social change'. (Meekosha 1993,
p181 and p188)

Social justice in sustainable development clearly implies not just
tackling poverty and inequality, but also tackling the exclusion
which accompanies it: poor people must be part of a wider community which includes us all. In France and Germany, and more
recently in the UK, there is increasing concern about social exclusion, and development and regeneration efforts, based on:

'*The philosophy of integrated social development, aiming*
to develop participative structures which transcend the old
administrative divisions, and in so doing to reinvigorate a
citizenship and social cohesion which is everywhere threat-
ened by unemployment and widening inequalities. This
involves a shift from outmoded forms of welfare targeted
on populations defined by needs (because these merely
reinforce marginalisation and in any case are no longer
relevant in today's patterns of poverty)'. (Cannan 1995,
p238)

In the UK it is still controversial to argue for mixed neighbourhoods (echoes of gentrification), but it is beginning. Chris Holmes,
as Director of Shelter, has argued in favour of integration in building community, in his analysis of the concentration of low income
households on council estates in future housebuilding
programmes. He says that 'Socially mixed neighbourhoods ... make
it more likely that people from all different backgrounds can share
in the benefits of a self-confident and mutually supportive community ... The key objective must be the development of socially
balanced communities' (Holmes 1997). Holmes quotes Aneurin
Bevan's evocation of 'the lovely features of English and Welsh
villages, where the doctor, the grocer, the butcher and the farm
labourer all live in the same street. I believe it is essential for the
full life of a citizen ... to see the living tapestry of a mixed community' (Bevan, in Holmes 1997).

Working with poor people to tackle poverty must continue to be the priority in sustainable development, and will require special resources. As has been pointed out elsewhere, 'there is nothing more unequal than the equal treatment of unequals ... Social justice must be seen as a precondition for sustainable wealth' (Mega 1996, p77). This requires a recognition that poverty is not just a problem for poor people, and there is no reason why poor people have to be separated out from the rest of humanity in tackling poverty and its many implications.

The basic assumption that 'community = poor, weak, vulnerable people' must continue to be challenged. In local community organisations I have personally been involved with, there have been well-known broadcasters, schools inspectors, academics, designers, internationally renowned architects, professors, local government officers, professional artists and musicians, scientists. In the same groups there were single mothers, black women, people with severe physical disabilities, unemployed people, people with no academic qualifications at all, people with mental illness. Very often, the characteristics in the second list applied to the people in the first list; some had lots of money and some had practically none.

The crucial divisions are not just between rich and poor; they are between those who are prepared to engage in these new ways of working and those who are not. Assumptions are easy to make, and without recognition of these assumptions, the danger remains that while *we* affluent(ish) professionals have democracy, *they* have community action. Not only does it yet again distance poor people from the mainstream political process (however flawed that may be), it drives yet another professionally-generated wedge between the 'poor' and the rest.

These assumptions must be disentangled so that clear statements can be made about tackling poverty as *the* priority of sustainable development, and about community development as a process of encouraging and supporting community-based sustainable development as an essential method for doing it. However, we can now go beyond that, to see community action, and the process of building communities, as not targeted only at poor people, but at everyone.

It has been argued that 'community is time-consuming and difficult to implement ... Far from protecting people from the unpleasant reality across the hallway or down the road, it forces them face to face with it' (Stock 1996) and this, I would argue, is its great strength. But this difficult and demanding effort cannot just be left to 'poor' people, when clearly the responsibility goes much wider (see Taylor, Chapter 9 this volume). Community is not an answer to poverty, it is a way of living and working which allows people to see what they have in common, not what divides them, and not only makes poverty more visible but also less acceptable. It also allows people to learn from each other in finding new ways of tackling poverty.

Capacity-building

Capacity-building has been identified in much sustainable development policy as one of the key strategies for increasing the potential for a community-driven approach to sustainable development. However, this concept also carries assumptions about what capacity is, who has it and who can build it.

Agenda 21 is eloquent on the issue of capacity-building:

> *'National capacity-building for implementation of the above activities (ie sustainable development) is crucial and should be given high priority. It is particularly important to focus capacity-building at the local community level in order to support a community-driven approach to sustainability and to establish and strengthen mechanisms to allow sharing of experience and knowledge between community groups at national and international level. Requirements for such activities are considerable and are related to the various relevant sectors of Agenda 21 calling for requisite international, financial and technological support'.* (Agenda 21, 3.12)

Given such a commitment to resourcing community-driven sustainable development, it may seem churlish to question the focus on capacity-building, but jargon always demands analysis to ensure it is not hiding oppressive assumptions.

There seem to be two basic approaches to capacity-building. The first may be summed up as: 'Capacity-building is training and other methods to help people develop the confidence and skills necessary for them to achieve their purpose' (Wilcox 1994, p31). Chambers prefers the term 'capability' to capacity; for him, capability is 'the quality of being capable; the ability to do something' (Chambers, Chapter 7 this volume). He suggests that 'Capabilities refers to what people are capable of doing or being. They are means to livelihood and fulfilment; and their enlargement through learning, practice, training and education are means to better living and well-being' (Chambers 1997, p11). Chambers asserts that the real targets of capacity-building are 'the poor, weak, vulnerable and exploited' (Chambers 1997, p11), reflecting the historic focus of community development. Both these approaches focus on individual abilities, latent or apparent and, here, motivation for and rewards from capacity-building rest with those whose capacity is being built.

The second approach is more instrumental: 'Capacity-building is a strategy whose starting point is to encourage, reinforce and build social capital. The challenge for the city manager is to increase trust and the enjoyment of social interaction, while minimising isolation and distrust; in short, to build "loyalty"' (Whitehead and Smyth 1996, 37). In this instance, capacity-building is used as an instrument to build successful communities by increasing social capital (based on concepts from Putnam 1993).

The questions raised by these two approaches are about whose capacity is being built, by whom, for what and who controls the process. Both approaches can, and do, coexist. However, they imply very different relations of power, albeit for the best motives in many instances.

In some analyses, there is an implicit assumption that 'ordinary people' cannot take action or responsibility unless and until they have their capacity built, presumably by someone else: capacity-building is sometimes seen as a precursor to participation. Some proponents of capacity- or capability-building fully recognise the professional dilemmas that these new relationships may create by establishing new forms of professionalisation which may raise more barriers between people and their control of their own circumstances (eg Chambers 1997 and Chapter 7 this volume).

Community groups may be seen as 'out of their depth' in participation or partnership initiatives, but that is because these initiatives are almost always set in institutional contexts which are controlled by a different group of people with different experiences and expectations. Some council officers (for example) may be equally out of their depth at an ordinary community meeting, and 'how many chief executives could run a children's tea party?' (Wilcox 1994, p32). It is just a question of which bits of the sum of human skills you happen to hold at any particular time, and how those skills are valued differently in different contexts.

Much has been written about devising and holding participation, consultation, involvement exercises with local communities, but the inherent imbalances of power and resources are not always articulated. This is often because, for the best of intentions, those writing want to see more participation, consultation and involvement – and quite rightly, because the more contact there is between these people taking different roles, and the more experience of participation that is created, the more chance there is of capacity-building on all sides. To be effective, capacity-building must be a two-way process.

Capacity-building implies potential, not skills, and focusing capacity-building on poor people can be seen as making a judgement about the abilities which poor people possess. We do not discuss capacity-building for stockbrokers, or bank managers, even though wealthy professional people are no more likely to be able to create responsible, supportive, caring, inclusive community relationships than their poor neighbours. Capacity-building is in some ways an offshoot of community development, and retains the historical focus on disadvantaged groups. However, capacity-building tends to focus primarily on individual growth and social development (always an aspect of community development) rather than on social change and political participation.

There will always be a small minority of people (rich or poor) who are unable to take up opportunities to improve their quality of life without help, but this does not apply to the vast majority of people who are labelled 'poor'. Anyone who has seen the extraordinary achievements of community organisations in neighbourhoods suffering from extreme disadvantage will testify – not to the 'capacity' of these people, but to their 'ability'; to their strength, their commitment, their clarity of purpose and their skills. There is a danger that capacity-building takes the place of recognising and meeting the real needs of poor people: access to the same educational, training, work, leisure and social resources and opportunities as the more privileged people in society.

Any additional resources given to poor people in deprived neighbourhoods must be welcome, and much community development has recognised that it is because participation has so often been denied to poor people that special efforts are needed to redress the balance. However, ways need to be found of ensuring that capacity-building links individual growth and development into collective action for social change, feeding personal growth back into enhanced collective action and enabling everyone to continue to learn new skills so that we are better able to help each other as well as ourselves.

In this analysis, there *is* something called society, of which we all form a part, and we take from and contribute to society as our abilities and circumstances allow. Of course, this is idealistic and there are many pitfalls. But idealism is an essential part of sustainable development; sustainable development is a hope for a better, fairer world. Gramsci argued for 'pessimism of the intellect, optimism of the will' (Hall 1988, p13), both of which will always be essential to sustainable development.

Capacity-building is a well-intentioned attempt to do something for the poor, without imposing solutions or removing the ability of people to choose their own futures, and it has many strengths. However, it exemplifies the dangers of warm words which hide implications which undermine their radical purpose. Any programmes of capacity-building must recognise that what is needed is not a redressing of the inequalities of *abilities*, but a redressing of the inequalities of *resources* and *opportunities* to practice and develop those abilities in ways which others in society take for granted.

Education for Sustainability

The concept of capacity-building also emphasises the need for education for sustainable development. The argument runs that if ordinary people do not care about development being sustainable, and change their attitudes and behaviour, any amount of policy programmes will fail. Learning about sustainability is important (see Fagan, Chapter 11 this volume), and the community approach to education for sustainability usually recognises that education and action in these circumstances are closely allied.

Participation in practical projects and policy discussions, as an experiential form of community education, is increasingly recognised as a learning experience which can reinforce positive messages about sustainable lifestyles and sustainable development. Participatory action helps build caring from knowledge and experience, and when people care about something, they will fight for it – whether that means doing practical work to plant trees, or protecting the places they care about by standing in front of bulldozers. Participatory action, like community development, is an educational process in the broadest sense, where participants learn by doing.

The radical approach to adult education has been characterised by Paulo Freire's concept of 'conscientisation' as the process through which people 'learn to perceive the social, political and economic contradictions, and to take action against the oppressive elements of reality' (Freire 1996). His analysis of the learning process has been highly influential (particularly in community development and community education in the UK and Latin America) and is based on the principles of dialogue between teachers and lay people for *mutual* liberation. The mutuality of the learning process is crucial – it is not learning at the feet of a master, but a process of joint learning in which the knowledge of all parties is respected, and which recognises that 'the educator himself needs educating'.

Freire argues that education is needed because 'no reality transforms itself' (Freire 1996, p35). However, that education must be based on a 'pedagogy which must be forged with, not for, the oppressed ... No pedagogy which is truly liberating can remain distant from the oppressed by treating them as unfortunates and by presenting for their emulation models from among their oppressors' (Freire 1996, p30). Once oppression has been recognised (through the radical, community-based educational approach Freire argues for), this pedagogy ceases to belong to the oppressed alone and becomes a pedagogy of all people in the process of permanent liberation.

Capacity-building in itself is not enough, it needs to be part of a wider educational process (in the broadest sense). Reflection, based on understanding, is essential to action so that future action is based on an understood and acknowledged experience and a learning about our own ways of understanding: Chambers calls this approach self-critical epistomological awareness (SEA) (Chambers, Chapter 7 this volume). Learning through debate and dialogue will always be essential to sustainable development. The new paradigm we are seeking is one which does not provide a fixed and final answer, but offers a way of thinking about change which is organic and flexible and continuously developing (Chambers, Chapter 7 this volume).

Learning from others should go beyond any idea that professionals or experts have the answers, but recognises that a negotiation can take place in which experts and lay people come together in an interactive process, reconnecting science and technical knowledge and their cultural context (O'Riordan, Chapter 6 this volume). Placing different knowledges and, possibly, values, alongside our own, allows us to re-evaluate our own knowledge and beliefs. It even supports the role of the professional or intellectual in bringing ideas to the process of change, following Gramsci's vision of the role of organic intellectuals in challenging dominant hegemonies (Gramsci 1971). Once the space has been established for this potential to be explored and understood, new solutions can begin to be found.

Not Community Alone

An increasing focus on community initiatives in government environmental and regeneration programmes leads to questions about the relationship between these initiatives and democratic

institutions. There are varying views on the balance between
community responsibility and traditional government, and there
is considerable potential for developing new relationships in this
area. Indeed, it may be that it is in working with local authorities
that the greatest opportunities for community-driven sustainable
development are located. David Donnison has pointed out that
'There is, in short, no magic about community. The age-old tasks
of government still have to be performed – creating legitimate
authority and transferring it to new leaders when necessary,
accounting for public money ...' (Donnison 1993). These tasks of
government have to be seen alongside the enthusiasm of some
local authorities (always recognising that it is not all) in promoting community-driven development and, more specifically,
community-based approaches to LA21 (see Webster, Chapter 10
this volume).

The balance in this relationship between community organisations and government is being developed through experience, and
by establishing new protocols of accountability and democracy,
answering questions about how accountable or representative
community organisations are, can or should be, and whether
community organisations can or should offer opportunities for
increasing involvement (see Stewart, Chapter 3 this volume).

Very often, these questions are raised by government and other
agencies which may find it easier to consult, or invite into participation, a neatly delimited 'community' or 'neighbourhood' as an
administrative block, but then have difficulties in establishing a
common 'community view', or finding one which does not fit the
parameters they had set for the exercise based on the (clearly
mistaken) view that community interests are homogenous (see
Taylor, Chapter 4 this volume).

The proper balance between public service responsibilities and
community participation is difficult to achieve, but it can certainly
be argued that:

> *'Every profession and public official should respect those*
> *who depend on their services and find ways of giving them*
> *a voice which cannot be disregarded. That calls for more*

> *sensitive and effective civic leadership, not less of it, from*
> *democratically accountable public authorities'.* (Donnison
> 1993)

These relationships are not fixed, and 'claims of autonomy and governing power are not absolutes, but make sense only in complex and ever-shifting structures of interlocking power, competence and legitimacy' (Mulgan and 6, 1996, p3). Movement and change may allow the space for new approaches to be tried and new balances found.

It can be argued that there is at present a unique opportunity for democracy and sustainability to revitalise each other:

> *'Revitalising local democracy depends crucially on the*
> *environmental policy agenda for two reasons. First, the*
> *emerging agenda of environmentally sustainable develop-*
> *ment requires strong local government if its goals are to be*
> *recognised. Second, the re-energisation of local democracy*
> *requires strong commitment to sustainable development.*
> *No other source of civic energy is a plausible contender for*
> *the task'.* (Christie 1996, p29)

Agenda 21 stresses extending participation and developing partnerships between all interests, while recognising the imbalances of power and resources which need to be addressed before such partnerships can begin to work. Developing the basic support for community participation is one of the key strategies proposed for redressing that balance.

Building Community-Driven Sustainable Development

Support in terms of policy and resources for community-driven sustainable development is vital. Much of this introductory essay has examined implied meanings in the warm words of community and capacity-building, in order to challenge oppressive assumptions, and to support the radical implications of community participation in sustainable development; to help ensure that, this time, the community approach retains its radical purpose and is recognised to be concerned with social and political change – as is sustainable development.

Building a creative relationship between the community approach and the public institutions which support it is vital. Few studies have examined what the recipients of capacity-building feel about the help and support they get from institutions. Chanan found that 'satisfaction with personal networks was high, with authorities was low, with influential individuals was moderate and with local groups was high' (Chanan 1992, pxvi). These findings, from a European-wide study of community action, are supported by a more recent study of public perceptions of participation in sustainability in Lancashire, which concluded:

> 'People display a pronounced degree of fatalism and even cynicism towards the country's public institutions, including national and local government. This is reflected in an apparently pervasive lack of trust in the goodwill and integrity of national government, and in doubts about the ability or willingness of local government to achieve positive improvements in the quality of people's lives (not least because local authorities' powers are seen as diminishing).' (Macnaghten et al 1995, p3)

The effects of this lack of trust on people's willingness to participate in sustainability initiatives, or 'even attend to information about the environment is strongly affected by their sense of "agency" – that is, by whether or not they feel a capacity to influence events associated with that information' (Macnaghten et al 1995, p3 and p17). This is bound up intimately with their continual negotiation of relationships with government, and their lack of trust in those institutions. As Macnaghten et al point out: 'It would be a serious mistake to judge people's capacity or motivation on specific initiatives ... without taking into account these less explicit dimensions and attempting to understand and address them' (Macnaghten et al 1995, p18).

The lack of respect and status accorded to community approaches is reflected in the lack of faith in community groups by many government institutions which, in turn, affects community participants' belief in their own ability to actually change anything. Capacity-building must not be seen as a precursor to participation, but as a process of development through action supported by programmes established according to certain principles. Good, effective participation or involvement programmes take this into account and make sure that principles of good practice are observed, including a 'commitment to working with communities as equal partners; commitment to share power with communities who are affected by its use; commitment to mutual respect, tolerance and trust' (Hart 1994, p10). Establishing ground rules such as agreeing shared objectives, openness and accessibility, honesty, relevance, achievements, and learning from experience helps often lengthy processes operate more smoothly and effectively (Bishop 1994, p4).

The ways in which progress is measured are also amenable to wide participatory action. If local people can be involved in creating visions of a sustainable future world, and in setting indicators for progress towards that goal, they can then be fully involved in deciding when an initiative has been successful: *their* criteria and judgement of success begin to matter (Lawrence Chapter 4; MacGillivray; Chapter 5 – both this volume).

Sustainable Development as a Social Challenge

> *'If we really are to help the Earth get better, and achieve a comfortable quality of life for all the people of the world, then sustainability must be deeply rooted in every local neighbourhood. Success can only come through active participation from all corners of the community, with individuals and organisations playing to their own particular strengths'.* (Baines 1995, p13)

It is now recognised that 'regeneration and renaissance is mainly about people, not about places ... Sustainability is most of all a social challenge ... Societies can flourish only if they are embedded in the local community and the cultural continuity that enhance a sense of place, of identity, of belonging. Cultural diversity and citizen participation are considered to be part of the richness of cities and regions in Europe at an historic moment' (Mega 1996, pp77–78, 88). The rhetoric of sustainable regeneration, at least, has recognised the importance of participation.

Collective action is required for sustainable development because of the nature of what is to be achieved. As Michael Jacobs points out:

> *'Environmental goods are public goods; it is collective not individual choice which they require ... individual wellbeing is dependent on the health and resilience of the things we share and must provide together'.* (Jacobs 1995, p17 and p19)

When we talk of community, we are not only talking about different groups of people, we are talking about a different kind of action, of political action, which relies on us operating in ways which incorporates all our professional knowledge (whatever that may be) but also our humanity; not only our technical skills, but also our affection for each other. This is because community action 'largely springs from the need of local inhabitants to solve joint problems of daily living' and uses the 'personal networks of family, friends and neighbours to help with a range of problems' (Chanan 1992, pxvi).

All institutions reflect their histories, and community action is no different: it begins with these sorts of personal relationships and informal networks which remain its foundation (see Judy Ling Wong, Chapter 12 this volume). Community action offers a space to experiment, personally and collectively. Technical expertise and new ideas and approaches will always be needed, but it must be provided by people who see themselves as the equals of those to whom they are providing it, and not as their superiors.

One key problem has always been how local community action can avoid being marginalised and actually contribute to social transformation and global change, without being co-opted into a minor role in the traditional political process (see Taylor, Chapter 9 this volume). One way forward is through new forms of collective action which are based less on the shared characteristics of specific groups, and more on coalition-building, networks and alliances between different groups who recognise a common cause. Networks which draw together groups and individuals concerned with traditional environmental concerns, tenants associations, youth groups and many others are beginning to show a way forward which builds on, but is not limited to, the local focus.

Networks can offer a different form of personal experience and create the space to develop new concepts: Melucci describes these networks as 'cultural laboratories' (in Scott 1992, p137). Networks can also be the means by which disparate social movements can gain a critical mass and begin to influence national and international policy, events and change. Reports of the increased networking of community protests in the UK support this idea: 'Communities are linking in common local protest at everything from toxic waste to asthma, electro-magnetic fields, airports, supermarkets and waste tips and are coming up with solutions' (Vidal 1995).

Sustainable development requires participatory action which has an identification with the democratic community because it depends on 'the legitimacy and trust with which governments are perceived and the sense of citizenship which enables individuals to participate in civic society. For this reason, sustainable development almost certainly implies a renewal and rejuvenation of the democratic process' (Jacobs 1995, p22). In future, it may be 'in the activities of non-governmental and community organisations ... that positive change is most evident ... such groups are finding creative and lasting ways of making their – and therefore our – world better' (Jacobs 1996, p5).

All the work on sustainable development, from the World Conservation Strategy, through the Brundtland Report and Agenda 21, to all the national and local government strategies, has recognised that more than protective legislation is required. Changed attitudes to individual and collective responsibility are needed and increasing participation is essential to this process. Community-based sustainable development offers an approach which can be holistic, which respects difference and individual growth and development, and which also recognises the need for collective action, for mutual learning and for poverty to be recognised as a problem for all of us, not just for poor people.

The way forward can be based on a new and passionate dialogue through which we can all listen to each other, learn from each other, care about each other, and care about the future of the world in which we all live.

References

Baines, C (1995) 'Local action for sustainability', *First Steps: Local Agenda 21 in Practice* presented to Global Forum in Manchester 1994; HMSO, London

BDOR (1991) *Countryside Community Action: An Appraisal* Countryside Commission, CCP 307, Cheltenham

Bishop, J, Davison, I, Hickling, D, Kean, J, Rose, J and Silson, R (1994) *Community Involvement in Planning and Development Processes* HMSO for Department of the Environment, London

Bishop, J (1994) *Community Participation in Local Agenda 21* LGMB, London

Campbell, B (1994) 'Praise the community, blame the mothers', in *The Independent*, 30.11.94

Cannan, C (1995) 'Urban social development in France', in *Community Development Journal*, Vol 30, No 3, July (1995), pp 238–247

Chambers, R (1997) *Whose Reality Counts? Putting the First Last* Intermediate Technology Publications, London

Chanan, G (1992) *Out of the Shadows Local Community Action and the European Community* Community Development Foundation/HMSO (with the European Foundation for Living and Working Conditions), London

Christie, I (1996) 'A green light for local people', in *The Return of the Local*, Demos Quarterly Issue 9

Church, C (1995) *Towards Local Sustainability. A Review of Current Activity on Local Agenda 21 in the UK* UNA Sustainable Communities Unit/Community Development Foundation, London

Clark, G, Darrall, J, Grove-White, R, Macnaghten, P and Urry, J (1994) *Leisure Landscapes. Leisure, Culture and the English Countryside* Centre for the Study of Environmental Change, Lancaster University, for CPRE, London

Clarke, G (1995) *A Missed Opportunity. An Initial Assessment of the 1995 Single Regeneration Budget Approvals and their Impact on Voluntary and Community Organisations in England* The Urban Forum, NCVO, London

Commission of the European Communities (CEC) (1990) *Green Paper on the Urban Environment* CEC, COM (90) 218 Final Brussels

Commission of the European Communities (CEC) (1992) *Towards Sustainability. Fifth Action Plan on the Environment* CEC, COM (92) 23, Luxembourg

Corden, A (1996) 'Writing about poverty: ethical dilemmas' in *Ethics and Social Policy Research*, Dean, H (ed) Social Policy Association, University of Luton Press

Craig, G and Mayo, M (1995) *Community Empowerment. A Reader in Participation and Development* Zed Books, London

Davidson, J and MacEwen, A (1982) *The Livable City* World Conservation Strategy Report No 5, Nature Conservancy Council, Peterborough

Department of the Environment (1986) *Evaluation of Environmental Projects Funded under the Urban Programme* HMSO, London

Donnison, D (1993) In *The Guardian*, 10.11.93

Flecknoe, C and McLellan, N (1994) *The What, How and Why of Neighbourhood Community Development* Community Matters, London

Freire, P (1996) *Pedagogy of the Oppressed* Penguin, London (originally 1970)

Gosschalk, B and Hatter, W (1996) 'No sense of place? Changing patterns of local identity', in *The Return of the Local*, Demos Quarterly Issue 9

Gramsci, A (1971) *Selections From the Prison Notebooks* Lawrence & Wishart, London

Gray, J (1997) 'Do we really want more US decadence?', in *The Guardian*, 27.1.97

Hall, S (1995) 'Culture, Community and Nation', in *Identity, Authority and Democracy* University of Sussex Culcom Research Papers, Vol 1

Hall, S, Lumley, B and McLennan G (1988) 'Politics and ideology: Gramsci', in *On Ideology* Centre for Contemporary Cultural Studies, University of Birmingham, Hutchinson

Hart, L (1994) *Creating Involvement. A Handbook of Tools and Techniques for Effective Community Involvement* LGMB, London

Hastings, A, McArthur, A, and McGregor, A (1996) *Less than Equal? Community Organisations and Estate Regeneration* Policy Press/Joseph Rowntree Foundation; Bristol/York

HMSO (1994a) *Sustainable Development. The UK Strategy* HMSO, London

HMSO (1994b) *Biodiversity. The UK Action Plan* HMSO, London

Holmes, C (1997) 'Faded tapestry', in *The Guardian* 12.2.97

Illich, I (1973) *Celebration of Awareness* Penguin, London

Jacobs, M (1996) *Politics of the Real World* Earthscan, London

Jacobs, M (1995) *Sustainability and Socialism* SERA (Socialist Environmental Resource Association), London

MacFarlane, R (1993) *Community Involvement in City Challenge. A Good Practice Guide* National Council for Voluntary Organisations, London

Macnaghten, P, Grove-White, R, Jacobs, M and Wynne, B (1995) *Public Perceptions and Sustainability in Lancashire. Indicators, Institutions and Participation* Lancaster University for Lancashire County Council

McConnell, C (ed) (1993) 'Community Development and Urban Regeneration' Special issue of *Community Development Journal*, Vol 28, No 4, October

Meekosha, H (1993) 'The bodies politic – equality, difference and community practice', in *Community and Public Policy*, Butcher, H, Glen, A, Henderson, P and Smith, J (eds), Pluto Press, London

Mega, V (1996) 'Highlights from the Foundation's works on urban environments', in *What Future for Urban Environments in Europe?* European Foundation for the Improvement of Living and Working Conditions, Dublin

Mulgan, G and 6, P (1996) 'The local's coming home: decentralisation by degrees', in *The Return of the Local*, Demos Quarterly Issue 9

Oakley, P (1991) *Projects with People. The Practice of Participation in Rural Development* International Labour Organisation (ILO), through IT Publications, London

O'Riordan, T (1981) *Environmentalism* Pion, London

Pahl, R (1995) 'Friendly society', in *New Statesman and Society*, 10.3.95

Phillips, M (1995a) 'The race to awaken sleeping duty', in *The Observer*, 2.4.95

Phillips, M (1995b) 'Time's up for the welfare state', in *The Observer*, 14.5.95

Phillips, M (1995c) 'Crocodile tears over crated calves', in *The Observer*, 12.2.95

Putnam, R D (1993) *Making Democracy Work Civic Traditions in Modern Italy* Princeton University Press, USA

Rahman, M A (1995) 'Participatory development: Towards liberation or co-optation', in *Community Empowerment* Craig, G and Mayo, M (eds) Zed Books, London

Roome, N (1993) 'Green perspectives in community and public policy', in *Community and Public Policy*, Butcher, H, Glen, A, Henderson, P and Smith, J (eds), Pluto Press, London

Scott, A (1992) 'Political culture and social movements', in *Political and Economic Forms of Modernity*, Allen, J, Braham, P and Lewis, P (eds) Polity Press with Open University, London

Scott, I, Denman, J and Lane, B (1989) *Doing by Learning. A Handbook for Organisers and Tutors of Village-Based Community Development Courses* ACRE, Cirencester

Scottish Community Development Centre (1996) *Policy for Practice* SCDC Seminar Series (1995)–96, Community Development Foundation, Edinburgh

Stock, F (1996) 'Time to hate thy neighbour as thyself', in *The Guardian* 26.11.96

Taylor, M (1992) *Signposts to Community Development* Community Development Foundation, London

Vidal, J (1995) 'The real earth movers', in *The Guardian* 19.3.95

Walker, M (1995) 'Community spirit', in *The Guardian* 13.3.95

Warburton, D, Mount, D and Roome, N (1988) *Making Community Action Work in the Environment* Losehill Hall, Derbyshire

Wates, N and Knevitt, C (1987) *Community Architecture. How People are Creating their own Environment* Penguin, London

Whitehead, A and Smyth, J (1996) 'Creating social capital', in *The Return of the Local*, Demos Quarterly Issue 9

WCED (World Commission on Environment and Development) (1987) *Our Common Future* Oxford University Press, Oxford

Wilcox, D (1994) *Guide to Effective Participation* Partnership Books, Brighton

Williams, R (1988) *Keywords* Fontana, London (originally published 1976)

Worpole, K and Greenhalgh, L (1996) *The Freedom of the City* Demos, London

Yeo, E and Yeo, S (1988) 'On the uses of community: From Owenism to the present' in *New Views of Co-operation* Routledge, London

Willmott, P (1989) *Community Initiatives. Patterns and Prospects* Policy Studies Institute, London

2

A Communitarian Perspective on Sustainable Communities

Amitai Etzioni

Until recently, the environmental and the communitarian movements have mostly progressed along parallel lines. The environmental movement often centred on the physical environment and the communitarian one on the body of society. It is important to note in this context, that the society is not a 'social environment' because society is not external to us but we are part of it and it is us; we are not an aggregate of individuals that constitute externalities to one another but we are interwoven, members in one another.

While there have been numerous environmentalists who showed great concerns and understanding of socio-economic and political factors, and there have been some communitarians who noted the parallel concerns with the common good that animates both movements, the focus has been rather different. When all was said and done, many environmentalists tended to focus on Mother Earth, the atmosphere, the seas (and lakes and rivers), and so on, the well-known lists of priorities. Communitarians mainly concerned themselves with societal building stones: families, schools, neighbourhoods, and the community of communities (the society), on moral and social values and the infrastructure that sustains them.

Recently there has been an increased awareness of the deep connection between the physical and the social dimensions of our shared existence. Reference is made to sustainable communities and not merely sustainable environments. To give but one example: in 1995 the Board of Trustees of the Johnson Foundation decided that 'our long standing interest in the environment should focus for the coming five years on...the development of sustainable communities' (Bray 1996). Sustainable communities are said to include '...not only the physical environment, but the economic, social, political, and human environments as well. Justice, equity, voluntarism, and philanthropy contribute to the sustainability of communities. Strong families, healthy and educated children, a competent workforce, and jobs with decent pay are essential' (ibid). And it is suggested that the indicators of the state of affairs should include not merely pollution levels, ozone depletion, and recycling but also measures concerning crime, poverty, and social justice.

The increased cross-fertilisation between the two movements seems to make good sense, given that both are dedicated to the common good. I turn next to provide an outline of communitarian thinking and then to discuss some of the issues that must be faced if the said cross-fertilisation is to be enhanced. In proceeding, I draw heavily on the *Responsive Communitarian Platform*, a manifesto of the communitarian movement (Communitarian Network 1991).

The Communitarian Platform was drafted in a specific context that deserves to be briefly highlighted because understanding the context will help to point out issues that must be taken into account if one is to draw on this approach in other contexts. The Platform was drafted during 1990 and 1991. It was endorsed by more than 70 American leaders from a wide variety of social and political backgrounds and served as the launching pad for the Communitarian movement. It was translated and adapted into German and UK English (Etzioni 1995).

The formulation of the Platform started in 1989, when I was teaching ethics at the Harvard Business School. I was deeply affected by the preoccupation of most of the students with 'making it' at practically any cost to others and often to self. A study came my way that reported that young Americans feel strongly about their right to be tried before a jury of their peers if they are charged with having committed a crime but, when asked to serve on a jury, they sought to avoid serving. This finding became a symbol that reflected much other evidence of excessive individualism, of a sense of entitlement to rights but shirking of social responsibilities. (The environmental equivalent may be those who wish to consume the earth's resources but not to contribute to its sustainability.) We hence argued that 'strong rights presume strong responsibilities' – note that the argument is not against rights but for assuming corollary responsibilities.

The context was American. Other societies differ from this viewpoint. As I see it, the UK and several continental societies have been drifting in the same direction but because they started from a higher level of social responsibilities, they have not become as individualistically obsessed as Americans. Asian societies, on the other hand, seem to be excessively duty bound and may well need a heavy dosage of individualism, especially recognition of rights. Moreover, under the influence of several factors, including the communitarian movement, the American society has become somewhat less individualistic since 1990. There is now a wide agreement, across most of the political spectrum, that individuals have to assume more personal and social responsibility: *Time* magazine reported in its September 9, 1996 issue that Clinton, Gore and Kemp all support the communitarian agenda; the Family Leave Act has been enacted; the character education movement has moved along significantly[1] and communities' role in providing social services has increased, to take just a few examples. The Communitarian Platform still applies, but a tad less so as part of its agenda has now been served.

The second issue the Platform addresses is the moral infrastructure. The basic assumption, spelled out in *The Spirit of Community* (Etzioni 1993), is that for societies to sustain a commitment to the common good – whether it is social, moral, environmental, or the very sustainability of the community – this concern needs to be undergirded with a set of social institutions. If

---

1 The 'character education movement' believes that public schools have tried too hard to advance a 'values-neutral' curriculum; not only is a 'values neutral' curriculum impossible, but moreover harmful when values are learned on the street rather than in the schools. The character education movement aims to reintroduce into the public school curriculum the education of basic, core values which build character: values such as self-discipline, truth-telling, and empathy.

these deteriorate they need either to be shored up or replaced, but one cannot simply do without them. They are to the body society what air, water, and nourishment are to the human body. It is here that the debate about the need for, nature of, and future of the family enters. It is the place historical commitment to the common good was first introduced to the new members of society. Schools were the second building stone for the last 1,000 years or so. And the conceptions of the role of the whole community as a social fabric 'it takes a whole village...', the third, and a view of society as a community of communities (rather than an aggregation of individuals), was the cap stone.

The Platform points out that to sustain a society one must:

> '...recognise both individual human dignity and the social dimension of human existence. A communitarian perspective recognises that the preservation of individual liberty depends on the active maintenance of the institutions of civil society where citizens learn respect for others as well as self-respect; where we acquire a lively sense of our personal and civic responsibilities, along with an appreciation of our own rights and the rights of others; where we develop the skills of self-government as well as the habit of governing ourselves, and learn to serve others – not just self.

> A communitarian perspective recognises that communities and polities, too, have obligations, including the duty to be responsive to their members and to foster participation and deliberation in social and political life'.
> (Communitarian Network, 1991)

The Platform stresses that the way to keep the balance between freedom and social order, the right to choose and commitments to the common – an essential balance if a community is to be sustained – is not to rely firstly on the state or merely on individual efforts: but we need to draw on the moral voice of the community, a factor often overlooked or shied away from. It never ceases to surprise me how many good people are willing to fine or jail those who violate the social good (say dump toxic waste into a river) but not shame them, for instance by publishing their name in the paper and on bill boards. The Platform says about this point:

> 'America's diverse communities of memory and mutual aid are rich resources of moral voices, voices that ought to be heeded in a society that increasingly threatens to become normless, self-centred, and driven by greed, special interests, and an unabashed quest for power.
>
> Moral voices achieve their effect mainly through education and persuasion, rather than through coercion. Originating in communities, and sometimes embodied in law, they exhort, admonish, and appeal to what Lincoln called the better angels of our nature. They speak to our capacity for reasoned judgement and virtuous action. It is precisely because this moral realm, which is neither one of random individual choice nor of government control, has been much neglected that we see an urgent need for a communitarian social movement to accord these voices their essential place'.

The Platform anticipated a common criticism made in reference to the moral voice of communities and responded:

> 'Communitarians are not majoritarians. The success of the democratic experiment in ordered liberty (rather than unlimited license) depends, not on fiat or force, but on building shared values, habits and practices that assure respect for one another's rights and regular fulfilment of personal, civic and collective responsibilities. Successful policies are accepted because they are recognised to be legitimate rather than imposed. We say to those who would impose civic or moral virtues by suppressing dissent (in the name of religion, patriotism, or any other cause), or censoring books, that their cure is ineffective, harmful, and morally untenable. At the same time divergent moral positions need not lead to cacophony. Out of genuine dialogue clear voices can arise, and shared aspirations can be identified and advanced.

Communitarians favour strong democracy. That is, we seek to make government more representative, more participatory, and more responsive to all members of the community. We seek to find ways to accord citizens more information, and more say, more often. We seek to curb the role of private money, special interests, and corruption in government. Similarly, we ask how 'private governments', whether corporations, labour unions, or voluntary associations, can become more responsive to their members and to the needs of the community'.

Maybe the point most often overlooked when communities are discussed is that they are not necessarily good or public-minded. One should not champion communities *per se* or hold that any set of group-values is *ipso facto* good merely because such values originate in a community. Indeed, some communities (say, neo-Nazis) may foster reprehensible norms. And all too often, communities glorify their own members and vilify those who are not members. Communitarians should, although they not always do, insist that communal values be judged by external and overriding criteria. How to establish these is a challenge I cannot deal with in the confines of this article (see Etzioni 1996, Chapter 8).

Probably the biggest controversies have resulted from the communitarian view as to what constitutes the specific infrastructure of communities. The Platform urges that:

'The best place to start is where each new generation acquires its moral anchoring; at home, in the family. We must insist once again that bringing children into the world entails a moral responsibility to provide, not only material necessities, but also moral education and character formation.

Moral education is not a task that can be delegated to baby-sitters, or even professional childcare centres. It requires close bonding of the kind that typically is formed only with parents, if it is formed at all'.

At this juncture the Platform makes a point of utmost importance for the coming together of traditional environmental thinking and communitarian thinking. It speaks in favour of setting non-consumeristic priorities for those who have the resources they need for basic creature comforts, in effect for voluntary simplicity. While the argument is made in the name of children rather than Mother Earth, in effect both approaches concern our future and that of future generations.

The Platform states:

> 'Fathers and mothers, consumed by 'making it' and consumerism, or preoccupied with personal advancement, who come home too late and too tired to attend to the needs of their children, cannot discharge their most elementary duty to their children and their fellow citizens.
>
> It follows, that work places should provide maximum flexible opportunities to parents to preserve an important part of their time and energy, of their life, to attend to their educational, moral duties, for the sake of the next generation, its civic and moral character, and its capacity to contribute economically and socially to the commonweal. Experiments such as those with unpaid and paid parental leave, flexitime, shared jobs, opportunities to work at home, and for parents to participate as volunteers and managers in childcare centres, should be extended and encouraged.
>
> Above all, what we need is a change in orientation by both parents and work places. Child-raising is important, valuable work, work that must be honoured rather than denigrated by both parents and the community'.

The discussion of schools, as the second element of the communitarian infrastructure, is more 'American' because European schools are still much more attentive to character building and transmission of values than American ones. It should, though, be noted that schools in general have an important role in sustaining communities even when families function perfectly. It is also the place many children get their first introduction to environmentalism and communitarian thinking and commitments.

In the US, suggestions that schools participate actively in moral education are often opposed, and the question is posed: 'Whose morals are you going to teach?' The Platform reasoned:

> 'We ought to teach those values all share, for example, that the dignity of all persons ought to be respected; that tolerance is a virtue and discrimination abhorrent; that peaceful resolution of conflicts is superior to violence; that generally truth-telling is morally superior to lying; that democratic government is morally superior to totalitarianism and authoritarianism; that one ought to give a day's work for a day's pay, and get a fair day's pay for a fair day's work; that investing in one's own, and one's country's, future is better than squandering one's income and relying on others to attend to future needs'.

The importance of sustainable communities clearly needs to be added to this list.

The fear that our children will be 'brainwashed' by a few educators is far-fetched. On the contrary, to silence the schools in moral matters simply means that the youngsters are left exposed to all other voices and values but those of their educators. For, one way or another, moral education does take place in schools. The only question is whether schools and teachers will passively stand by, or take an active and responsible role.

Turning to the third building stone, communitarians note that a person who is completely private is lost to civic life. The exclusive pursuit of one's self-interest is not even a good prescription for conduct in the marketplace; for no social, political, economic, or moral order can survive that way. Some measure of caring, sharing, and being attentive to others and the community, is essential for society to thrive.

Here, the Platform evoked a principle which today is often referred to as devolution:

> *'Generally, no social task should be assigned to an institution that is larger than necessary to do the job. What can be done by families, should not be assigned to an intermediate group, school, etc. What can be done at the local level should not be passed on to the state or federal level, and so on. There are, of course, plenty of urgent tasks (including environmental ones) that do require national and even international action. But to remove tasks to higher levels than is necessary weakens the constituent communities. This principle holds for duties of attending to the sick, troubled, delinquent, homeless and new immigrants; and for public safety, public health and protection of the environment—from a neighbourhood crime-watch to community-wide emergency resuscitation training, to sorting the garbage to enhance recycling. The government should step in only to the extent that other social subsystems fail, rather than seek to replace them'.*

One may readily question the merit of the last point, and see a larger and earlier role for the government, and still accept the importance of the community as a key partner.

Communitarians have much work to do when it comes to the question of the connection between equality and the sustainability of communities. It is too easy to declare that equality is essential or should be achieved. One must clarify what one means by equality: economic only? Also social? Does one mean that everyone will get the same share of everything, which even kibbutzim in their heyday could not achieve? If not, what degrees and kinds of inequality is one willing to condone? And does all equality advance sustainability?

The Platform left most of these questions open for future deliberations stating:

> *'At the heart of the communitarian understanding of social justice is the idea of reciprocity: each member of the community owes something to all the rest, and the community owes something to each of its members. Justice requires responsible individuals in a responsive community.*

Members of the community have a responsibility, to the greatest extent possible, to provide for themselves and their families: honourable work contributes to the common-wealth and to the community's ability to fulfil its essential tasks. Beyond self-support, individuals have a responsibility for the material and moral well-being of others. This does not mean heroic self-sacrifice; it means the constant self-awareness that no one of us is an island unaffected by the fate of others'.

For its part, the community is responsible for protecting each of us against catastrophe, natural or man-made; for ensuring the basic needs of all who genuinely cannot provide for themselves; for appropriately recognising the distinctive contributions of individuals to the community; and for safeguarding a zone within which individuals may define their own lives through free exchange and choice.

Communitarian social justice is alive both to the equal moral dignity of all individuals and to the ways in which they differentiate themselves from one another through their personal decisions.

'At the same time, vulnerable communities should be able to draw on the more endowed communities when they are truly unable to deal, on their own, with social duties thrust upon them.

Many social goals, moreover, require partnership between public and private groups. Though government should not seek to replace local communities, it may need to empower them by strategies of support, including revenue-sharing and technical assistance. There is a great need for study and experimentation with creative use of the structures of civil society, and public-private cooperation, especially where the delivery of health, educational and social services are concerned'.

Turning to the society at large, the cap stone, it is easy to start with the polity. Being informed about public affairs is a prerequisite for keeping the community from being controlled by demagogues, for taking action when needed in one's own interests and that of others, for achieving justice and a sustainable future.

Voting is one tool for keeping the polity reflective of its constituent communities. Those who feel that none of the candidates reflect their views ought to seek out other like-minded citizens and seek to field their own candidate rather than retreat from the polity. Still, some persons may discharge their community responsibilities by being involved in non-political activities, say in volunteer work. Just as the polity is but one facet of interdependent social life, so voting and political activity are not the only ways to be responsible members of society. A good citizen is involved in a community or communities, but not necessarily active in the polity.

If the environmental and the communitarian movements are to learn more from one another, idealism will have to be mitigated with a sense of political, social, and economic realities; of priorities and strategies. There is reason to envision a world in which people and nature will learn to live in easy harmony, and the society will be just, peaceful, and beautiful. Such visions inspire and guide our endeavours. They can also lead to gross disappointments, if we seek to jump so high and make so little progress (or even fall back) in our attempts to reach for the brass ring, if not the moon. Specifically, stringing one virtuous goal next to another, compiling lists of indicators that measure reality against a perfect model, may not be the only or even always the best way to proceed.

One question that needs to be addressed, an issue which both movements struggle with daily, is what can be achieved in the near future? Given our limited capabilities, how are they best focused? Answering this question requires a major analytical exercise, as well as a moral dialogue to ensure that the normative implications of such priority-setting are both explicated and shared. And one must answer the question: How can the natural compatibility of the environmentalists and communitarian endeavours be drawn upon to enhance the sustainability of the earth and its communities?

The essay draws on *The New Golden Rule: Community and Morality in a Democratic Society*. Basic Books, New York 1996.

References

Bray, C W (1996) 'Fostering sustainable communities' in *Wingspread Journal* 18:2 (Spring 1996) p3

Communitarian Network (1991) 'The Responsive Communitarian Platform: rights and responsibilities', in *The Responsive Community*, 2:1 (Winter (1991)[2]

Etzioni, A (1993) *The Spirit of Community* Simon and Schuster, New York

Etzioni, A (1996) *The New Golden Rule: Community and Morality in a Democratic Society* Basic Books, New York, USA

Etzioni, A (1995) *The Spirit of Community* Fontana Press, London 1995 Also, 'Dei Stimme der Gemeinschaft horbar machen: 'Ein Manifest amerikanischer Kommunitarier: uber Rechte und Verantwortung in der Gellschaft', in *Frankfurter Allgemeine Zeitung*, Dienstag, 8 Marz 1994, Nr 56/Seite 37

---

2 The Platform is available by calling or writing to The Communitarian Network, 2130 H Street, NW Suite 714J, Washington DC 230052, 1–800–245–7460. The entire text can also be found on the world-wide-web at http://www.gwu.edu/-ccps

3

Accountability in Community Contributions to Sustainable Development

Murray Stewart with Philippa Collett

A key feature of the whole sustainable development debate – and the central theme of this volume of essays – is the espoused commitment to community involvement in the development process. Agenda 21 is predicated on a community-based approach to local action which safeguards the natural and built environment. This is reflected in other national and international initiatives. The Healthy Cities initiative emphasises community-based programmes supporting personal and public wellbeing through local education and life styles change. Safer Cities policy relies on local actions which enhance community safety and protection. Local economic development practice increasingly recognises the importance of supporting local business and of creating long term jobs for local people. Housing policy has increasingly acknowledged the role of local management and devolved ownership and control.

In this apparent reassertion of the importance of a community input, and in the face of considerable cynicism about the commitment to it of both central and local government, it is essential that the values which underlie the community contribution are made explicit and adhered to. Community legitimacy derives only from the extent to which community organisations sustain the functions of articulating and pursuing community goals.

Accountability is therefore crucial, and it is with accountability that this chapter is concerned.

A central characteristic of current community involvement is its institutionalisation in formal programmes of physical renewal of neighbourhoods and estates, of economic and social regeneration, and of environmental protection and management. The new watchwords of this espoused community approach are empowerment and partnership, both highly ambiguous in terms of definition and application.

Empowerment ranges from a tokenistic and almost therapeutic manipulation on the bottom steps of Arnstein's famous ladder (Arnstein 1969) to a more positive empowerment of individuals and communities where control of resources and decisions passes to local interests. Empowerment involves resisting the isolation of individuals and reducing their dependency as service users, but it also means reducing the marginalisation of communities by enhancing their role in radically new structures of area governance (Stewart and Taylor 1995).

Partnership conceals a variety of collaborative relationships as varied and sometimes competing interests assemble consensual alliances and coalitions. Partnership is increasingly a required condition of access to European or national funding and the establishment of a partnership is the prerequisite for entry to the ever more competitive world of local place marketing. If urban and rural regeneration and the revalorisation of run down estates provide the exemplars of the partnership approach, the creation of Agenda 21 alliances follow the same model. But within the new partnerships the 'rules of engagement' between partners are often only implied and seldom written down.

The 'community' is a key stakeholder in these new multi-organisational structures. There is community representation on partnership boards, committees, and forums, and community involvement is a key feature of the new processes of coalition and strategy-building at local level. There is thus the potential for a considerable shift of power in the new structures of area governance as communities are invited to become players in a bigger game, but equally this potential for empowerment is offset by problems and indeed dangers for the community. Representation on a partnership committee is fraught with difficulties and is vulnerable to manipulation; the skills of bargaining, negotiation, and coalition-building are more complex than those of complaining or demanding; participation in partnerships is hard work for community representatives; the language and discourse of the new coalitions can confuse and obfuscate.

Indeed, in one survey of the new arrangements for joint working it is suggested that over three-quarters of those interviewed felt the public had only a limited influence on joint working – and indeed half of these (38 per cent) thought there was no influence at all (Hambleton et al 1995). Others have pointed to the difficulties of community organisations in City Challenge (Macfarlane 1993) whilst the first experience of community involvement in the Single Regeneration Budget process highlights the absence of community from partnership leadership (Mawson et al 1996).

For all these reasons, the new politics and structures of partnership can offer both significant empowerment to local communities but can also carry the threat of marginalisation in an even larger arena than hitherto. They increase the risk of exposing and exacerbating divisions within the community. Insofar as partnership demands consensus, traditional community activism may be seen as the unacceptable rocking of the boat.

In this new context of multisectoral initiatives, and with special reference to accountability in sustainable development, this chapter illustrates three main themes. First there is the continuing, indeed growing, need for accountability within the community sector. Participation in, and empowerment through, new structures carries responsibilities as well as benefits, and it is essential that these responsibilities are seen to be exercised on behalf of the interests of local people.

There is a danger, however, that community organisations are stereotyped as being somehow less accountable in terms of representation, financial management or service delivery than the more established organisations of local governance. The second theme therefore is that of highlighting the demands which new forms of working make for the accountability of formal organisations. Local authorities must rethink (as many are doing) the ways in which new forms of accountability must supplement the traditional, if infrequent, accountability of the ballot box, whilst the many other agencies and organisations involved in local development must reflect on the extent to which they offer any public accountability at all.

Lastly, there is the need to examine how accountability can work in the new multi-organisational structures. Joint action and co-funding cloud the responsibilities and obligations of participant organisations in partnership and traditional expressions of accountability become opaque. Accountability to the partnership machinery becomes confused with accountability to the 'original' local government, private sector or community interest represented in the partnership structures. Representative responsibilities become confused with executive roles in new, often informal organisational forms.

In the remainder of this chapter, differing definitions of the term accountability are rehearsed. Thereafter there is discussion of the significance of such definitions within the sustainable development debate. Lastly, we draw some conclusions about the application of accountability principles within joint or partner structures.

Concepts of Accountability

One hallmark of the past Conservative government was the dominance of an ideology which recognises the market as the most effective mode of resource allocation. Traditional forms of service planning and provision have been radically shifted. No longer is need identified through bureaucratised rules of eligibility, provision dominated by unionised labour, performance assessed in terms of inputs rather than outcomes, users treated as clients rather than as customers. For local communities this has been a mixed blessing.

Users have a greater say in service planning and delivery, the imposition of professionally determined standards has been challenged, the monolithic town hall has been decentralised, the public are treated as important. These all represent community gains, but there is a down side. The new public management promotes managerial accountability, whilst the fragmentation of agencies together with the separation of purchaser from provider splits the politics of service planning from the technicalities of provision. There are important implications for the accountability of the local councillor (Walsh 1995).

In general terms the purchaser-provider split has been symptomatic of a wider dilution of local authority autonomy. The diminishing nature of public accountability in recent years has been highlighted by the emergence of the quango state in general and of the local quango state in particular (Stewart, Greer and Hoggett 1995). The basis of appointment to non-elected bodies, the lack of accessibility of the public to information about procedures and outcomes, the absence of routes of complaint or redress, and the inability to remove those responsible for decisions have all drawn criticism. The appointment by central government (as opposed to direct election) of board members, directors and governors of local organisations begins to create if not a new elite, at least a 'new magistracy' (Morris 1990). It has been estimated that the new extra-governmental organisations (EGOs) involve 70,000 appointed and self appointing positions, of which 70 per cent are at local level (Weir and Hall 1994). The 50,000 new local 'magistrates' are more than double the number of local councillors (Stewart, Greer and Hoggett 1995).

The accountability of local decision-makers to democratic control through election, however, represents only one route through which accountability can be demanded or proffered. There are many situations in which local accountability may be expected. These occur wherever decisions are required which involve the legitimate interpretations of national policy, where local priorities have to be set for the allocation of resources at local level, or where standards of provision of public services can vary according to local discretion. There is, in addition, the distinction to be made between decisions which reflect contested social or political values and those which rely more clearly upon technical considerations. Although both must be subject to proper accountability, the latter may in some instances be less controversial and hence sheltered from public scrutiny. But the distinction between political and technical is a fine and dangerous one, to which experience with choices in health, education and increasingly the environment bear witness.

There are thus multiple structures of accountability. In considering the relationship between sustainability, community and accountability it is appropriate to recognise this variety and complexity:

- *Professional* accountability is inculcated through professional education and experience, reinforced by restricted entry to employment, policed by the profession itself and/or by professional inspectors, and enforced by peer group codes of conduct.
- *Financial* accountability is determined by accounting and audit practice (also a professional activity), exercised through checking financial behaviour or by reference to proper use of funds. Financial probity is usually subject to external investigation, in the case of public bodies through the Audit Commission, the National Audit Office, and ultimately Parliament.
- *Legal* accountability embodies the obligation to behave within the law and to be brought to account in the courts if the law is broken. A characteristic of recent years has been the more frequent recourse to the law in relation to 'illegal' public administration.
- *Procedural* and/or administrative accountability is evident in the extent to which organisational processes conform to statute or to the rules and precedent of natural justice. Judicial review of process and/or recourse to the ombudsman represent new forms of legal redress.
- *Managerial* accountability is defined in terms of the performance of those who allocate resources or manage services in terms of the achievement of targets and conformance with the internal managerial objectives of the organisation.

These forms of accountability are in general generated from the perspective of the provider. Though designed to offer accountability to the public their thrust is towards the technical, professional, managerial and administrative processes of service planning and delivery, and to the legal and financial environments within which activity must be undertaken. They contrast with other forms of accountability which can be characterised as being more closely oriented to non-provider interests. Four forms of this latter accountability are immediately evident.

1) *Market* accountability deriving from the centrality of the market as the arbiter of allocation of resources, and operationalised through price, competition, and freedom of information. Accountability to consumers (the accountability which has challenged democratic accountability in the last fifteen years) is often reinforced by consumer charter mechanisms and market regulation.
2) *User* accountability is exercised through the ability of users of services (increasingly termed clients or customers) to demand provision of services and/or to determine the volume and nature of such services, through the increased obligation on service providers to provide information about service standards, and through the right to complain and/or seek redress.
3) *Political* accountability is exercised through the democratic electoral processes which underpin representative democracy as well as by the political structures which seek to ensure adherence to political position and loyalty to party, and through the enforcement and disciplinary procedures of whipping and party groups.
4) Finally there is a *temporal* accountability of generation to generation. In often non-specific and non-enforceable ways the present generation is accountable both retrospectively to past generations and prospectively to the future.

Accountability in Sustainable Development

In established areas of public interest – education, health, policing and so on – there exists in respect of each of these strands of accountability a set of conventions which are reflected in the actual practice of making and receiving 'accounts'. As argued above, the values which underpin the relationship between state and civil society in recent years have altered, and continue to alter, the relative importance of the different strands. Moreover the application of concepts of accountability to sustainable development is problematic.

Sustainable development remains ambiguous, inexact, ill-defined, unbounded, and unmeasurable. Hence the identification of professional or technical standards against which achievements may be judged is difficult, whilst the absence of appropriate rules or precedents has up till now made the application of legal or procedural accountability harder. The value laden and often contentious nature of sustainability as a political objective renders political accountability hard to identify. Furthermore the multiplicity of organisations and agencies involved in sustainable development, together with the absence of clearly defined organisational responsibilities, makes the application of appropriate forms of accountability more difficult.

Given the complexity and ambiguity of the whole debate about accountability, and its peculiarly opaque nature when applied to sustainable development, a window of opportunity is open through which the negotiation of appropriate new forms of accountability can be developed. Given also the widely acknowledged expression of commitment to community empowerment in sustainable development, those negotiations can, in principle at least, be conducted on the basis that the aim is to enhance community-based values in the accountability process.

It is clear that sustainable development offers immediate scope for shifting the basis of some interpretations of accountability. Most obviously, it is the sustainability debate which has highlighted the whole question of temporal accountability (the obligations to future generations as well as the present) and which in practical terms has demanded reassessment of a number of technical issues (the rate of discount in investment appraisal for example).

It is also clear that the nature of professional accountability is altering and in particular that the claims which the traditional professions have made about their monopoly of knowledge have been successfully challenged. A number of these challenges have come from local communities. They have refused to accept the established wisdom of how neighbourhoods can or should be managed and – sometimes with technical professional support which is subservient to community priorities – have demanded changes in the way in which services are delivered. Local preferences – for community safety, environmental improvement, traffic management – can challenge the conventional wisdom of professionals.

The scope for these challenges is greater in the field of sustainable development because there are few established conventions which would determine precisely what good accountable professional practice actually is. Sustainable development is often led from planning or environmental health departments, with a new emergent 'profession' of environmental coordinators beginning to draw together Agenda 21 activity. If indeed such a new profession is beginning to emerge, there is every reason why local communities should impose upon it new professional values and demand a different style of professional accountability – locally present in the community, responsive to local needs, listening rather than 'professing', supporting rather than imposing.

There is also scope for communities to influence even financial accountability. The Audit Commission (1996) has suggested that the total value of expenditure in England in those activities to be covered by its new 'environmental stewardship' audits amounts to £3.6 billion of which over £1 billion is local authority expenditure. The environmental audits, incorporating publicly available indicators will offer a useful new route for community interrogation of public services.

There are close links between professional, financial and managerial accountabilities in relation to the development and use of sustainability indicators. The Local Government Management Board has supported a project examining the scope for appropriate indicators and this work illustrates the scope for community involvement in what some might have seen as a largely technical issue. Fife Regional Council (and now the new Fife unitary authority) used the sustainability indicators exercise as the opportunity to test the potential for developing locally specific indicators for differing localities within the authority. Widespread community consultation in three localities is leading to an indicators system which aims to provide local communities with indicators suited to local needs and chosen by local people (Rowan 1995).

Agenda 21 provides the ideal opportunity for the generation by the community of local profiles, local diagnosis of issues and problems, local solutions and locally relevant indicators of achievement. A community specific approach to sustainability can be generated in other ways. In Bristol and South Gloucestershire the Bristol Recycling Consortium has initiated a scheme under which five local communities in differing socio-economic areas develop locally specific approaches to waste reduction. Local surveys and local forums support this initiative and GIS methods are being used experimentally to assess the variations between areas. The interesting feature of this initiative is the intention to provide community-specific information about progress and success in terms of waste reduction targets. The community-based approach has a number of benefits.

Some of the information gathering processes are developed from within the community itself (eg surveys of the practice of local shops in waste reduction), whilst surveys and follow up leafleting have been carried out by local groups. The feedback of locally generated information supports decision-making by community groups which become better able to suit and reflect local conditions and local preferences. Such information may act as an incentive to communities to raise their rates of waste reduction in competition with other areas, but more importantly represents the provision to local people of a measure of local achievement of sustainability objectives.

Much of the criticism of past efforts at community involvement focus on the failure of large organisations to demystify the processes of consultation. Too often the language of community involvement is incomprehensible to normal people, procedures bureaucratic, the location unfriendly and the agenda imposed. The experience of community involvement in waste management planning in Hampshire (Petts 1995) illustrates both the potential and the pitfalls inherent in community participation.

There are of course instances when the processes of community consultation run counter to the law, and in such instances there is redress to legal accountability – the challenge to authority through the courts, through judicial review, or through use of the ombudsman where the offence is more one of procedural rather than legalistic injustice. More often, however, there is the simple failure to treat local people as though they were equals in the process. Too often also initiatives in community involvement start off with genuine commitment and high hopes only to descend into routine and formalised meetings. The experience of the four major Urban Partnerships in Scotland (Stewart et al 1996) illustrate the difficulties of sustaining participation over a number of years, with the processes of involvement becoming increasingly symbolic rather than real. The second Standards in Public Life report (Nolan Committee 1996) on local public spending bodies highlighted the need for codes of conduct which regulate the relationships between such bodies and the community and other interested parties. Enhancing such procedural accountability is perhaps the most important route through which community empowerment may be achieved, not least because this creates a long term and sustainable basis for relations between the community and other bodies. Much of the 1980s was taken up with the management of short life organisations and initiatives which had little motivation for the establishment of lasting rapport with communities. Building stable and accountable structures for the long-term sits uneasily with the preparation of exit strategies, and discussion of closure and/or succession.

There are therefore a number of routes through which improvements in accountability might be pursued in order to enhance the role of the community in sustainable development. Contemporary policy offers greater consumer power and account-ability through market structures and through the systems of regulation and consumer protection which surround the quasi-markets of the new public management. But market accountability is limited not simply because many environmental services are public goods but also because disparities in income inhibit the exercise of choice through markets. There have, however, been widespread improvements in the rights of users to seek informa-tion about and to demand better or quicker services. Dominated by shifts in the structure of housing provision and by the emergence of estate management boards and cooperatives as well as by the growth of locally based housing associations, the commu-nity has gained more control over repairs, improvements, lighting and safety. There is widespread involvement of users in the redesign of neighbourhoods. Health and education services have also begun a slow shift towards a more local orientation. The fragile community business movement offers some local accountability; the Department of Employment has opened job centres in porta-cabins on construction estates to assist local labour recruitment. Only the poverty services (welfare benefits) appear to remain impervious to local control.

Political accountability remains, however, the main focus for debate with the key issue being the relative merits of representative versus participative democracy. It is in relation to political accountability that there re-emerge the three themes identified at the outset of this chapter – accountability within the community, accountability to the community and accountability in multi-organisational structures.

Participative democracy by definition raises fewer questions about accountability. As more are joiners, the need for secondary routes which legitimate action through recourse to the approval (retrospective or prospective) of 'representatives' recedes. Structures which permit universal participation (the parish meeting for example) allow access to all who wish to require political accountability. But not everyone wants to be involved in planning and running services and a more passive loyalty remains an option for many residents in addition to voice and exit (Hirschman 1970). Where representative community organisations exist there are inevitably accusations about unrepresentativeness, usually from those who for whatever reason find accommodating the wishes of the community difficult. As communities become better resourced, more articulate, and more influential, and as the multitude of community interests and organisations in a neighbourhood become funnelled through multisector partnership initiatives, so the need for accountability within the community becomes more important.

The experience of recent years is of the need to make much more explicit and transparent the arrangements for community representation (and in particular the growing number of umbrella bodies). Thus there need to be clear processes for electing or appointing representatives, to enforce openness in information gathering and recording, to develop codes of conduct, and to establish the methods of whistle-blowing should malpractice appear. These are all, of course, the elements of best practice in standards of public life that Nolan recommends for local public spending bodies. They apply equally to the community which should pride itself in giving a lead in expressing the principles not only of sustainability but of open and accountable ways of working.

It would be quite wrong, however, to demand more from the community in terms of its internal accountabilities than is demanded from the larger, and better resourced, formal organisations of local governance. Earlier parts of this chapter have highlighted the challenge to the more technical (professional and managerial) accountabilities embodied in the officer structures of local public bodies, and there a range of ways in which greater accountability to communities can be built into the language, behaviour and culture of organisations. The Local Government Management Board (LGMB) for example (Stewart and Taylor 1993) pointed to the need to develop a professional and managerial ethic which incorporates a community orientation and within which officers should amongst other things:

- avoid reference to administrative or bureaucratic norms as the necessary source of legitimacy;
- enhance one or first stop shopping as the basis for normal practice and develop community presence, responsiveness and accountability in decentralised and devolved working;
- build community experience into criteria for annual staff review, promotion and performance pay.

The main emphasis in developing new forms of accountability to communities rests, however, with elected members. The long-standing resistance of many elected members to community organisations is grounded in the 'I was elected for this ward and I'm the one who knows best what it needs' line. The Hampshire experience again illustrated the concerns of elected members about the legitimacy of the consultative exercise (Petts 1995). Councillors have been under considerable stress in recent years as their traditional responsibilities in service areas such as housing, education and social services have been stripped away. Compulsory competitive tendering also made the role as guardian of service quality more complex as the councillor's role appeared to recede into a crude contract management function. These shifts, however, can enhance the role of at least some members as the link between community and authority develops and there does appear to be scope for enhancing new community-related roles (at both ward and strategic level) as offering real political return. Councillors need to give greater priority to 'external relations', recognising that chairing or sitting on internal service committees should be matched by being 'out there' in accountable representative roles. Power shared can be power enlarged.

New forms of decentralised and hopefully devolved administration are becoming widespread in both traditional two-tier counties and in unitary authorities (old and new). Indeed one of the few gains from the local government review has been that existing authorities were at least temporarily galvanised into recognising the interests of smaller neighbourhoods (and of parish councils as institutions). It is to be hoped that the promises made by larger authorities about new forms of cooperation and delegation will be actively pursued and formally monitored. The responsibility for improved accountability lies firmly therefore with existing public organisations.

Finally, there are complex issues involved in the accountability of the new partnerships, coalitions and alliances which characterise current local politics and into which the community is increasingly drawn. Partnerships involve political, financial, and professional accountabilities, many of which are exercised within a new culture of company status. Directors or partnership board members from the community sector carry individual as well as collective responsibility and there is an acknowledged tension between accountability within a specific partnership (eg as director, trustee or board member) and accountability to the community organisation(s) from which a partner comes. The potential dilution of accountability within joint structures is evident in the post-abolition experience of the metropolitan county areas (Leach et al 1992) and public, private and community 'representatives' are all uneasy about the challenge to accountability which partnership working poses. Nevertheless, whilst new forms of priority-setting and decision-making are emerging, the principles of proper accountability, such as access to information and regular reporting, can be maintained and respected within partnership working.

The institutionalisation of sustainable development which is emerging in the structures established for Agenda 21 replicates much of the experience of joint working which is already visible in economic development, in leisure and recreational provision, in the arts and cultural development, and in urban and rural regeneration. It is clear that the success of many of these short life initiatives will be judged not simply by what is achieved in the period of their organisational life but what is left afterwards as longer term local capacity. Sustainability is a value which must be applied, not simply to safeguarding and preserving the environment, but to the institutions of state and civil society. If the objective of partnership in neighbourhood regeneration is to empower communities and recreate a lasting sense of ownership of, and pride in, locality, then enormous effort must be put to ensuring that the local community welcomes and owns the changes now in progress. Enhanced accountability is central to that process.

References

Arnstein, S (1969) 'A ladder of participation in the USA' *Journal of the American Institute of Planners* July Vol 35, pp 216–24

Audit Commission (1996) *Environmental Stewardship*, Audit Commission, London

Gummer, J (1996) *Local Government Reorganisation (England)*. Statement to the House of Commons, Hansard, 2nd March 1996, Col 1183–1185 HMSO, London

Hambleton, R, Essex, S, Mills, L and Razzaqne, K (1995) *The Collaborative Council; A Study of Inter-Agency Working in Practice* Joseph Rowntree Foundation, York

Hirschman, A (1970) *Exit, Voice and Loyalty: Responses to Decline in Firms, Organisations and States* Harvard University Press, Harvard

Leach, S, Davis, H, Game, C and Skelcher, C (1992) *After Abolition: The Operation of Post-1986 Metropolitan Government in England* Institute of Local Government Studies, University of Birmingham

Macfarlane, R (1993) *Community Involvement in City Challenge. A Policy Report* National Council for Voluntary Organisations, London

Mawson, J, Beazley, M, Bentley, G, Burfitt, A, Collinge, C, Hale, S, Lee, P, Loftman, P, Nevin, B, Srbljanin, A (1996) *The Single Regeneration Budget: Stocktake: A Review of Challenge Round II* Centre for Urban and Regional Studies, University of Birmingham

Morris, R (1990) *Central and Local Control of Education after the Education Reform Act* Longmans, Harlow

Nolan Committee (1996) *Local Public Spending Bodies* 2nd Report of the Nolan Committee's Second Report on Standards in Public Life Cm 3270-1 HMSO, London

Petts, J (1995) 'Waste management strategy development: A case study of community involvement and consensus-building in Hampshire' in *Journal of Environmental Planning and Management* Vol 38, No 4

Rowan, L (1995) *Sustainability Indicators for Fife: Study Report* Fife Regional Council

Scottish Office (1996) *Partnership in the Regeneration of Urban Scotland* HMSO, Edinburgh

Stewart, J, Greer, A and Hoggett, P (1995) *The Quango State: An Alternative Approach* Commission for Local Democracy, Research Report 10, CLD, London

Stewart, M and Taylor, M (1993) *Local Government Community Leadership* Local Government Management Board, Luton

Stewart, M and Taylor, M (1995) *Empowerment in Estate Regeneration* Report to the Joseph Rowntree Foundation, The Policy Press, Bristol

Walsh, K (1995) *Public Services and Market Mechanisms: Competition, Contracting, and the new Public Management* Macmillan, Bristol

Weir, S and Hall, W (1994) *EGO TRIP: Extra-Governmental Organisations in the United Kingdom and their Accountability* Democratic Audit, University of Essex and the Charter 88 Trust

4

Getting the Future That You Want: The role of Sustainability Indicators

J Gary Lawrence

Sustainability indicators can be an important tool in helping individuals, institutions, communities and societies make different and better choices about their futures. They are not by themselves 'the answer', but they can lead us to better answers if they provide trustworthy information about those things in life that we value.

Sustainability indicators are supposed to help one understand what is happening to those attributes of the earth which make existence possible and pleasurable. Knowing more is critical to our future. But unless the knowledge compels us to examine our lives and change our own individual and collective unsustainable behaviours, knowing more will not be particularly helpful. In this brief examination of the subject I hope the reader will keep in mind the following:

- In order for indicators to be effective in creating change it is necessary that you first decide upon the future you would prefer; you need to be able to compare what *is* to what *ought to be* so you know if you are headed in the right direction.
- Science needs to be presented in a way that is rationally and emotionally accessible to people – people need to know what it means to them, not to some abstract future.
- Be humble: most of the facts with which you try to encourage change have a lot of subjectivity built into them.

What are Indicators of Sustainability and Are They Important?

The concept is really pretty simple. Indicators of sustainability are intended to answer the question, for a variety of audiences: 'how might we objectively know whether things are getting better or worse?' To answer this question, quantitative and/or qualitative techniques are used to provide the basis upon we can deduce the status of the attributes of our lives, including the direction and rate of changes.

Each of us has an intuitive sense upon which we rely to answer the 'better or worse' question for ourselves, our families and our communities. Through this subjective process we develop a set of beliefs which guide our behaviours. Since the beliefs we develop are not likely to be informed by omniscience, we occasionally, as individuals, institutions and societies, develop beliefs which are inconsistent with what might be concluded from more complete information. Many of those concerned with the ability of our planet to sustain our species believe that one of the principal causes of our self- and planet-destructive behaviour is the reliance upon errant beliefs as guides to action. Indicators are supposed to help us reduce our reliance upon errant beliefs.

Proponents of indicators also assume that sources of more objective information, which we can understand and which we are willing to trust, either exist or can be developed. Indicators are intended to provide the quantitative or qualitative measures from which we can deduce the current state, direction and/or rate of change for attributes of our existence – to provide us with those 'facts'. Once this information is easily accessible to societies, communities and/or individuals, it is reasoned, we will reduce reliance on intuition and increase reliance on more objective information and, therefore, make better, more sustainable decisions.

There are a number of different types of indicators, some of which I will discuss in the next section. But before we get to them, perhaps an examination of some things one ought to consider when developing or using indicators is in order.

Indicators will only be as good as the data that supports them. Yet, even the most objective indicators based in solid science have subjective aspects. The decisions on what to measure, how to measure it, where the measurements will take place, and how to describe the results, all have subjective components. Even more subjective is the choice one makes about which data to include as the basis for developing indicators. Does the lack of perfect objectivity mean that we ought not rely on data or experts? Of course not. Without the gathering of good data we would be lost. It does suggest, however, that those developing indicators need to be deliberate in their choice of sources, accept that reasonable people can disagree, and acknowledge the risks associated with being absolutely certain about anything.

Once you have good data, who gets to decide what the data mean? Often we rely upon our institutions and experts for that. They decide what data to collect, how to organise the data into information, tell us what the data ought to mean to us and then tell us how we ought to change our behaviours in response. The only difficulty with this method is that it doesn't seem to change people's behaviour very much.

For example, public health and air quality experts have been quite good at collecting data on the public health consequences of automobile emissions. They regularly issue reports that describe the situation, present alarming statistics, and tell us that we need to use single occupant automobiles less and less harmful alternatives more. They have translated their data into information that identifies causes and recommends alternative behaviours. In many cases they also develop indicators to measure our progress toward better air quality and reduced congestion. In the meantime, the vehicle miles travelled and trips per household continue to increase in the developed world. Why doesn't our understanding of the consequences lead to behavioural change? In a large part it is because few of us are willing to change our behaviours based upon someone else's determination of meaning.

Successful indicator projects will necessarily involve the community in deciding how to translate the data into information that is accessible to those whose behaviours need to change. Too often the data get translated into information that is accessible only to the people who collected the data in the first place. This results in information that is poorly suited to communication with those who aren't experts.

Once you have data in a form that the community can access, successful indicator projects will invite the community to decide what the information means to them and how they ought to act in response. People are pretty good at figuring out solutions when they feel the problem is theirs to solve. Giving them the opportunity to translate the information into meaning for their own lives will give them 'ownership' of the problem. When the community 'owns' the problem, they are much more likely to act than if they believe that it is someone else's problem to solve.

People should be encouraged to let their emotions be engaged in deciding what the data mean to them. Too many indicators projects are exercises in accounting. Few people get passionate about spreadsheets. For indicators to lead to change there needs to be emotional content: people need to care in their hearts as well as in their minds.

Many scientist friends are no doubt horrified at this apparent abandonment of rationality as the basis for indicators. Fear not, I continue to believe that there are things we can actually know that ought to inform our choices. What I am suggesting is the need for an interface between the science and the individual, something that helps make the information personally meaningful.

The example of a Graphical User Interface in computing is a good example of the point I am trying to make. Most of us are not particularly interested in the millions of lines of code that lie behind the graphics which come up on our screen. We are perfectly happy with icons (symbols) that represent all of the data. Could the icons exist without the code? No. Could you get at the code (data) if you really wanted to? Yes.

Similarly, it is possible to create community icons for indicators that symbolise what the data mean in terms of community values. In Sustainable Seattle's (1992) work for instance, the indicator for water quality is the number of wild salmon that return to the rivers and streams each year. We could have measured turbidity, temperature, percentages of oxygen, chemical composition and/or any number of scientific measures, but people don't get emotional about things like 'parts per billion'. In the Pacific Northwest people do get emotional when their major cultural and economic resources, salmon, are in decline. Since the number of wild salmon is related to the quality of our surface waters, any

solution to the salmon problem will necessarily involve improvements to water. Using our icon example, the icon here represents
not only the fish but all of the externalities which relate to the
habitat.

As you consider indicators, think about what causes people to
have pride in their community and what unique attributes are part
of their identity. Then think about how the data relate to undesir-
able changes in those things which they value. Develop indicators
which link people's hearts and minds and it is likely that the
indicators will be a much more effective tool.

Types of Indicators

There are a number of different types of indicators. Each has its
own strengths and each can be very useful if one knows during
project design the purpose toward which they will be used. I generally categorise indicators into three types – distinct, comparative,
and directional.

DISTINCT INDICATORS

The tables in the United Nations Development Programme's (UNDP)
annual Human Development Report, the Oregon Benchmark's and
governmental statistical reports on population, employment, and so
on are examples of distinct indicators. They measure one thing (eg
unemployment among white males aged 14 to 16 in Yorkshire) and
have no normative content (there is no determination whether the
number is good or bad, it just is). Selecting at random from the 1996
Human Development Report (UNDP 1996), we find that 30.7 per
cent of the total land area of Costa Rica was forest and woodland in
1993 and deforestation in Costa Rica in 1993 equalled an annual
rate of 3.1 per cent, and so on.

In many cases these measurements are indexed so as to make
comparisons across time a little easier. For example, let us say that
a total of 18 cats resided on your street in 1990. If we decided that
1990 was our base year and that 18 cats was the normal number of
cats, we could say that those cats equalled a value of 100 on your

street's Feline Companion Index (FCI). If, in 1995, the FCI were 105, we would know that there were five more cats than is 'normal'.

Distinct indicators are beloved by many governmental institutions, economists and others who are interested in making sure that we have good data which allows for comparison across time. The best of this kind of data allows for investigation beyond knowledge that the number has changed to understanding something of what conditions and forces were behind the change. Often, however, the reader just has the number with which to work.

My favourite example of a distinct indicator comes from Douglas Adams' *Hitchhiker's Guide to the Galaxy*. In one portion of the book the largest computer in the Universe's answer to the question 'What is the meaning of life, the universe and everything?' (the ultimate sustainability index) is '42!' Because the meaning was not in the least bit obvious, it became necessary to build an even larger computer to answer the question 'What does 42 mean?' Many of us look at distinct indicators with the same comprehension as those in the *Hitchhiker's Guide* had for the answer '42'. Most distinct indicators are numerical representations of a condition that do not arouse the layperson to act; that is, they lack the mechanisms which allow individuals to intuitively conclude 'and, therefore, I should do something about this'.

There are many sustainability indicators projects which count things without knowing what counts for the future of the community. In the developed world, we often have more data than we can ever use. What is lacking is not data but resolve. In many parts of the developing world there is a legitimate need to develop distinct indicators projects as the basis for change. But here again, knowing something and deciding to do something about it are two different steps.

COMPARATIVE INDICATORS

One way to start supplying meaning to distinct indicators is to compare them to similar indicators in other places. A good example is *The European Sustainability Index Project* which set out to 'develop indicators which can be measured in cities throughout Europe, thus enabling a comparison of sustainability levels between cities' (Institute for the Urban Environment 1994). The comparison, it is suggested, is a 'valuable leitmotiv for development, analysis, adjustment and improvement of local policies' (ibid). This project compared, among 12 European cities, things like the percentage of registered companies which are involved in recycling, the average usage of water in litres per capita and the average number of trips per annum by means of public transport per inhabitant.

There are at least two advantages and one disadvantage to the development of valid indicators of comparison between governmental bodies. One advantage is that the leaders in any category validate that making progress is plausible. Most public institutions are unwilling to take political and/or financial risk. Knowing that it is achievable increases the likelihood that others will try to achieve the same ends, plus a little bit more. The other advantage is that being last in a quality of life measure carries significant political risks as well. No elected official or bureaucrat has made a successful career out of being 'the worst'. If it can be demonstrated that your community has the worst air quality or the worst water quality or lowest educational attainment, it is very likely that voters will hold local officials accountable for remedying the situation. The rebirth of Chattanooga, Tennessee in the US is directly related to being named 'the most polluted City in America' in the recent past.

The disadvantage with comparisons is that those in the middle often conclude that being in the middle is good enough. It is often politically safest to be average. If your city was 'the best' and someone does better, then you are, in a very public way, getting worse. This is true even if you are maintaining the status quo: you were the best, now you aren't and you have some explaining to do. And, if you aren't the worst, then all you need to do is avoid becoming the worst and most of your constituents will probably think you are doing well enough. Those communities which find themselves to be doing OK will need something more than comparisons to get them going.

DIRECTIONAL INDICATORS

Directional indicators are less focused upon numerical representations and more focused upon action. Some measure progress in relation to specific standards and/or benchmarks. Some measure change in relationship to the state of nature which existed when the indicators were first developed. Each is more concerned with direction than with absolutes. Some good examples of directional indicators are Rescue Mission Planet Earth's *Indicators for Action* (Peace Child International 1994) which were developed as part of Habitat II, and Sustainable Seattle's *Indicators of Community Sustainability* (Sustainable Seattle 1992).

To illustrate the first type – directional with standards – let us return to the Feline Companion Index. Pretend that we have just completed the census of cats for our block. We have just learned that the 1996 FCI is 95. Because of the value system on our street, we have concluded that an FCI of 95 is not just an interesting fact, it is a problem which must be remedied. WE NEED MORE CATS! But, how many more cats will be enough? We previously established that an FCI of 100 is normal. We could develop strategies targeted at returning us to normal.

Given the need for a process to find cats which the indigenous tabbies will not find disagreeable, it will not be possible to get back to normal all at once. A Feline Companion Integration Strategy is called for which establishes benchmarks or interim goals. We could decide that, given all of the other stuff we have to do each month, that we can add no more than two cats per month. Therefore, since we started at an FCI of 95, the benchmark against which we would measure our progress at the end of month one would be an FCI of 97. The benchmark for month two would be an FCI of 99. If we have achieved our established benchmark for the first two months we need to get only one more cat in month three to get back to normal. To let everyone know how we are doing, we develop indicators to measure our progress in implementing the Strategy. In this case, we are measuring action, but against previously agreed upon benchmarks and standards.

In many cases, the distinct indicators end up being used as standards and/or benchmarks in directional indicators projects.

Using the Costa Rican examples above, let's say that the people of
Costa Rica decide that the acceptable standard for the percentage
of land area in forest and woodland is 40 per cent rather than the
30.7 per cent they had in 1993. Further, they have decided that
there should be a 1 per cent increase each year. Their indicators
would measure change toward the annual benchmark as well as
change against the standard.

In the second type – directional without standards or benchmarks – we have not been able to reach agreement on how many
cats is the right number. All we can agree on is that we need to have
more than we have now. If the index is going down, that is even
worse. If the index is going up, good for us. Is it possible that we will
end up with too many cats? Maybe some people will think so and
others will not. We'll need to keep checking back with one another
to see and we'll also need to monitor the societal cost of each
additional cat. We may decide that an FCI of 105 is perfection given
the people who reside on the street at that time but that the effect
on the Bird Companion Index is too severe at that level. It will be
important, no matter what kind of indicators you choose, that you
remember that they will not stand alone. Complexity matters.

Questions can certainly be raised about the value of indicators
without standards and benchmarks. Most revolve around concern
that unless we determine in advance what we are trying to achieve
we will not be able to know when we are done. Advocates for
indicators which measure direction without benchmarks take the
view that the most important attribute of sustainability indicators
is agreement on what direction the community should be going
and that arguments over standards are barriers to getting the agreement upon direction.

One Size Does Not Fit All:
The Seattle Experience

1991 was a very exciting time to be in Seattle if one liked planning
processes. The City of Seattle, all of the suburban communities
within King County and the County itself were all engaged in
developing comprehensive plans. That all these entities were

planning at once was not some cosmic accident. In its 1990 legislative session, the State of Washington had adopted new laws which required every jurisdiction in the State that was of a certain size or greater, and/or growing faster than a certain rate, to do a comprehensive plan which addressed land use, transportation, housing, capital facilities and utilities. In some areas, like Seattle, the law required that economic development be included as well.

The plans had to be internally consistent, consistent with the plans of adjacent jurisdictions, consistent with regional plans and developed with the maximum feasible public participation. New administrative law courts were created to review the plans and the processes involved in developing them. These courts had the power to remand the plans to the responsible jurisdiction and instruct them to do things differently or better. Once adopted, the plans themselves became laws. Where these plans exist the local government is prohibited from making any decisions which are inconsistent with the plan and its goals. If a court finds that the plans are inconsistent, then monetary damages can be sought from the jurisdiction.

This law, the Washington State Growth Management Act, shares attributes of both dreams and nightmares. The dream is that it is possible to develop a shared vision for the future of the community and take consistent and coordinated action to achieve that future. The nightmare is that many of the questions that had been, for years, too complex or too politically difficult to address were now unavoidable.

As the city government of Seattle was embarking on growth management planning, some residents were starting to consider the concept of sustainability as an organising and action tool for civic action in support of environmental protection. These folks, including Alan AtKisson, Sheila Kelly, Nea Carroll, Richard Conlin and Steve Nicholas, who were to become the nucleus of Sustainable Seattle, were independently and collectively involved in dialogue with like-minded individuals around the world on the relationships between civic education, civic involvement and environmental protection. They recognised that the mandated planning process created a tremendous opportunity to increase civic understanding about the relationship between economic, social and environmental choices. They also recognised that, because the plans had a legal component, there was a real chance that an active and informed citizenry could have a significant role in determining the community's future.

Along with the Global Tomorrow Coalition, these individuals organised a series of community forums to discuss the concept of sustainability within a community context. Through these forums Sustainable Seattle was born. This voluntary network and civic forum works to improve the region's long term cultural, economic, environmental and social health and vitality. Sustainable Seattle's first project was to develop indicators for the community.

WHY INDICATORS FIRST?

It was recognised early on that one of the major barriers to the development of good comprehensive plans was the lack of a shared understanding about what changes were actually taking place or what could be predicted with some certainty. Another of the barriers was a lack of agreement within the community about what mattered most if we were to sustain our environment, our civility and our economic security. Indicators came first because the process of developing indicators created opportunities to build the shared understanding required about what was happening and what mattered. Development of the tool, though very important, was not the driving force. The need to reach agreement was.

After a couple years of process involving environmental, business, neighbourhood, institutional and other interests, agreement was reached on the first 20 of the ultimate 40 indicators. The choice was made to work with directional indicators without benchmarks. This allowed people to commit to improvements without protracted debates about how much improvement was enough. A simple graphic device, the use of arrows, was adopted so that anyone picking up the report could immediately get a sense of what was happening with regard to the matters that he or she cared about. Arrows pointing to the right meant that things were getting better. Arrows to the left meant that things were getting worse. A line meant that there was no discernible change. What follows is a partial list of the first 20 indicators:

- ◀▥ Wild salmon runs through local streams
- ▥▶ Number of good air quality days per year
- − Percentage of Seattle streets meeting 'pedestrian friendly' criteria
- ◀▥ Percentage of children born with low birth weight
- − Adult literacy rate
- ◀▥ Percentage of children living in poverty

The important part of the Sustainable Seattle indicators' process was and is that members of the community, not the institutions of government, have decided what's important and what to keep track of if you want to know what is happening. Less important is the indicators we selected. The Sustainable Seattle indicators are built upon local values, the nature of our society, economic opportunity, our relationship to nature and a variety of conditions that, in combination, are unique to this part of the US. Those things that people in Berlin or Dubai would choose to measure would be very different, but just as valid.

Conclusion

There is no one 'right' way for a community to develop sustainability indicators. There are a variety of models from which one might choose, and there are more models all of the time. Communities all over the world in vastly different economic, political, social and environmental circumstances are experimenting with ways and means to develop indicators for the neighbourhood, community or nation. In my experience there are some attributes of indicators which increase their chance of legitimacy and effectiveness. They are:

- the data upon which they are based must be as objective as is possible;
- the people whose behaviour needs to change in order for the community to have a more sustainable future must have a role in translating the data into information that is accessible to the diverse elements of the community;

- the people whose behaviour needs to change in order for the community to have a more sustainable future must be allowed to decide what the information means to them;
- the things that get measured should evoke happiness when they are improving and unhappiness when they are getting worse – if the change doesn't matter to the community then you are not monitoring the right thing;
- if the process of developing the shared knowledge, shared understanding, and shared vision for the future of your community isn't enjoyable, then you should figure out a different way to do it.

We did not get ourselves into this unsustainable mess overnight, and we will not get out of it quickly. The community will need to maintain their introspection and efforts for improvement over a long period. If it isn't fun, it is unlikely that the people you need to have involved will stay involved.

References

Adams, D (1991) *Hitchhiker's Guide to the Galaxy* Pan MacMillan, London

Institute for the Urban Environment (1994) *The European Sustainability Index Project* International Institute for Urban Environment, Delft

Peace Child International (1992) *Rescue Mission Planet Earth* Peace Child International, Buntingford, UK

Sustainable Seattle (1992) *Indicators of Community Sustainability* Sustainable Seattle, Seattle

UNDP (United Nations Development Programme) (1996) *Human Development Report 1996* Oxford University Press, Oxford

Special thanks to Sarah Phillips and Rumi Takahashi for their editorial assistance

5

Turning the Sustainability Corner: How to Indicate Right

Alex MacGillivray

Let the People Decide...

'What are indicators?'
'Things on cars.'
'Anything else?'
'Things to communicate between people.'
Interview with Elizabeth Gomez (aged 9), 1994

Those famous salmon of Seattle have inspired counties, cities, towns and villages throughout the UK to develop their own sustainability indicators. From Longformacus, a village of 200 in the Scottish Borders, to the county of Lancashire's 1.4 million, ten per cent of the UK's population are already covered by these initiatives (whether they know it or not). The common element is an attempt by normal people to find something meaningful to say about trends in their communities. Supported by community activists, researchers, environmental organisations and local government, these communities are using their own indicators to simplify, measure and communicate information across the spectrum of social, environmental and economic concerns known as Local Agenda 21. The goal is action: to protect what is valued, and to improve trends that are all too often negative.

Reaching the goal relies on overcoming two major obstacles. The first is empowering people to recognise that jargon words like 'sustainable development', 'quality of life', 'wellbeing' actually mean something(s) that people truly value. The second is the inertia, mistrust and cynicism that people feel with conventional economic indicators.

Getting to Grips with Sustainability

You can't eat sustainability: when it comes down to it, what people really want is cash income.

It sounds plausible enough, but there is good evidence from some of the 'poorest' communities in the world that this is not how people really see things. A well-known example comes from N.S. Jodha, who in 1988 asked farmers and villagers in two villages in Rajasthan, India, for their own categories and criteria of changing social, environmental and economic status. They named 38 indicators. Comparing data from his fieldwork over 20 years earlier, he found that 36 households had become more than 5 per cent worse off in per capita real income. Yet they ranked themselves as better off in 37 out of 38 indicators. Improvements included quality of housing, wearing shoes regularly, eating a third meal a day, and being able to sleep in different rooms to animals. The one exception was the availability of fresh milk, which was now being sold outside the villages (Jodha, 1988).

The gap between income and sustainable quality of life is becoming more accepted in research and political circles. Economists such as Andrew Oswald have examined linkages between growing national income and happiness or well-being. In a broad range of industrial countries, Oswald concludes:

> *'Well-being appears to rise as real income grows. But the rise is so small as to be sometimes almost undetectable. Unemployment, however, seems to be a large source of unhappiness. In a country that is already rich, policy aimed at raising economic growth may be of comparatively little value'.* (Oswald, 1995)

Even in 'hard-nosed' and depressed UK cities, there is a strong appreciation that there is much more to happiness, welfare or quality of life than cash income. Robert Rogerson at the University of Strathclyde has undertaken an important series of opinion surveys asking people about what they value. In the UK, more people rate health (70.3 per cent) and security (68.7 per cent) as 'very important' to them; more than the standard of living (58.8 per cent) or housing (49.4 per cent). A survey by New Economics Foundation for the *Independent on Sunday*, one of a series of rankings of UK localities, used these components to rank the UK regions (Nicholson-Lord et al, 1995). Even quite 'woolly' features such as tranquillity and community spirit are highly valued by a significant part of the population (see Table 5.1).[1]

Table 5.1 *Key components of sustainable communities*

Component	Per cent saying 'very important'
Health	70.3
Security	68.7
Standard of living	58.8
Education	57.1
Environment	56.1
Culture, recreation & leisure	49.5
Housing	49.4
Transport/access to goods and services	36.1
Tranquillity	29.2
Community spirit	22.2

Source: New Economics Foundation

There are, not surprisingly, significant regional differences in priorities. Rogerson finds that twice as many Scots value community spirit as people in Yorkshire and Humberside (Rogerson, 1995 and

---

1 Cited in: *Quality of Life in Cities: an overview and guide to the literature*, Lesley Grayson and Ken Young, British Library in association with London Research Centre, 1994 'Quality of Life: a nationwide survey', David Nicholson-Lord, Alex MacGillivray, Maaike Schouten & Mike Dowding, *Independent on Sunday*, 19 November 1995 For a similar exercise, see *Top Towns: the Guinness guide to finding the best places to live in the UK*, C Focas, P Genty & P Murphy, Guinness Publishing 1995

1997). Similarly, it depends who you ask. The researchers in Lancashire found that young unemployed men will tend to value 'having a job and a proper wage' above 'safer streets and a proper community'. Even so, in-depth studies again and again confirm the same basic pattern, so long as people are given the space to articulate their own views (see Box 5.1 and Box 5.2).

Working With the Feel-Bad Factor

'They only tell us what they want us to know. And that's the end of that, so you're left with a fog in your brain, so you just think – what have I to worry about? I don't know what they're on about'. (Macnaghten et al 1995)

The big puzzle for politicians and economists in the 1990s is the failure of the so-called Feel-Good Factor to return with the

Box 5.1 Life in the Borders

In the small villages of Cranshaws and Longformacus, in the Scottish Borders, a survey of all 100 households was undertaken, asking what priority they gave to a number of features of the community which had been identified by 'brainstorming' by the community council. The results were analysed and reported back to the community at a village hall meeting within two weeks. Some villagers were surprised to discover just how highly they valued the local environment. 'Living in a pleasant, clean and safe area' came out as the top priority. Preserving the quality of the natural heritage was also important. 'That's why I live here', said one local. Safer roads, more affordable heating, and more benches to enjoy the scenery would be major improvements. But there were differing views on the importance of public transport and car ownership – as one person said: 'a fundamental issue for the community as a whole'.

'Sadly lacking' was one comment about community spirit; 'It would be wonderful', said another. Many suggestions were put forward, such as more events and a cheap community newsletter. And over a third of respondents said that it would help if people could regularly find out if the community was making progress towards its goals. Hey presto: time to start selecting indicators, gathering information and communicating the results.

Source: New Economics Foundation

Box 5.2 Results from Longformacus

Here is how they ranked the 12 aspects of life and selected comments

Priority

| ■ Top | ▨ Medium | □ Low |

Living in a pleasant, clean and safe area
'How lucky we are'
'The area is pleasant, clean and safe, but as far as road safety, the 30 mph signs are too close to the village'

| 36 | 12 |

'The quality of the natural heritage should be maintained and improved'
'The natural heritage is in excellent condition and doesn't need meddling'
'What is the natural heritage doing for Longformacus at the moment? It is an attractive village but no facilities for tourists'

| 26 | 14 | 7 |

Adequate income to cope with heating, transport, food etc
'Heating is a very high cost in this area as cottages take more to heat than modern houses'

| 23 | 18 | 5 |

The availability of local employment
'Employment is needed, however, development should take into account the environment locally and planning conditions'
'With good roads nowadays and little traffic, people are willing to commute elsewhere'

| 23 | 13 | 11 |

A vibrant community spirit and shared values
'Probably the hardest to achieve is the desire for a community spirit'

| 20 | 14 | 13 |

Better roads
'Our roads are reasonable'
'We need to improve roads to cope with the heavy traffic'

| 20 | 11 | 17 |

Having a village school which is open and stays open
'We need to keep the schools open because we need a mixture of ages in the area and less distance for the children to travel'
'There is no school and never will be one now'

| 20 | 10 | 18 |

Easy access to shops, schools, health and leisure for those without cars
'I suspect a fundamental issue for the community as a whole'
'People without cars should not live in rural areas where they know there is no public transport'

| 16 | 18 | 14 |

Affordable and comfortable local housing
'Half of the houses in Longformacus are holiday homes and I can't see any point for building any more'

| 13 | 22 | 13 |

Community activities (eg leisure and culture) for both young and old
'No after lambing or Hogmanay do's, where are they now?'
'This would be very important in developing a shared community spirit'

| 3 | 32 | 12 |

Good value and reliable public transport
'When people get retired and can't afford to keep their car, they are pressured to move into Duns because of no other transport. If there was, they could see out their days in an area they love'
'Because most people own cars, public transport is not viable'

| 6 | 22 | 19 |

Attracting more people to live in the area
'The area is not able to sustain more inhabitants'
'Yes, but what kind of people?'

| 4 | 6 | 37 |

| 0 | 20 | 40 | 60 | 80 | 100% |

economic upturn. In the UK, the phenomenon has become a cliché, covered in all media, from *Bella* magazine to *The Financial Times*. Britons are told to think themselves lucky with a jobless count of 'only' 8 per cent. The economy is growing, inflation is low, productivity is up... people should count themselves lucky. Think of Spain – there unemployment is 23 per cent!

The problem is that people ignore these conventional economic indicators. They see instead a new economic context, and don't like what they see. Those in work put in the longest hours in Europe. Job security is (at least felt to be) a thing of the past. Gloomy predictions are made about an ever-shrinking job market, under the onslaught of new technologies. Jeremy Rifkin and others warn that more and more workers (whether blue, white or striped pink collar) will be chasing fewer and fewer 'real' jobs (Rifkin, 1996).

The gulf between how people feel and what they are told reflects a dramatic decline in the confidence people feel in national institutions, according to opinion poll research by the Henley Centre and Gallup. Yet government and its agencies are the major source of information on social and environmental trends. The problem is that official statistics tend to be boring, confusing, suspicious or all three. Sometimes there is good reason for mistrust: the methodology for calculating unemployment rates has changed *thirty* times since 1979, for example. In general, initiatives for 'open government' should be welcomed. But all too often, the indicators that result, whether on railway punctuality or urban air quality, simply don't match people's everyday experience. The cynicism about this bombardment of official indicators has been confirmed in a recent study by Lancaster University (see Box 5.3).

Again, the answer to this alienation is to empower people to devise their own indicators, which are common sense and have the trust of the community. As one rural person put it:

> 'It comes back to local knowledge. People have said that the beaches are more polluted than what they've been for years. I could have told you that. Because I've seen from upstairs for 30 years and looked out the window every day and seen the colour of the sand change colour. Whereas it used to be like everyone imagines sand, it's now a browny colour'.

Box 5.3 Alienating Indicators

In a study commissioned by Lancashire County Council, researchers at Lancaster University held a series of 'focus groups' to investigate public perceptions about sustainability – and the institutions and indicators being used to tackle it. The groups were made up of eight to ten members of the general public: young men on government training schemes; Asian women; mothers; unemployed men; retired people; rural professionals; working class women and young professionals.

The discussions in the focus groups revealed a disturbing degree of cynicism, even fatalism, towards the indicators originating from the country's public institutions: 'Whilst people do in fact use a variety of indicators in their day to day lives (eg weather forecasts, body temperature as an indicator of health, exam marks as an indicator of educational progress), it appeared to be difficult for people to reflect on the role of current indicators in their lives.

Moreover, the majority of the groups not only considered the idea of indicators an abstract and difficult concept, but more generally were suspicious of official statistics and information ...The further removed indicators were from people's immediate realities, the less likely they were to find them credible. '...[M]ost participants not only felt ignorant about wider social and environmental matters, but were also of the opinion that this state of ignorance was perpetuated by institutions carefully and cynically presenting their own biases...'.

Source: Macnaghten, P. et al 1995.

Measuring Sustainable Communities

Given the opportunity, people can and do identify effective indicators and take sustainable quality of life seriously. Indicators are like flags, used to simplify, measure and communicate information, and to rally support for action. An indicator is nothing mysterious; it is simply a way of measuring and making understandable something that is considered important. Hours, minutes and seconds are indicators of passing time. A high temperature is an indicator of sickness. And a leaping salmon is an indicator of clean water. Community indicators arise from a process which can, like in Seattle, take years, but which can also take a fortnight (see Box 5.4).

Community indicators have been tried at a wide variety of scales, from regions of over two million inhabitants, down to single villages and parishes (Table 5.2).

Box 5.4 Don't tread in it, flag it up!

This example comes from the city of Reading. A local park was being ruined by the large amounts of dog mess on the paths and grass. Local people had become concerned about the issue, and the ineffectiveness of controls on dog-owners. One day, red flags were placed over each dog mess in the park by a team of volunteers. There were lots of onlookers. The press was invited to come and see, and took photos of over 900 flags!

This vivid indicator literally 'flagged up' the problem and communicated it effectively to the readers of the local papers. When the exercise was repeated a few weeks later, only 250 flags were needed. The indicator was certainly effective in galvanising action among dog-owners.

Source: WWF UK 1995

The processes, people and products have come in all shapes and sizes. They are far too various to summarise here. But because of the narrowness and alienating quality of official statistics, it is no surprise that the common element in all successful exercises is the principle of popular participation.

There is no off-the-shelf approach to a community-based indicators exercise. Local people debate and reject standard lists of sustainability themes. As many as 300 separate sustainability indicators have been proposed; none of them perfect (MacGillivray and Zadek 1996). Some communities like a few 'headline' indicators; others favour 30 or more in a basket. In some communities, only good quality data is acceptable; others prefer more anecdotal evidence of trends. Sometimes the indicators are launched at an event, while in other communities a report or scorecard works better. Some communities know what action is needed; others have to work towards the answer. In a recent project supported by the Local Government Management Board, ten communities were assisted with a common set of themes, a menu of 101 indicators and ideas for data gathering and communication. At least ten different approaches emerged!

It is however possible to identify a series of stages that community projects generally go through. Box 5.5 suggests ways of maximising popular participation at each stage.

This is by no means a blueprint for a successful project; rather

Table 5.2 *Community indicators: types of community and population*

Pilot	Type of locality	Population
Bedfordshire	county	540,000
Cardiff	city	297,000
Fife	region (plus 3 small communities)	350,000
Hertfordshire	county	976,000
Jacksonville (USA)	city	700,000
Lancashire	county	1,414,000
Leeds	city	724,500
Leicester	city	270,000
Longformacus	village	243
Mendip	rural district (parish case studies)	95,000
Merkinch, Inverness	district	3,500
Merton	London Borough	168,000
Middlesbrough	city	144,000
Oldham	Metropolitan Borough	220,000
Peterborough	city	153,000
Pilton, Edinburgh	estate	25,000
Seattle (USA)	city	500,000
Strathclyde	region	2,290,000

Source: MacGillivray and Zadek 1996.

it is an outside analysis of what seems to have happened in a range of different projects. Nor need these stages be sequential.

If there is a common lesson, though, it is that if participation falters at any stage, it is increasingly difficult for the project 'champions' to regain it at a later stage. One typical bottleneck is at the data gathering stage, where the technocrats in every community like to take control (see Figure 5.1). This is unfortunately why so many exciting projects have such dull outputs (typically an A4 report full of graphs and pie charts) which are not well enough known in the community. Even worse when the project team try to recoup printing costs by charging £5 for the report – the average

Box 5.5 Stages in an indicators process

Getting started

Raising awareness about the project, planning the next stages, and enlisting help. Who do you need to reach, and how will they receive the information? What timescale is there, and what resources are needed/available? Are there local champions?

Deciding issues

Helping the community to think through and reach agreement on the issues that are of most concern and interest. Questionnaires, interviews and workshops can be used to get people involved. Conflicts of interest need to be negotiated. All members of the community should be included. At the very least, make sure that everyone can attend meetings. Disabled people, the elderly, those who work in the evenings won't turn up at a typical 6.30 public meeting on a wet February evening.

Choosing indicators

Working from the list of common issues, try to identify one or more indicator ideas for each issue. A basic list of criteria (eg meaningfulness, resonance) will assist selection. The best indicators will strike a chord in the community. Sometimes they are quite controversial or embarrassing: in Jacksonville, Florida, inhabitants are asked to name two local council members (accurately!).

Gathering data

Harness the resourcefulness of the community to gather information for itself. In Oldham, people looked at how many ponds had frogs in them. In Merton, a disabled person did a survey of disabled facilities in local buildings. Schoolchildren are good (and cheap) researchers. Identify worthwhile data from official sources, too, and start thinking about what targets the community can realistically set.

Communicating indicators

Turning the information that has been gathered into understandable indicators for the community. This is a crucial but often neglected stage. Use relevant media: newspapers, local radio etc, exhibitions, displays, publications, and material for schools. And be inventive!

Galvanising action

The indicators are for education and action: to grab people's attention, make them think, get them arguing and spur them on. The audience includes the 'powers that be' outside the community, who become more accountable. It's also time to start the whole process again – this could be a long-term project!

Source: MacGillivray and Zadek 1996

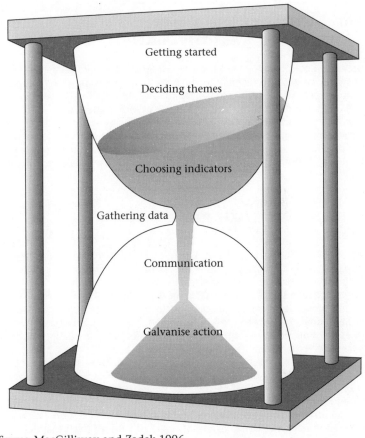

Getting started

Deciding themes

Choosing indicators

Gathering data

Communication

Galvanise action

Source: MacGillivray and Zadek 1996

Figure 5.1 *The indicators egg timer*

Briton only buys two books a year and they will not be sustainable community reports.

In contrast, a range of techniques can be used at each stage of the process to build interest and excitement (see, for example, New Economics Foundation 1998). Whether these are parish maps in the Mendips, community theatre in Northern Ireland, Planning for Real in Kyle of Lochalsh, street surveys by schoolchildren in Peterborough or barbecues in Seattle, they are a mixture of old and new, familiar

Box 5.6 Not your typical indicators project: Future Search in Sutton

Brainchild of US facilitators Marvin Weisbord and Sandra Janoff, Future Search is an exciting technique which brings together up to 64 people from diverse backgrounds for an intensive two and a half day shared exploration of the past, present and future of their community.

An event in the London Borough of Sutton brought together 50 citizens and policy makers. Eight key 'stakeholder' groups (such as young people, business) were identified by the Local Agenda 21 steering group. Well over 100 hours were spent in recruiting people who satisfied three criteria:

- that had information;
- that would be affected by events; or
- that could affect events.

When the participants arrived on Friday evening, they found three strips of paper marked 'global', 'Sutton' and 'personal'. Each strip was 24 feet long and covered the last three decades. Everyone wrote down their key events for each decade; the results were then discussed and summarised. At the global level, many people had been influenced by, or at least remembered, the same events. The personal strip, even more, showed people's similarities, in terms of the rhythms of birth, education, work, relationships and family.

On a strip of paper 8 foot by 12, a 'mind map' was then created to show the trends influencing Sutton now. A shared view was developed, with different groups of people asked to say what trends they were proud of, and those they were sorry about.

By the end of the event, almost every inch of the large Tudor hall was covered in paper: evidence of the principle of Future Search that everyone's views are equally important. This unleashed such energy and shared vision that ten action groups were formed on the spot, with concrete plans set out and agreed. The plans ranged from developing a register of holistic health practitioners to setting up a telecottage. Some identified timetables, barriers and ways to overcome them. The action groups are now busy working towards their targets.

Source: Walker, 1995

and exotic, easy and difficult. Some work only for a particular part of the process. Others, like the visioning work in Sutton (see Box 5.6) are a community project in microcosm.

One puzzle for sustainability professionals (all 50,000 of us) is to find a role for themselves in these local initiatives. Every community facilitator knows that this is a delicate balancing act. Are they 'hands-off' dead-weights that turn up to hear about progress every so often (and then take the credit in learned papers for all the hard work done by the community)? Or are they bossy, indomitable 'champions' that drive their vision through the community roughshod? In the most successful cases we have examined, the 'community' does have (and probably needs) one or more champions who get gripped with 'indicators fever'. Such champions have the energy to see things through in the dark hours when a couple of hundred community questionnaires need to be analysed by Monday evening. And they need to come from within the community.

The role for research and training organisations like New Economics Foundation is to lay the groundwork in a community so that such champions can come forward. There is also a role for the outsider in checking that the champions do not get carried away, and to give constant ideas and encouragement to ensure that community involvement is maximised at all stages.

But Does it Work?

'Measure what can be measured, and make measurable what cannot be measured'. (Galileo Galilei cited in Gaardner 1995)

'Another 'green herring' is the current pre-occupation with indicators ... How on earth can anyone decide on a set of indicators before objectives have been determined?' (Wright 1996)

Critics have seen the recent enthusiasm for sustainability indicators as a 'green herring': as part of the old measurement obsession, words and numbers instead of action. Even worse, local communities, left to themselves, might act selfishly, choose 'soft options' and ignore the pressing global problems that face us.

Despite the potential pitfalls, we have seen from the park in Reading that community indicators can work. US cities like Seattle, Chattanooga and Jacksonville report an improved self-image and the attraction of inward investment. In the UK, most projects are still too young to be yielding spectacular results. The first signs of success are not likely to be a dramatic fall in air pollution, a big increase in cycling to work, or European Commission funding.

Instead, such initiatives are a potent way of building 'social capital'. Social capital is the new jargon term given to those elusive but fundamental qualities of community spirit, civic engagement, vibrancy, robust local democracy, and so on. We noted above that they are highly valued in communities, and often felt to be under siege.

In a benchmark study of Italian regions, Harvard Professor Robert Putnam found that membership of choral societies is one of the three best predictors of a robust and effective local democracy and economy – alongside membership of soccer clubs and cooperatives (Putnam 1993). According to Putnam: 'Communities don't have choral societies because they are wealthy; they are wealthy because they have choral societies – or more precisely, the traditions of engagement, trust and reciprocity that choral societies symbolise'. In the US, Putnam notes the decline in bowling clubs as an indicator of the decline in social capital. He blames TV. In the UK, attendance at football matches is talked about as a measure of community spirit.

As the people of Longformacus mourn the dwindling numbers who attend village hall events, they have hopefully begun to find in their indicators project a new way to galvanise community spirit. Interestingly, the wheel comes full circle: literally participation for participation's sake. Does it work? New Economics Foundation certainly believe so, which is why, with the support of the Worldwide Fund for Nature and Environmental Action Fund, we have worked with other community groups throughout the UK. These are often small communities such as Longformacus, where participation can be very broad. But at the rate of four communities a year, it would take us 69,000 years to cover the UK population. That is why we have developed a community indicators resource pack, to provide enthusiasm, examples and encouragement to the many community groups who are ready to get started.

References

Gaardner, J (1995) *Sophie's World* Phoenix Books, London

Jodha, N S (1988) 'Poverty debate in India: a minority view', *Economic and Political Weekly*, special number 2421–2428, November 1988

MacGillivray, A and Zadek, S (1996) *Accounting for Change: Indicators for Sustainable Development*, New Economics Foundation, London

Macnaghten, P, Grove-White, R, Jacobs, M and Wynne, B (1995) *Public Perceptions and Sustainability in Lancashire: Indicators, Institutions, Participation* Centre for the Study of Environmental Change, Lancaster University/Lancs County Council

New Economics Foundation (1998) *Participation Works! 21 Techniques of Community Participation for the 21st Century.* New Economics Foundation, London

Nicholson-Lord, D, MacGillivray, A, Schouter, M and Dowding, D (1995) 'Quality of Life: a nationwide survey' *Independent on Sunday* 19 November

Oswald, A (1995) *Happiness and Economic Performance*, Andrew Oswald, Centre for Economic Performance, London School of Economics, London

Putnam, R D (1993) *Making Democracy Work. Civic Traditions in Modern Italy* Princeton University Press, Princeton

Rifkin, J (1996) *The End of Work: the Decline of the Global Labor Force and the Dawn of the Post-Market Era* Tarcher/Putnam, New York

Rogerson, R (1995) 'Environmental and health related quality of life: conceptual and methodological similarities', in *Social Science and Medicine*, Vol 41, pp 1373–82, Pergamon, London

Rogerson, R (1997) *Quality of Life in Britain* University of Strathclyde, Glasgow

Walker, P (1995) 'Turning dreams into concrete reality' *New Economics*, Winter 1995

Wright, G (1996) 'Getting to the Heart of Local Agenda 21', in *EG Local Environmental News*, Environment Resource and Information Centre, University of Westminster, London

WWF-UK (1995) *Working in Neighbourhoods: WWF and Local Agenda 21* WWF-UK, Godalming

6

Civic Science and the Sustainability Transition

Tim O'Riordan

Apparently if you surf the web, you will find between 50,000 and 250,000 citations to some aspect of research or publication regarding sustainable urban development alone. There is an exploding industry of consultants and specialists in the field. Possibly as many as 50,000 individuals are involved full time in the European Union alone (Wolff 1996). This could mean almost anything. But it suggests that there are plenty of people in search of a mission, that sustainable development is a wide open arena to explore and to make a living in, and that a modern, non-sustainable economy creates sufficient spare wealth to finance research into its radical redirection. Academics jump on lucrative bandwagons, lumbering by, regardless of destiny. Urban managers, seeing Local Agenda 21 popping up on the political horizon, feel compelled to set up a small working group to puzzle it out. Industry, faced with eco-audits that mostly encourage good public relations and sensible housekeeping, hire consultants who are only too willing to oblige, regardless of experience. And because nobody really knows what sustainable development is, there are plenty of candidates for seminars, workshops and conferences, all of which need speakers, administrators and public relations.

Sustainable development is not any nearer. But it is a money-spinner and a job generator. Maybe this is a sign of the times in the rich nations. They can afford to siphon off a few per cent of growth income in think tanks, sustainability indicator studies and project coordinators without causing much of an additional ripple on the turbulent surface of business as usual. The sustainability transition may have begun in the sense that the concept is being over-studied and endlessly redefined. But effective practical action remains the stuff of brave people and comforting dreams.

This book is essentially about communitarian politics. Etzioni (Chapter 2) emphasises the significance of bonding, fair treatment and the exuberance of collective action in this vital realm of civic activity. Others reveal the extent of constructive activism that certainly has the potential to be a truly revolutionary force in the sustainability transition. But civic action, indicator assessments and minority mobilisation are not sufficient in themselves. They are a vital stimulant to a political economy that has to be responsive to a more sustainable and caring age. This chapter looks at the scope for civic activism in the sustainability transition. To do so, it first looks at what really is meant by sustainable development, and why the transition has to be all encompassing for all the institutions guiding human destiny.

What is Sustainable Development?

Sustainable development ought to mean the creation of a society and an economy that can come to terms with the life support limits of the planet in a way that enables the most vulnerable peoples to survive with dignity in a self reliant manner. Long before the advent of social organisation sophisticated enough to accumulate wealth and political power, subsequently to conquer and to import slaves, human societies meddled with their surroundings. The evidence is well examined by Bennett (1976) and by Simmons (1993). Humans, like all living beings, are continually negotiating with natural chance. Sometimes climate change or fire would reduce their capacity to survive without removing excessive numbers, sometimes peoples migrated, or developed new skills. More often than not early 'sustainable' societies suffered terrible privation in the struggle for existence. Sustainability was neither pleasant, nor equitable, nor guaranteed. It is no wonder that it is essentially in the human condition to triumph over subsistence and seek to manipulate the planet for security and comfort. Maybe 'true' sustainability never was in the human condition. After extensively examining the evidence, the famous American geographer Y.F. Tuan (1972) found that sustainable existence was an 'equilibrium not of this world'.

Modern humanity gets round this uncomfortable prospect by defining sustainable development to mean almost anything we want it to mean (see, for example, Fischer and Black 1995). The very ambiguity, not to say contradiction, of the term allows interests from many different walks of life to debate it and to seek to achieve it. Because sustainable development is seen as a 'good' thing, its interpretation is stretched to accommodate almost any unrequited social goal from minority rights to debt relief. As Lele wryly remarks:

> 'Sustainable development is a 'metafix' that will unite everybody from the profit-minded industrialist and risk minimising subsistence farmer to the equity-seeking social worker, the pollution-concerned or wildlife-loving First Worlder, the growth maximising policy maker, the global orientated bureaucrat, and, therefore, the vote counting politician'. (Lele, 1991, p613)

Sustainable development is beginning to adopt the mantle of a new renaissance idea that covers the whole of human endeavour and planetary survival. Who could possibly oppose it? The various sustainable development round tables that have sprung up in a number of countries, such as Australia, New Zealand, Canada and the UK, survived for surprisingly long, given that they had no power and were not seriously listened to by governments and their power-brokers. This dogged determination is one form of institutional commitment to a process that is seen to be good and worthwhile, even when progress is painful and the language unintelligible. The only hope for a successful transition towards more sustainable development may be that the notion becomes such a powerful energising force that it might come to have the same momentum as creative evolution itself. We are not at all sure where we will end up, but we keep on trying, almost as if a greater force is propelling us. That may prove to be the most important driver towards envisioning sustainable futures.

Sustainable Development and Social Change

For sustainable development seriously to be contemplated, it has to fit into the mainstream of social and political change as it is already occurring in the late twentieth century. Much of this change is already commented upon in companion chapters to this volume, notably in the ideas of communitarian politics, new social movements, decentralising tendencies, and deep distrust of governing institutions at all levels of non-delivery. (See, for example, Putnam (1993) for an excellent discussion of citizen's distrust in governance.) It is profoundly important to bear all these in mind when contemplating the upheavals necessary for any realistic transition towards sustainable development.

The fascinating experiments in designing common futures now being conducted in Seattle, Lancaster and Longformacus, to name a few, show that people do care about their 'place' and are willing to work to make it more secure for them and their children. The key to this is to create a communal 'science' of effective reality.

What are the overriding social and practical dynamics to all the changes that bear on this sustainability transition? Here are three that emerged from a detailed study of the responses in European countries to the UN Framework Convention on Climatic Change (O'Riordan and Jäger 1996, pp351–360). This was a detailed study of how various countries and the European Community as a legal entity sought to come to terms with the reduction of atmosphere warming gases.

1) Lasting institutional adjustment takes place best when the response is triggered by a number of policy developments, acting co-operatively, but not necessarily with the same political starting guns. Essentially, however, these propulsive forms must have an economic component (eg privatisation, tax reform, fiscal rectitude), and an industrial support base (eg ecoauditing, business ethical responsibility, consumer sensitiv-

ity, product stewardship), but also are resonant with the groundswell of popular support (via polls, pressures on politicians, campaigning successes of non-governmental bodies, working in concert).

2) Robust institutional adjustment to more sustainable futures has to be backed by economic ministries and economic policy strategies. Tackling the roots of conventional micro-economic philosophy will fail, no matter how out of step that is with eco-purism, or with any environmental agenda, unless the two approaches can be made to reinforce one another. The trouble is, in essence, environmentalists do not talk enough to the business community, the financial services sector, or the finance industry and its economic advisors. Curiously, there is a common agenda for them to discuss, notably on the dangers of 'hot' money chasing desperately unstable short-term economic returns. But the two groups do not have sufficient of a common language to communicate.

3) Policy communities were described by political scientists (originally Jordan and Richardson 1985) as stable collectivities of interests that fed information and receptiveness to policy-makers in return for a reliable policy response to suit their interests. Nowadays, political theorists (eg Rhodes 1985; Sabatier 1987) talk of issue networks and policy coalitions. Issue networks are constructions of potentially reinforcing policy areas which serve to generate new political perspectives. Policy coalitions are the coalescing groupings of interests who may not have talked to each other before, but find common interests in issue networks. Rhodes (1990) talks of 'policy chaos' to reflect a state of great indecision about the role of policy in a rapidly reconstructing policy environment when no particular recombination of objectives and procedures seems likely to last. This offers an opportunity to approach the economic policy fray with new social and environmental demands. But it is also a danger, because instability creates uncertainty and ill-tempered bedfellows in both coalitions and networks. Nevertheless, it is in such a time of institutional flux that the power of organisations with resources and influence is being reconstructed, while the

evaluative and regulatory means of dealing with awkward social choices are being reconsidered. This is very much the institutional environment that favours civic science, as we shall see below.

So we are entering turbulent and insecure times. The awesome power of economic and information globalism is creating 'collateral social and cultural damage' amongst a growing number of vulnerable populations. People fear for their economic security; social values are in flux and the traditional regulatory devices of parenting, schools, the church, and peer responsibility are breaking down. Alienation is on the increase as a growing number of people have no social anchors to hold them to comforting (or subjugating) positions. One outcome is a surge of criminality in a context in which social morality no longer regards theft or vandalism against the rich or powerful as anything other than justice. This in turn adds another layer of insecurity, the insecurity of possible personal violation or property damage. On top of both economic and social insecurity lies ecological insecurity, manifest in threats of toxic assault on the body or the unborn, and in its distant thunder of climate change and irreversible damage to the biological functioning of critical ecosystems. One of the factors promoting the drive to sustainable development therefore arises from this triple layering of insecurity.

So we see that there are two external propulsive conditions in the drive towards sustainable development, ambiguously interpreted as it is. One is the scope for radical restructuring of the economy and society simply because the institutional conditions are in sufficient flux to accommodate really dramatic new arrangements (Fischer and Black 1995). Of course, for this to happen there would have to be a set of shoves in particular directions; of that, more below. The other is the instability of insecurity that causes a number of people to search for combinations of policies that hopefully unite communities in more secure economic, social and environmental futures. This is introduced in a paper by the UN Research Institute for Social Development (1995). These are both exciting and potentially very profound initiating conditions of the transition to sustainable development.

What is the Sustainability Transition?

There is no agreed definition of a sustainability transition except that it must be how we progress from our present, substantially non-sustainable state, to some future, more sustainable existence. As has been discussed earlier, the precise image of that future is hugely dependent upon value biases towards power, equity, technical innovation, political accountability and economic reform. A more sustainable future should be more resource efficient, less waste generating, more fully costed to reflect the potential damage of the price of living, more cooperative and altruistic, more collectivist and more indentured to tend the global commons. Fischer and Black (1995) cover much of this ground, but the reading list is simply enormous.

The point about the transition is its purposefulness, its directability and its accountable initiatives. This is the essence of Agenda 21, the requirement for every country to present a sustainable development strategy, progressively leading to a better world. As yet there are few good Agenda 21s, mostly because the idea is too new, and few governments are prepared to commit themselves too soon to what would be a very difficult political radicalism. For the sake of this analysis, one could identify seven pointers to assess how far the sustainability transition is being addressed (see O'Riordan and Voisey 1997).

1. The Use of Language

Language reveals much. Look to the rhetoric of any national debate on sustainable development and see how much the phrases 'reliable economic growth', 'durable economy', 'stewardship of nature', 'taking care for future generations', 'protecting life support', and 'empowering the vulnerable' come up. In the earlier part of this essay, sustainable development was characterised by the triple notions of economic security, stewardship or husbanding for the future, and empowering people by giving them real opportunities for self-respect and effective involvement. In general, most of the rhetoric remains embedded in the first two of these concepts, not so much the third. This is why this book is so important; it specifically addresses the language and practice of empowerment. The sustainability transition is, in fact, the steady shift in confidence from economic necessity, through stewardship, to empowerment. It is neither easy nor desirable to push all three at the same time. Hence the progressive qualities of the sustainability transition, but also the seeming dismissal by government officials of empowerment as an 'environmental' theme.

2. Policy Integration

Joining policies together is always more difficult to achieve than is commonly supposed. Again, for the reasons cited earlier, policies are shaped by direct interests and governmental structures. They are creatures of bias and interest, not for the public good in some undifferentiated way. So a real test of the sustainability transition is the reconstruction of both policy communities and governing structures to enable the 'piggy-backing' of economic, social and environmental objectives into a more unified focus. Don't hold your breath, for this will be a slow transition. The signs are, however, there. Look at the transport debate in the UK: it combines urban vitality, human health, a decentralised economy and fresh perspectives on non-market ecological accounting in a manner that would have been unheard of outside academic circles 20 years ago.

3. Interdepartmental Coordination

This is the bureaucratic variant of policy integration, but involves shifts towards more cooperative and compatible approaches to policy evaluation and cost-benefit justification. For example, stewardship means giving weight to the non-market valuation of future interests and to the life-support functions of geophysiological mechanisms such as carbon cycling in sediment or nutrient absorption in biomass. Such concepts may be embraced in environmental departments, but not necessarily so in economic institutions such as finance houses or banks or industry. Again the signs are that some meeting of the methodological minds is taking place as fresh approaches to economic analysis appears in policy documents. (See for example the UK approach in the Department of the Environment's 1991 position paper.)

4. Sustainability indicators

Sustainability indicators form a particularly good measuring tool for the sustainability transition. These are calculated trends in key variables such as changes in air or water quality, the efficiency of energy conversion and the state of environmental health generally. The UK Department of the Environment published an enormously impressive list of such indicators in March 1996, much to the envy of other European nations. But, in general, most serious minded nations are coordinating their data for this purpose, and subsequently producing targets for performance accounts. Though by no means comprehensive, or legally demanding, nevertheless the collection of the indicators and their role in target setting will form a vital aspect of the sustainability transition. Again, this book offers heartening experiences (see Lawrence Chapter 4, and MacGillivray Chapter 5). Indicators cannot be dictated to us all through official (and sometimes dubious) statistics. Indicators must sense the pulse of community concern if they are to mean anything for the sustainability transition.

5. Ecotaxation

Ecotaxation means not just the levying of taxes against resource depletion and polluting or toxic substances or discharges, but also the redirection of revenue specifically in favour of sustainability objectives. Both the theory and the practice of ecotaxation are reviewed by O'Riordan and colleagues (1997). They conclude that this is an area of political and economic change that will prove a crucial indicator of the sustainability transition. At present, governments have faced difficulty in levying environmental taxes without ensuring that their highly competitive economies do not suffer in the face of other economies which do not incur such costs. The key is therefore the recycling of the revenue into jobs and into technological or social innovation that creates a more sustainable economy and an improved democracy. We are many years away from all this at present. But the debate over environmental cost 'correction' and the need to find new revenue for socially supportive initiatives are likely to promote the cause of ecotaxation as a policy measure generally over and above the needs of sustainability.

6. Compatibility of Business and Environment

Business and environment are becoming more compatible as businesses are forced into full and published ecoaudits, and as consumers and environmental organisations increase their demands for more ethical and environmentally-friendly business practices. The result is a growth in such regulations as ecolabelling, as well as the spread of informal regulatory devices such as the accreditation of products that meet particular sustainability objectives. For example, many firms will not buy wood from any supplier who is not accredited by the Forest Stewardship Council. Other firms, notably high profile retailers such as B&Q and Tesco, are beginning to work with all their suppliers to ensure that their products are manufactured from suitably protected natural and social regimes. This is not always easy to ensure. And, of course, once a firm embarks on this course, the road ahead is endless and increasingly rocky. So we have to be patient; product stewardship is very difficult to guarantee. Nevertheless, the fact that all this is happening in the highly competitive world of commerce, and that market analysts and finance institutions are beginning to take a serious interest in environmental issues, is part of the signs of the sustainability transition. Business is also now taking an interest in caring for its employees' welfare, the needs of the local community, local sourcing and promotion of cooperative stewardship schemes: just the kind of indicator issues discussed in companion chapters.

7. Local Agenda 21

Local Agenda 21 (LA21) is the transfer of Agenda 21 to the local level. Under Chapter 28 of the Rio document, all local governments were supposed to submit a report on LA21 by 1997. In practical terms this means little more than their own ecoauditing, recycling and energy efficiency efforts. But the more adventurous are addressing empowerment, especially for the marginalised and most vulnerable elements of society whose futures need the benefits of ecotaxation revenue and the linkage to social care and community uplift. In the UK, an enormous range of responses are taking place with regard to LA21. This is mostly because there is a lively pressure group involved, the Local Government Management Board, and because many local authorities see in LA21 a chance to develop their own political, social and economic futures separate from the restraining influences of central government. In financial terms, such wresting of independence is most unlikely. But the struggle is certainly on, so LA21 is one of the key indicators of the sustainability transition (see O'Riordan and Voisey, 1997).

These seven themes are by no means the only elements of the sustainability transition. But they provide a useful set of yardsticks by which to recognise a coordinated and constructive national response to Agenda 21. There is no doubt that, in the UK at least, all of these seven arenas of action are active and progressively evolving. Cynics may look in vain for particular signs of real movement. But the transition must be slow, if for no other reason than that it requires multiple levers generating cohesively over a prolonged period before the evidence becomes observable. That is what is now happening in the UK (O'Riordan and Voisey, 1997).

Linking Economy, Society and Environmental Security

All this suggests that there are a trio of conditions that underpins any serious analysis of a transitional pathway towards sustainable development.

1. Continuation, Reliability, and Durability of Economic Performance

The future economy cannot afford to be undermined by avoidable costs of ecological restoration or social reconstruction, or the search for renewable resource substitution, all in a hurry. This would destabilise any economy and might lead to great social hardship just at a time when citizens' rights were being given political prominence. Even now, economists (for example, Leipert and Simonis 1987) who look at the ecological costs of conventional growth estimate that these could exceed 6 per cent of gross product. This means an effective doubling of economic performance simply to stand still, or an entirely different form of economy and accounting system. The most accessible summary of this position can be found in Jacobs (1996).

2. Stewardship, Trusteeship and a Duty of Care Towards Vulnerable Ecosystems and Peoples

Vulnerability is a culturally-framed term. It has no absolute meaning. It applies to conditions where the physical basis for survival in food, shelter, sanitation, health generally, education and gainful employment cannot be provided at a rate sufficient to allow a culture to adapt. Different cultures tolerate environmental hardship in varying ways. One fruitful form of adjustment is the self-help, informal economy, that may account for up to half all transactions in many threatened societies. Stewardship means recognising that conditions of future vulnerability should be avoided, if necessary by the application of the precautionary principle, and that policies towards the planet take into account a duty of care for people who might otherwise create their own vulnerability out of desperation. Only cared for people will care for the planet. For a very heartening analysis of different cultural interpretations of sustainable development, see Nagpal and Foltz (1995) and Smith (1996).

3. Localism, Democratic Empowerment and Greater Self-Reliance

This, to some extent, comes from the stewardship condition. But it is an additional factor. Localism is very much the theme of this volume, it is a code for paying attention to people at the local level, to cultural differences that matter and which help shape a communal future, and to a sense of shared ownership in this future. Empowerment is not so much demonstrating the acquisition of power, as it is the creation of conditions for social and individual self respect and for a willingness to listen with care and flexibility to the interests and aspirations of others (Schwerin 1993). Self-reliance is a possible paradox. It means granting greater opportunities for people to work together for a common goal. But it also means adjusting to the needs of others to create a shared outcome. This, surely, is the basis of true democracy. The real paradox is that, for many at present, such opportunities are not yet sought, even though for a minority, say 50,000 in the UK today, self-help is proving a life-saver (Nicholson-Lord 1996).

Let us take stock. There is a tremendous flux in institutional performance in the modern state. This involves repositioning organisations, resources for mobilisation, and effective power. It is also putting pressure on traditional evaluative and regulatory mechanisms, such as cost benefit analysis, risk management, ecoauditing and community empowerment techniques to transform them to meet the conditions of economic reliability, stewardship and empowerment mentioned above.

But there are still not sufficient conditions. Nagpal and Foltz sum up the dilemma in a perceptive manner

> 'The paradox we face is: how do we help the poor if their survival is repeatedly put at risk by those who say they wish to help them, but whose primary concern is capital accumulation and exploitation of raw materials? There exists a far reaching force of importing alien models of corruption and behaviour – in sum changing indigenous customs – with no purpose other than foisting the western market model on these peoples ... or to make these people useful tools for enriching others'. (Nagpal and Folz, 1995, p163)

There we have it: what and who is sustainable development actually for? If it is for the gradual victory of capitalism in some eco-moderated form, then the equity and cultural integrity dimensions get short shrift. If the objective is greater social justice leading to empowered self reliance, together with more effective sharing of the global commons, then much of the case for ecoefficiency based on quasi-market principles will be treated with circumspection.

Envisioning sustainable futures will mean, at the very least, clarifying these underlying value premises. It will also entail discovering, even more than we do at present, why such value premises are formed and through what processes of revelation they may be accommodated into larger and more coherent social structures. This in turn opens up another dilemma. Sustainable development has to be visualised at various scales of space and time, culture and economy, ecosystem and biochemical flux. We do not have the psychological apparatus, nor the institutional means, of coordinating these scales of envisioning. We appear temperamentally and constitutionally capable of connecting only a small number of these scales at a time. If it is to progress, the sustainability transition will have to help us all connect up scales of perception and consequence that are almost unnatural to us now.

Civic Science and the Sustainability Transition

The term civic science was termed by Kai Lee (1994) to denote a form of interactive partnership between resource managers and constituent citizens' interests in guiding a programme of environmental and social change. Many scientists are nervous of any adjective before science, claiming that science is a culturally accepted practice of clear rules (see especially Rosenhead 1989 and Lidskog 1991). These apply to the validation of laws, the testing of hypotheses, the trial of falsification, the acceptance of peer review, the use of models to abstract reality and the weighing of uncertainty via probability and sensitivity functions. For this well-established group of analysts, science is an objective exercise, seeking truth and informing citizens and policy makers alike of the likely implications of certain outcomes.

But for Kai Lee and those who concern themselves with the social construction of science, it is meaningless to talk of socially disconnected scientific function. There are genuine uncertainties in the data record, in the sensitivity of ecosystems to changes in the vulnerability of societies to stress, and in the tolerances of political institutions to random social change. The engagement in scenario building, with the active help of interested parties, is not only sensible. It is also a form of empowerment in its own right, and hence a crucial part of the new democratic process. This is why civic science is such a vital concept in the creation of visionable future conditions of economy, society and environmental securities and insecurities.

From the discussion so far, the application of civic science to the sustainability transition involves four interpretations of sustainable development, each of which is essential to its achievement, and each of which can only be identified in the presence of the others. This is a slightly expanded version of the points raised above, but it is in keeping with the argument nevertheless.

1) 'Markets' refer to arrangements in the competitive economy to ensure that ecological and social tolerances to expansion and change are not exceeded. Though the mechanism of control may also be regulatory, the process of implementation is primarily competitive and market driven. This is in part a process that encourages innovation and entrepreneurship. But it cannot guarantee social responsibility or social accountability, part of the stewardship.

2) 'Regulations' apply to patterns of control and guidance, imposed either by the state in the form of legal rules, or various formal restrictions, or by voluntary agreements, supported by a commitment to collective norms. Stewardship has to some degree to be supported by rules: it cannot be left to conscience alone, for this is a flimsy guarantee of social responsibility. In any case, markets actually work better when regulated by open and accountable regulatory procedures. This is also the necessary environment for voluntary self-regulation.

3) 'Equity' relates to distributional fairness in dealing with both non-human and human life. It is an important part of

stewardship. But it is also a crucial element of empowerment. Equity encompasses both rights and duties towards future as well as present generations and ecosystems. Within the principle of equity will be legal norms that guide institutional arrangements such as monitoring, protecting, evaluating, compensating, either in cash or by 'no worse off' compensatory agreements. As with markets and regulations, equity requires socially sanctioned rules and norms that guarantee that the final distribution of power and responsibilities is socially sanctioned. For this to be the case, there has to be vast improvement in, and respect for, governing institutions and their policy packages and procedures. Hence the significance of the introductory criteria for continuation, stewardship and empowerment in the institutional design of civic science for sustainable development.

4) 'Revelation' is a code word for 'going beyond empowerment'. It is aimed at capturing the spirit of communal obligation and citizenship that enables individuals and groups to relate to each others' needs. Revelation is therefore the sum of the processes for discourse and negotiation. When consensus has been reached, initial presuppositions will have altered, and insurmountable policy blockages or inappropriate evaluative procedures will have been exposed and addressed. This is the purpose of revelation. It is a precondition for empowerment.

According to various conceptual analyses, for the most part undertaken by economic theorists, political scientists and sociologists, each of these four components of civic science in the sustainability transition contain attributes that mutually compensate for each other.

The notion of civic science involves two connected themes. One is the suggestion that there is no 'science' outside of culture, and that different cultures interpret science in their own ways. Obvious examples include the apparent impossibility of dealing with high-level radioactive waste without an enormous fight (see Kemp 1993), and the emerging fear over toxic chemicals that may endanger fertility (Colborn et al 1995). In these and many other examples, 'science' has to be an interactive process between 'lay' and 'expert' judgements based on mutual respect and trust. Irwin (1995) provides a fine and accessible analysis of this aspect. The other element is the empowerment referred to earlier, namely the desire for many people to control their own more secure functions through direct and constructive involvement. This in turn has led to the point of the informal, active, society outlined by Nicholson-Lord (1996) in the UK. This element of activism is, or can be, extremely exhilarating and strengthening. But it requires support in official circles, including resources, training and opportunity. This is where the points of interaction would come in, should or when the revenues become available.

At present neither aspect of civic science is so well developed as to be effectively set against the more traditional mechanisms of participation and consultation. In general the traditional approaches have been influenced by a reluctance on the part of those who hold power to relinquish their control with any relish. The whole point of civic science and empowerment is the actual transfer of both respect and power to grassroots levels. So far that remains an elusive relationship, as analysed by the German sociologist Ortwen Renn and his colleagues (1995). What follows is based partly on their work, but also on some interesting conceptual ideas presented by Steve Rayner (1995), and sadly not followed up in terms of this all-important link between civic science and the sustainability transition. To follow this, one way forward is to show how a dialogue of civic science might be broken down along the four themes outlined earlier. For the sake of this analysis, the points that interacting groups of envisioning citizens might address amongst each other are:

- myths of nature, or views of natural tolerances, and vulnerabilities;
- social justice values, in respect of social tolerances, and vulnerabilities;
- policy orientations, or views on the appropriateness of policy instruments for certain socially and economically desired outcomes;
- distributional, or redistributive, arrangements, or beliefs as to how compensation should be shared and in what manner;

- generating consensus by reaching acceptable negotiated outcomes;
- intergenerational responsibilities; views on the rights and needs of future generations;
- liability arrangements, or perspectives on the basis of losses and responsibility for compensation.

Table 6.1 *The promotion of civic science in the sustainability transition*

	Market	Regulatory	Equity	Revelatory
Myths of nature	expandable limits	precautionary limits	breached limits	negotiated limits
Social values	enterprise	protection of vulnerable	citizenship	community
Policy orientations	price signals	rules to contracts	equality of opportunity	inclusion
Distributional arrangements	markets	by agents of rule-makers	by democracy	by negotiation
Generating consent	compensation	by agreed rules	negotiation and compensation	by reasoned discourse
Inter-gener-ationality	future looks after itself	future helped by present	future planned by present	future envisioned
Liability	spread losses	fine redistribution	burden-sharing	by negotiation

In diagrammatic form, the processes of discourse that might frame the promotion of civic science in the sustainability transition might look as suggested in Table 6.1.

From this one can see that there are many variations of the sustainability transition, each of which require serious debate amongst social groups as to how such interests define their objectives and respond to the views and positions of others. It is quite possible to arrive at future visions that are coherent but inherently diverse and unobtainable. This is when the drivers of the sustainability transition outlined at the outset, namely forging new policy correlations with economic interests, may come into play. This of course will be a tremendously difficult task, because many of the positions adopted, notably with regard to equity and revelation, are at serious cross-purposes with mainstream economic thought and institutional practices.

Here is where we return to the 50,000 consultants and practitioners currently operating in the politics of the sustainability transition in a variety of ineffective and effective ways. Hopefully some of these people can be encouraged and enabled to debate more seriously these policy discourses and identify both conceptual reinterpretations of outlook and zones of policy, or evaluative and regulatory incompatibility, that need addressing at various fundamental scales. It is surely only this process of examination, usually via a host of pilot schemes, that such a fundamental change might begin.

One hope is for Local Agenda 21 to be this valuable driver. Right now LA21 is very much a pilot project to allow local governments, of extremely widely varying political and social circumstances, to address the sustainability transition for their local communities. In the UK, all local governments were asked to do just this. About a third are taking this seriously (Tuxworth and Carpenter 1996) by hiring coordinators, instigating sustainability indicator studies, developing performance criteria, and facilitating social and environmental uplift schemes in particularly disadvantaged areas. Of course, local authorities have few discretionary powers and even less discretionary money. There is a lively debate about this policy blockage that in itself is healthy for the sustainability transition.

Some are beginning tentatively to try out visioning exercises using round tables of local interests. The trouble here is obvious. The interests have to be representative, the participants articulate and trained in negotiating skills, and the outcomes that they agree on must be deliverable in policy and cash terms. In practice, none of these crucial conditions for empowerment applies. Pushing civic science into place in the sustainability transition is a tough nut to crack. But at least a start has been made, and that is the spirit in which this chapter is written. There is every point in trying, and in sharing the successes and failures of a truly worthwhile endeavour. Let us hope that this book assists this noble cause.

References

Bennett, J W (1976) *The Ecological Transition: Cultural Anthropology and Human Adaptation* Pergamon, New York

Colborn, T, Dunamoski, D and Myers, J P (1995) *Our Stolen Future* Dutton, New York

Department of the Environment (1991) *Policy Appraisal and the Environment: A Guide for Government Departments* HMSO, London

Department of the Environment (1996) *Indicators of Sustainable Development for the United Kingdom* HMSO, London

Fischer, F and Black, M (eds) (1995) *Greening Environmental Policy: The Politics of a Sustainable Future* Paul Chapman, London

Habermas, J (1987) *A Theory of Communicative Action* Beacon Press, Boston

Irwin, A (1995) *Citizen Science: A Study of People, Expertise and Sustainable Development* Routledge, London

Jacobs, M (1996) *The Politics of the Real World* Earthscan, London

Jordan, G and Richardson, J (1985) *British Politics and the Policy Process: An Arena Approach* George Allen & Unwin, London

Kemp, R V (1993) *The Politics of Radioactive Waste Disposal* Manchester University Press, Manchester

Korten, D (1995) *When Corporations Rule the World* Earthscan, London

Lee, K (1994) *Compass and Gyroscope: Integrating Science and Politics for the Environment* Island Press, New York

Leipert, C and Simonis, V (1987) *Environmental Damage and Environmental Expenditures* IIWG Discussion Paper 87–11, WZB Institute on Environmental Policy, Berlin

Lele, S (1991) 'Sustainable development: a critical review' *World Development* vol 19, no 6, pp 607–621

Lidskog, R (1991) 'In science we trust: on the relation between scientific knowledge, risk consciousness and public trust' *Acta Sociologica* vol 39, no 1, pp 49–58

Meadows, D H, Meadows, D L and Randers, J (1992) *Beyond the Limits: Global Collapse or Sustainable Future* Earthscan, London

Nagpal, T and Foltz, C (eds) (1995) *Choosing our Future: Visions of a Sustainable World* World Resources Institute, Washington DC

Nicholson-Lord, D (1996) 'The veggie-box economy' *Resurgence* vol 177, pp 4–7

O'Riordan, T (ed) (1997) *The Transition to Sustainability: The Politics of Agenda 21 in Europe* Earthscan, London

O'Riordan, T and Jäger, J (eds) (1996) *Politics of Climate Change: a European Perspective* Routledge, London

O'Riordan, T and Voisey, H (1997) 'The political economy of the sustainable development' *Journal of Environmental Politics* (in press)

O'Riordan, T and Voisey, H (eds) (forthcoming) *Institutional Responses to Sustainable Development* Earthscan, London

Pickvance, C and Preteceille, E (eds) (1991) *State Restructuring and Local Power: A Comparative Perspective* Pinter Publishing, London

Putnam, R (1993) *Making Democracy Work: Civic Traditions in Modern Italy* Princeton University Press, Princeton, NJ

Rayner, S (1995) *Observations on Global Governance* Battelle Institute, Washington DC

Renn, O, Webler, T and Wiedermann, P (eds) (1995) *Fairness and Competence in Citizen Participation* Kluwer Publishers, Dordrecht

Rhodes, R B W (1985) 'Power dependence, policy communities and intergovernmental networks' *Public Administration Bulletin*, vol 49, pp 4–13

Rhodes, R A W (1990) 'Policy networks' *Journal of Theoretical Politics* vol 2, no 3, pp 293–317

Rosenhead, J (ed) (1989) *Rational Analysis for a Problematic World: Problem-Structuring Methods for Complexity, Uncertainty and Conflict* John Wiley, Chichester

Sabatier, P A (1987) 'An advocacy coalition framework of policy change and the role of learning policy orientated learning therein' *Policy Studies*, vol 21, pp 129–168

Schwerin, E A (1993) *Mediation, Citizen Empowerment and Transformational Politics* Praeger, New York

Simmons, I (1993) *Environmental History* Blackwell, Oxford

Smith, F D M (ed) (1996) *Environmental Sustainability. Practical and Global Applications* St Lucia Press, Delray Beach, FL

Tuan, Y F (1972) *Topophilia: A Study of Environmental Perception, Attitudes and Values* Prentice Hall, New Jersey

Tuxworth, B and Carpenter, H (1996) *Responses to LA21 in England and Wales* Local Government Management Board, Luton

UN Research Institute for Social Development (1995) *States of Disarray: The Social Effects of Globalisation* Earthscan, London

Weisbrod, M and Janoff, S (1995) *Future Search: An Action Guide to Finding Common Ground in Organisations and Communities* Bennett-Kuckler, San Francisco

Wolff, R (ed) (1996) *Sustainable Urban Development: A Research Proposal* Division of Environmental Sciences, Gothenburg University, Gothenburg, Sweden

7

Us and Them: Finding a New Paradigm for Professionals in Sustainable Development

Robert Chambers

The Context of Change

In the last years of the twentieth century, change seems to be accelerating. Most ages have their contemporary historians who see themselves living through times of exceptionally rapid and potentially catastrophic change, often more rapid and acute than ever before; and change is a natural condition of physical, biological and social systems. But the late 1990s really do seem to be different.

In almost every dimension recent changes have been dramatic. Power, poverty and wealth are concentrated and polarising at the extremes, with a global overclass and a global underclass. Politically, the effects of the end of the Cold War have transformed international relations and mindsets, leaving power concentrated in Washington DC. Ideologically, the North is no longer inhibited by post-colonial guilt and neoliberalism has become a sort of global monoculture. Technologically, computers and communications seem set on ever faster innovation and obsolescence, both shrinking

This essay is an edited extract from Robert Chambers' latest book *Whose Reality Counts?*, published by Intermediate Technology Publications, 103 Southampton Row, London WC1B 4HH. 1997. ISBN 1 85339 386 X.

and expanding the world of those who are linked in, and creating a new class of the excluded. Environmentally, human impact continuously increases. Socially, the values and behaviours of different generations diverge more and more, especially in the North, and the experience is of increasing unemployment, job insecurity, crime, drug abuse and anti-social anomie. More seems to be changing and changing faster than before, and changes seem to be more interconnected and more and more instantly communicated.

The faster the change, the harder the future is to foresee; and the quicker and more global the communication, the greater are the costs of error. Futurologists are discredited. They have been spectacularly wrong, and the errors of economic forecasters have not been few. William J. Baumol has expressed the uncertainty that many feel with his statement that 'I feel obliged to confess that I can offer with any degree of confidence only one prediction – that the future will surprise me' (Baumol 1991, p1). New humility, sensitivity, nimbleness and willingness to change are needed for the more fluid and transient conditions of contemporary life.

Any balance sheet of human development shows achievements and deficits, and any vision of the future presents both problems and opportunities. Current problems have many levels – international, national, regional, community, household, and individual; many dimensions – gender, class, caste, age, occupation, and physical and mental capacity; many implications in domains which are political, legal, economic, social, psychological and ethical. At the same time, concentrations of power mean that huge opportunities exist to make a difference for the better.

I have chosen to focus on 'we' and 'us', as development professionals with power, and to ask about failures, errors and learning, about what we do and do not do, and how we can do better. The argument is that we are much of the problem, that it is through changes in us that much of the solution must be sought. I have written before about 'putting the last first' (Chambers 1983). But to put the last first is the easier half. Putting the first last is harder. For it means that those who are powerful have to step down, sit, and listen, and learn from and empower those who are weak and last.

The polarisation into 'us', development professionals, and 'them', local people, oversimplifies, when the reality is a contin-

uum with ambiguities and crossings over. At the field and community level there are usually people who belong both to 'us' and to
'them'. The point, though, is that those with more power have
more responsibility. There is a sense in which there are upper and
lower systems. The radical activist in a remote village in Bihar may
not identify with the president of the World Bank, nor he with
her. But both are actors, as will be all or almost all who read these
words, in the same upper system of organisation, communication
and power which is ever better linked; and our decisions and
actions impinge on those in the lower systems of local rural and
urban people and places. We are all trying to change things for
others, we say for the better. We are all development professionals.

So the analysis in this essay is concerned more with those who
are first, with 'us' and our errors, omissions, delusions and
dominance, than with 'them', the last. We are many. We are from
both North and South. We include political leaders, writers,
lawyers, film-makers, businessmen, and bankers; students and
teachers in schools, colleges, polytechnics, training institutes and
universities; researchers in all development disciplines; all who
influence or work for and with the multilateral agencies – the
International Monetary Fund (IMF) and the World Bank, the
regional development banks and many others; all those, too, who
influence or work for and with bilateral aid agencies and NGOs;
we include senior decision-makers in all countries; and, most
numerous of all, those who are closest to the action, the field-
workers and headquarters staff of government departments and
agencies and of NGOs who are directly engaged with poor people
and development.

The context of past errors, current rapid change, and an unpredictable future, presents all development professionals with
challenges which are both personal and professional. The most
basic challenge is a need for concepts on which to base action.

An Emerging Consensus on Concepts?

Faced with many dimensions which shift, change and vary, the
temptation is to simplify or despair. However, much can grow on

and out of failures and uncertainties. Past errors as well as achievements contribute to current learning. In the late 1990s, a consensus may be evolving on concepts, objectives and methods which promise a basis for better performance in future.

It is bold to assert that in conditions of accelerating change, concepts may be stabilising. Ideas for development policy and practice have continuously changed, not least in response to the conditions from which they derive and on which they act. With the spread of instant over-communication on the cybernetic superhighway, and with new concentrations of intellect and power in central places, Northern and donor-driven lurches of policy can now spread faster.

At any time there has coexisted a range of vocabulary, concepts, and values, some considered old-fashioned, some current, and some *avant garde*. So it is only to be expected that the frontier words of the late 1990s, such as accountability, ownership, stakeholder and transparency will be followed and perhaps superseded by others. All the same, certain words, concepts and phrases have gradually grown in usage and have a generality and utility which seem to fit them for survival in volatile and turbulent conditions and debates.

At an overarching level, there is the concept of *putting people first*, featuring in the titles of at least two books (Cernea 1985, Burkey 1993). A massive shift in priorities and thinking has been taking place, from things and infrastructure to people and capabilities. Consonant with this shift, five words, taken together, capture and express much of an emerging normative consensus. These are well-being, livelihood, capability, equity and sustainability (see Figure 7.1). Each is linked with the others, and each word represents both ends and means. But well-being has primacy as the overarching end.

- *Well-being:* The objective of development is *enhanced* and *responsible* well-being for all people. Well-being can be described as the experience of good quality of life. Responsible well-being recognises obligations to all others, both alive and of future generations, and to their quality of life.

    Unlike wealth, well-being is open to the whole range of

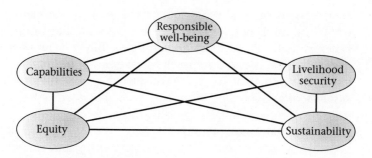

Note: The overarching end is well-being, with capabilities and livelihood as means. Equity and sustainability are principles which qualify livelihood to become livelihood security, and well-being to become responsible well-being.

Figure 7.1 *The web of responsible well-being*

human experience: social and spiritual as well as material. It has many elements. Each person can define it for herself or himself. Perhaps most people would agree to include living standards, access to basic services, security and freedom from fear, health, good relations with others, friendship, love, peace of mind, choice, fulfilment and fun. Extreme poverty and ill-being are strongly linked, but wealth and well-being are not. Reducing poverty diminishes ill-being, but amassing wealth does not assure well-being.

- *Livelihood:* Gaining a secure living is basic to well-being. Livelihood can be defined as adequate stocks and flows of food and cash to meet basic needs and to support responsible well-being. A secure living refers to secure rights and access to resources, food and income, and basic services, and includes reserves and assets to offset risk, ease shocks and meet contingencies.

- *Capabilities:* Capabilities, what people are capable of doing, are means of livelihood and fulfilment and are basic to both well-being and livelihood. Their enhancement through learning, practice, training and education can be means to better living and to well-being. I am using capability in its normal dictionary sense of 'the quality of being capable; ability' (*The Collins English Dictionary*, second edition 1986).

- *Equity:* The poor, weak, vulnerable and exploited, especially women, should come first. Equity qualifies all initiatives in development. This includes human rights, intergenerational and gender equity, and the levelling reversals of putting the last first and the first last being considered in all contexts.
- *Sustainability:* Good conditions and good change must be sustainable – economically, socially, institutionally, and environmentally. Long-term perspectives should apply to all policies and actions, with sustainable well-being and sustainable livelihoods as objectives for present and future generations.

A New Basis for Policies and Practices

When it comes to policies and practice, less consensus can be expected. What ought to be done, and how it should be done, is sensitive to changing conditions. Any tentative outline of consensus here is more open to challenge, and more likely to shift. Still, some elements in a late 1990s view of how to achieve well-being, livelihoods, enhanced capabilities, equity and sustainability, might include:

- balancing *the state and the market*, to benefit, serve and empower the poor;
- seeking *livelihood-intensity* in social and economic change;
- securing *human rights* for all, including peace, the equitable rule of law, and secure rights of property and access for the poor;
- ensuring *means of livelihood* for all, comprising access to livelihood resources and/or employment and/or safety nets;
- providing *basic services* for all, including health, education, water, housing;
- facilitating *participation*, with approaches which are bottom up with processes of learning, rather than top-down with blueprints.

On policies and actions, as on concepts and objectives, there is no final word. There are, as it were, two polarised paradigms: one with a structure which is linear, organised, predictable and converging on equilibrium, and one with a form which is non-linear, chaotic, unpredictable, divergent and non-equilibrium. In the latter, everything is provisional and subject to review. Change and learning know no boundaries. Realities are multiple. But some elements of learning do persist, and time will show whether those above will indeed be among the survivors.

The key is personal choice. The actions of transnational corporations (TNCs), of currency speculators, of UN agencies, of governments, of NGOs are all mediated by individual human decisions and action. People are complex and diverse. People can choose how to behave and what to do. The assumption of pervasive selfishness and greed in neoliberal and male-dominated thought, policy and action has misled with a simplistic view of human nature. This overlooks or underestimates selflessness, generosity and commitment to others, and the fulfilment that these qualities bring. Development theorists have neglected the drives and pleasures of generosity and altruism, and the personal trade-offs between satisfactions.

As words go, *altruism* is a Cinderella of development. Human motivation is many-sided, and almost any act can be seen in a good or bad way. Whatever other negative interpretations may also apply, there is a level at which part of the motivation for many actions is to help others, to make things better for those who are less fortunate or in need. Altruism is a fact of human behaviour, and can be chosen. The huge improvements in health in recent decades had many causes, but the desire to reduce suffering, to cut infant mortality, to make life better for those who are deprived, was surely one. No one is fully determined, and no one is immune from altruism.

The problem is how, in conditions of continuous and accelerating change, to put people first and poor people first of all: how to enable sustainable well-being for all. The thesis of this essay is that solutions can be sought in a new paradigm and a new professionalism.

Basic to a new professionalism is the primacy of the personal. This recognises the power of personal choice, the prevalence of error, and the potential for doing better. The personal, professional and institutional challenge is learning how to learn how to change, and learning how to organise and act.

The new paradigm needs change and adaptability in its genes: for if nothing is permanent but change, then managing and coping with change has to be inherent in the paradigm itself. In this respect, it is a meta-paradigm, a paradigm about paradigms. Different elements will have different degrees of robustness and permanence. Which will endure is not knowable. That they will change is the only certainty. The analytical challenge is to frame a practical paradigm for knowing and acting, and changing how we know and act, in a flux of uncertainty and change.

Myths and Errors

Development experience has been full of errors and myths. These have been serious in almost all domains. To illustrate with only a few examples, these can be found in macro-policy, as with bad lending and then structural adjustment which so badly hurt the poor; in the failures of so many large-scale integrated rural development projects; in scientific beliefs about human nutrition; in the misunderstanding of famines and what should be done to prevent and mitigate their effects; in the development and attempted transfer of agricultural technologies which did not fit poor farmers' conditions and needs; in the imperious introduction of inappropriate management systems for rural development; and in widespread misunderstandings of the relationships between poor people and their environments (for which see Leach and Mearns 1996).

Errors and myths have persisted through decades, reinforced and reasserted by intelligent, highly educated people across the range of disciplines and professional occupations. Learning and change have been slow and often resisted. Some changes and modifications, as with errors in macro policy and projects, were provoked by feedback and failures, learning from experiences and effects in the field. Some were so deeply entrenched that it required long-term, meticulous and versatile research and lobbying to overturn them.

In many professional domains, new understandings are now quite widely accepted. The puzzle is how and why errors were so deeply entrenched in the first place in the beliefs, thinking, values, and actions of development professionals. These included managers, scientists, planners, academics and consultants, of many disciplines, and working in many organisations such as aid agencies, national bureaucracies, research and training institutes, universities and colleges and private firms. How could they all have been so wrong, and wrong for so long? How were so many errors possible, and why were they so sustained?

Different observers would give different answers. There are multiple shifting realities. We choose answers which fit our constructs and predispositions. I am no different from others in having a personally idiosyncratic view and wanting to believe some things more than others. The mix of explanations can be expected to vary.

A first answer lies in the political economy of received narrative, in who gains materially from what is believed. When myth supports policies, projects and programmes, many uppers stand to gain. These are both individuals and organisations: bureaucrats, politicians, contractors, consultants, scientists, researchers and those who fund research; and their organisations – national and international bureaucracies, political systems, companies, firms of consultants, research institutes and research funding agencies. Any one, or several, or all of these, can benefit from the acceptance of wrong ideas, projects or policies.

Conditions vary. Where commercial and political interests dominate in large projects, myths may scarcely be needed. Where commercial and political interests are weaker or combine less, myth and bureaucratic interests can play a bigger part. With natural resources, those who seize land and exploit forests can divert attention from their rapacity by blaming the poor for erosion and deforestation.

Conventional Professionalism Challenged

Professionalism is concerned with our knowledge, and how we learn, analyse and prescribe. Erroneous beliefs were embedded in the concepts, values, methods and behaviour normally dominant in disciplines and professions. Those who have been wrong have had long education and training, whether as macro-economists, engineers, agronomists, ecologists, foresters, administrators or social scientists. Most were highly numerate. Most were specialists. All were linked in with other professional colleagues around the world. Through letters, the telephone, workshops, conferences, professional journals and papers, they were in touch with their professional peers and with current dominant values and beliefs. Their learning, then, was more likely to come laterally or from above, than from below, and to follow current ideologies and fashions. Most of them believed that their professional training and qualifications meant that they knew what was best for local people.

Distance blocks, blurs and distorts vision, and distance is institutionalised. Most of those who were wrong were physically, organisationally, socially and cognitively distant from the people and conditions they were analysing, planning and prescribing for, and making predictions about. Physically, they were centrally placed, in headquarters, in offices, in laboratories and on research stations far from and isolated from local, complex, diverse, dynamic and unpredictable local realities. Organisationally, they were trapped by norms of behaviour, by routines and by resources or their lack, which kept them in central places and rewarded them for working there. Socially, they were different and apart from local people. Their contact, if any, was confined to short special occasions, as development tourists. Cognitively, they were distant, having different categories, criteria, values and life experiences.

Being distant, they relied on secondary data. They calculated with the figures that were to hand, and treated numbers as reality. Analysis, planning and action were top-down and centre-outwards. Centrally determined packages could be transferred to and imposed on local conditions; centrally conceived and constructed realities were transferred.

Power hinders learning. Those who were wrong were powerful. They were senior, almost all men, mostly white, and influential, whether through age, professional authority, control of funds, or position in a hierarchy. Their very power conditioned their perceptions and prevented them from learning. However, power deceives.

Professionalism, distance and power can combine with vested interests to offer spirited resistance to new insights. Old professionals deny new understandings and realities. At the same time, the acceleration of change, the concentration of power and the diversity of people and conditions now make error both easier and more dangerous. It is easier because through new communications, professionals in central places have more instant power, and still little direct contact with the realities their actions affect. It is more dangerous because those who may be affected are more numerous and likely to be affected more quickly. So being right matters more now than ever before.

The question remains how correct, in their turn, new insights are. One conclusion has to be self-doubt. We have to ask how and why we construct our realities, how and why we learn and mislearn. 'Self-critical epistemological awareness' is an ungainly phrase but its acronym fits – SEA. For when faced with the complexity, diversity and dynamism of human and local conditions, there is no normal bedrock on which to anchor and few fixed points. Rather we need a repertoire of skills for staying afloat, steering, finding our way and avoiding shipwreck on a turbulent and transient flux.

So much we thought we knew we did not know, or were wrong about (and very likely much we now think we know we still do not know, or have got wrong): what we need to know is constantly changing. The realities of life and conditions are elusive: they are local, complex, diverse, dynamic and unpredictable. Central professionals are pervasively ignorant, out-of-touch and out-of-date about these realities.

It is not 'them', those who are peripheral, poor, weak and vulnerable, who are responsible for these problems of knowing, acting and error. For it is not they who have been wrong, but us. The first step is then humbling. It is to recognise our ignorance and error. Gradually, and none too soon, development professionals are coming to see that the problem is more 'us' than 'them'. It is with ourselves that we have to start.

Normal professionalism – the ideas, values, methods and behaviour accepted and dominant in professions or disciplines – is a means to status, power and wealth. Commonly, its elements derive from and fit *things* more than *people.*

The highest status disciplines and professions are concerned with things or with people as though they were things. For example, physicists are pre-eminently concerned with the physical world. Biotechnologists are concerned with genetic engineering, with treating living matter as composed of molecules and genes, reduced close to the level of being things. Surgeons need anaesthetists to reduce people to 'things' so that they can operate.

In contrast, the lowest status disciplines and professions are concerned with people as people. Social workers, nurses and agricultural extensionists are confronted by and have to cope with, variously, individuals, families, communities, and farming and livelihood systems.

The working environments of higher status disciplines and professions are standardised, controlled and predictable. Laboratories for physics and biotechnology, greenhouses for plant-breeding, operating theatres for surgery, are indoors and usually sealed off, providing environments which are clean, sterile and dust-free, with controlled temperature and humidity, and specially protected from human contamination: scientists wear white coats or protective clothing; surgeons wear face masks.

In contrast, the lower status disciplines and professions work in environments which are diverse, dynamic and uncontrollable. Social workers, community health workers and agricultural extensionists face the open, dirty and polluted conditions of slums, and poor dwellings, dealing with unpredictable families, sick people, communities, conflict, and risk-prone farming at the mercy of the seasons.

The academic disciplines confirm these polar dimensions of things versus people, and of quantification versus judgement (see Table 7.1). Hard physics has high status, with things as its subject matter. Economics comes next, quantifying, and dealing with people as numbers and their behaviour as describable in laws and equations; and the other social sciences, dealing though they do

Table 7.1 *Two paradigms: things and people*

Point of Departure and reference	Things	People
Mode	Blueprint	Process
Keyword	Planning	Participation
Goals	Pre-set, closed	Evolving, open
Decision-making	Centralised	Decentralised
Analytical assumptions	Reductionist	Systems, holistic
Methods, rules	Standardised, universal	Diverse, local
Technology	Fixed package (table d'hote)	Varied basket (a la carte)
Professionals' interactions with local people	Motivating	Enabling
Local people seen as	Beneficiaries	Partners, actors
Force flow	Supply-push	Demand-pull
Outputs	Uniform infrastructure	Diverse capabilities
Planning and action	Top-down	Bottom-up

Source: Adapted from the work of David Korten
(Korten 1980, 1984, 1995)

with the greater complexities, diversity and uncontrollability of people, have lower status, with social work which tries to help people as people in society lowest of all.

So those, often men, in the clean, controlled and comfortable conditions of the centre, in their dark suits, white coats and black shoes, receive recognition and reap rich rewards for their work with things, and with people as though they were things; and those, often women, in the dirty, chaotic and uncomfortable conditions of the periphery, in their work-a-day clothes and sensible shoes, are poorly paid, looked down on, and little recognised or rewarded for their work with people as people. In the things-people contrast, the gender dimension is pervasive. Were this paradox not so universal and familiar, its unfairness would seem grotesque.

Perhaps the most pervasive value of normal professionalism concerns measurement. Within and between professions, status and respectability are sought and can be gained through quantification, mathematical techniques, and precision. Professions or disciplines which develop or adopt skilled techniques of measurement move upwards. Many physical things are amenable to measurement. The problem is that the idiosyncratic attributes of people are difficult to measure. Their individual behaviour is unpredictable, and the approaches and methods for handling them are in continuous evolution and change.

Quantification and statistics can mislead, distract, be wasteful, simply not make sense, or conflict with common values. What is measured may also not be what matters. Real per capita gross domestic product (GDP) is still widely used as an indicator of how well a country is doing, yet much ill-being contributes to GDP. In the accounts, much of the bad life is counted as positive.

These criticisms do not question the power, relevance and utility of science, measurements and mathematics in many domains. The point is that their proven utility and the reverence attached to them also enables them to be misused and to mislead. In power and influence, counting counts. Quantification brings credibility. But figures and tables can deceive, and numbers construct their own realities. What can be measured and manipulated statistically is then not only seen as real; it comes to be seen as the only or the whole reality.

Not all normal professionalism suffers these defects. High status professionals also have to exercise judgement; and social workers sometimes make measurements. Nor do all academics accept the values which prevail as normal and prestigious. Some reverse them. But professionally they tend to be scattered and peripheral, usually a dispersed and marginal subculture looked down on for their lack of logic and rigour. Meanwhile, the traditional concepts, values, methods and behaviour of their conventional colleagues continue to dominate.

The Professional Prison

Much normal professionalism creates and sustains its own reality. A core magnetic pull draws people inwards towards cities, offices, libraries, laboratories, hospitals, research stations and computers, and then holds them there. For many, this is the road to advancement. To get on, you have to stay in. So professional methods and values set a trap. Status, promotion and power come less from direct contact with the confusing complexity of people, families, communities, livelihoods and farming systems, and more from isolation which permits safe and sophisticated analysis of statistics.

The normal reflex of professionals faced with complexity – of people, environments, farming systems and so on – has been to extract, process and analyse data and use that to decide what to do to those people, environments and farming systems. The processing and analysis of data are private activities under the control of professionals: power, in the name of planning and science – the project plan, the district plan, the farm plan, even the national plan – is retained in their hands and expressed in prescriptions for others.

The methods of modern science then serve to simplify and reframe reality in standard categories, applied from a distance. Social cost-benefit analysis, poverty lines, and production and employment thinking all do violence to complex, diverse and dynamic realities, and mutilate, massage and mould them to make countable packaged units. Those who manipulate these units are empowered and the subjects of analysis disempowered: counting promotes the counter and demotes the counted. Top-down, centre-outwards patterns are then self-reinforcing through rewards, status and power. It is then the reductionist, controlled, simplified and quantified construction which becomes reality for the isolated professional, not that other world, out there.

> *'In the final analysis, power is the right to have your definition of reality prevail over other people's definition of reality'.* (Rowe 1989)

To blame the victim is perhaps the most widespread and popular defence of professional failures. It flatters uppers and flattens

Table 7.2 *Acceptability of explanations of error and failure*

Explanation	Prescription
Lowers' moral defects: lazy, stupid...	They reform themselves
Lowers' ignorance	We teach them
Lack of resources	Increase resources
Our ignorance	They teach us
Our moral defects: ego, greed, short-sight	We reform ourselves

lowers. There is a hierarchy of acceptability to uppers of different explanations of error and failure (see Table 7.2).

With environmental degradation, for example, the normal reflex is to blame the long-term victim, not the short-term exploiter. The photograph on the dust cover of the archetypal green book may show a farmer in the foreground with a smoking, charred forest behind, burnt for shifting cultivation. But such farmers are often victims, moving in only after much of their forest has been destroyed. There is no photograph of the globalised or global person, corpulent, male, middle-aged, suited and cigar-smoking, who grows wealthy on the huge hardwoods that were cut out of the forest first. Fat contractors, corrupt politicians, international companies, and consumers of the North, are hidden from sight.

The environmental damage by the upper is an irreversible act which is hidden or passes out of sight. The damage to the victims is lasting and manifest, a stigma or loss for which they are held responsible. So farmers are blamed when they do not adopt packages of practices, instead of asking whether the packages are wrong; so too staff of multinational banks may blame poor countries which resist policies of structural adjustment, instead of campaigning for the abolition of debts incurred through the banks' own past lending policies. Better to blame the victim than to bear the responsibility oneself.

Whose Reality Counts?

Much has been done that is good. But so much has been so bad that to dispel and correct myth and error remains hugely important. Myths have led to massive misallocations of funds and human resources, to misguided programmes, to missed opportunities, and among professionals to deception, cynicism and loss of commitment.

In seeking to do better, criticism is easy. To be constructive is harder. Taking responsibility and accepting risk by actually doing something is hardest of all. But much of the best learning is through self-critical commitment to action, to engagement with the world, to learning by doing.

Self-critical commitment demands personal insight and reflection. If believing is seeing, we have to question belief in order to see well. Learning is then through doubt, self-examination, and willingness to change; seeking self-correcting engagement with dynamic realities, and making learning a way of life. In a phrase, this is epistemological awareness, awareness of how we learn, how that affects what we think we know, and how we perceive and distort the realities of others. We not only see what we are prepared to see, we create what we want to see; and the more powerful we are, the more we do this, and the more it is done for us. At the cost of their reality, and of pluralism, diversity and truth, others reflect our reality back to us.

The challenges are personal, professional and institutional. The evidence, arguments and conclusions may be modified or rejected. But if they are substantially accepted, then 'more of the same' will not do. Radical change is required on a wide front.

Participatory Rural Appraisal

The errors and myths of the past have challenged professionals to develop better ways of learning and better approaches in development. As they have become more aware of the misfit between the reality they construct, and the reality others experience, some professionals have sought and developed new approaches and methods. Insights and developments in many fields have contributed to the evolution of participatory approaches to learning and action, including the development of participatory rural appraisal (PRA).

PRA can be described as a growing family of approaches, behaviours and methods to enable local people to share, enhance and analyse their knowledge of life and conditions, and to plan, act, monitor and evaluate. Its extensive and growing menu of methods includes visuals such as mapping and diagramming. Practical applications have proliferated, especially in natural resources management, agriculture, health and nutrition, poverty and livelihood programmes, and urban contexts.

PRA has evolved so fast, and continues to evolve so differently, that no final description can serve. At one stage PRA was called 'an approach and methods for learning about rural life and conditions from, with and by rural people', with the emphasis on learning by outsiders. The prepositions were then reversed to read 'by, with and from', as the analysis and learning shifted from 'us' to 'them'.

Then the term PRA came to cover more than just learning. It extended into analysis, planning, action, monitoring and evaluation. It was also used to describe a variety of approaches as they evolved in different countries, contexts and organisations. To cover these, PRA has more recently been described as: 'a family of approaches and methods to enable rural people to share, enhance, and analyse their knowledge of life and conditions, to plan and to act' (Absalom et al 1995). 'Behaviours' can now be added to approaches and methods, and 'to monitor and evaluate' to the activities.

The essence of PRA has been induced from practice and what has been found to work, not deduced from a priori principles. It has three pillars (Mascarenhas et al 1992):

1) The behaviour and attitudes of outsiders, who facilitate, not dominate.
2) The methods, which shift the normal balance from closed to open, from individual to group, from verbal to visual, and from measuring to comparing.
3) Partnership and sharing of information, experience, food and

training, between insiders and outsiders, and between organisations.

PRA as it exists in the late 1990s has many historical roots. It has
evolved from, draws on, and resonates with, several sources and
traditions including activist participatory research. Activist participatory research refers to a family of approaches and methods
which use dialogue and participatory research to enhance people's
awareness and confidence, and to empower their action. It owes
much to the work and inspiration of Paulo Freire, and to the
practice and experience of conscientization in Latin America
(Freire 1970 and 1974). The Freirian theme, that poor and
exploited people can and should be enabled to conduct their own
analysis of their own reality, and take action to change it, has been
widely influential, even though it has remained a minority view
among development professionals as a whole.

In practice, PRA has similarly been concerned with poverty and
equity. The contributions of the activist participatory research
stream to PRA have been more through concepts than methods.
They have in common three principles:

1) Poor people are creative and capable, and can and should do
   much of their own investigation, analysis and planning;
2) Outsiders have roles as convenors, catalysts and facilitators;
3) The weak and marginalised can and should be empowered.

In the mid 1980s, the words 'participation' and 'participatory'
entered the official development vocabulary: participation was a
recurrent theme in the contributions to Michael Cernea's book,
edited for the World Bank, *Putting People First* (1985) which drew
on experience from earlier years.

In the late 1990s, activities described as PRA are being practised
in over 100 countries and there are many PRA-related networks.
Applications have become legion, in almost every sector of field-
level development. Not only NGOs and government departments,
but also training institutes and universities are increasingly using
PRA methods and approaches.

PRA has also shifted and spread in other dimensions:

- In emphasis, moving from stressing methods to stressing behaviour and attitudes.
- In impact, moving from methods to professional change, from behaviour and attitudes to personal change, and from field applications to changes in organisational procedures and cultures.
- In focus, moving from appraisal to analysis, planning, action and monitoring and evaluation.
- In location, moving from rural to include urban.
- In analysis, moving from practice to theory, finding what works, and then asking why?

The popularity of PRA has generated huge problems and widespread bad practice. Quality assurance has become a massive concern. Nevertheless, PRA or PRA-type activities continue to evolve and spread on an astonishing scale. The validity and reliability of information shared through PRA approaches and methods have usually been high. Done well, these shifts and reversals reinforce a shift of power, from extracting to empowering. Local analysts then own the outputs in a process leading to planning and action.

PRA is not a panacea, and will not solve all the problems of the world, but it does open up some ways of trying to tackle these challenges.

Why Did it Take us So Long?

If PRA approaches and methods are so powerful and popular, the puzzle is why it has taken until the 1990s for them to come together, for the menu of methods to achieve what appears to be self-sustaining growth; for so many applications to become evident.

At a personal level, others who like me are middle-aged can be bemused to understand how for decades we have been working in development without knowing about all this. More generally, it is astonishing that it has taken so long, despite earlier pioneers, for the development community as a whole to 'discover' the richness not just of the knowledge of local people, but of their creative and analytical abilities.

Much of the mystery disappears if we look for explanation not in local people, but in ourselves, as outsider professionals. Our personal and professional concepts, values, methods and behaviour have prevented our learning. Our beliefs, behaviour and attitudes have been similar all over the world. Scientists, medical staff, teachers, officials and others have believed their knowledge to be superior and that of farmers and rural people to be inferior; and even when the richness and validity of much local knowledge began to be recognised, we still believed that we had to be the ones who did the analysis.

So as outsiders most of us dominated: we lectured, holding sticks and wagging fingers; we interviewed impatiently, firing rapid questions; we interrupted, and did not listen; we 'put down' the poor and weak. Our reality blanketed that of local people. Our beliefs, demeanour, behaviour and attitudes were then self-validating. Treated as incapable, poor people behaved as incapable. They reflected the beliefs of the powerful, and hid their capabilities even from themselves. Nor did many outsider professionals know how to enable local people to express, share and extend their knowledge. The ignorance and inabilities of local people were then not just an illusion; they were an artefact of our outsiders' behaviour and attitudes, of our arrogant and ignorant manner of interacting.

For participatory approaches and methods to take off, a stage had also to be reached when different conditions could come together: recognition of past error and inadequacy; greater confidence and professionalism in NGOs; the contribution of new approaches and methods; and the emergence of an international community of communication. This has required a critical mass and momentum in which approaches and methods could be shared between disciplines, countries, and organisations.

Most important of all has been the insight that, in facilitating PRA, 'our' behaviour and attitudes matter more than the methods. Perhaps then it is understandable that it has taken until now for these new participatory approaches and methods, in their many forms and with their many labels, to cluster, to coalesce and to spread, as philosophy, repertoire and practice. Done well, they are still a small proportion of all rural and urban development activity. But they have spread and evolved, and continue to spread and evolve. We can ask ourselves whether, at last, their time has come.

At the same time, there is a case for careful and critical analysis, and for evaluating and understanding what happens. PRA seeks and stresses power reversals between uppers and lowers. Initiative and control are passed to local people. The shifts have built-in tendencies towards reversals of power, knowledge and ownership. Four linked practical and ethical issues then arise.

1) *Modes of facilitation:* It is difficult for a facilitator to avoid influencing outcomes. The transfer of reality can take place unintentionally. There is no complete escape from this trap, but solutions are sought in personal behaviour – transparent honesty, respect, sitting down, encouraging, listening, not interrupting.

2) *Who is empowered:* The easy, normal tendency is for those local people who participate and who are empowered to be those who are already more powerful – the better-off, elites, officials, local leaders, men, adults and the healthy, rather than the worse-off, the underclasses, the vulnerable, lay people, women, children and the sick. When this occurs, the weak and poor may end up even worse off. With women, the problem is compounded by their many tasks which make it hard for them to find blocks of undisturbed time long enough for some participatory modes of analysis. Deliberate steps have been repeatedly needed to offset such biases, identifying different groups in a community, finding out the times most convenient for them (Euler 1995), and encouraging and enabling them to conduct their own analysis and express their own priorities (Welbourn 1991).

3) *Who owns the information and what it is used for:* The unselfconscious sharing of information by local people through participatory methods is open to abuse by outsiders. PRA methods could be a clever trick for luring unsuspecting local people into parting with their knowledge. There is also the issue of who owns the physical output of the analysis. Most PRA practitioners have a strict code that the outputs belong to

those who created them and that only exceptionally, if at all, can outputs be borrowed.

4) *Empowerment and process:* The ideal sought by some PRA practitioners is a process in which people, and especially the weaker and poorer, are enabled not just to express and analyse their reality, but to plan and to act. The outputs of the process are enhanced knowledge and capability, an ability to make demands, and action and change.

All this fits together through the popularity and power of PRA. Conditions are not always right. But when they are, local people, and especially poorer people, enjoy the creative learning that comes from presenting their knowledge and their reality. They gain confidence, finding that they can do things they did not know they could, showing and analysing their complex realities.

Things are then seen together and differently. It is not just that local people share knowledge with outsiders. They themselves learn more of what they know, and together present and build up more than any one knew alone. It is not the reality of the outsider which is transferred and imposed, but theirs which is expressed, built up, and shared, and their confidence and capabilities which are strengthened. In a practical way, it is the reality of local people that comes to count.

Rigour, Relevance and Quality

The purpose of rigour is the assurance of quality. As traditionally conceived in the social and natural sciences, rigour is linked with measurements, statistical tests, and replicability. However, the simplifications which result, even if the measurements are accurate, miss or misrepresent much of the complexity, diversity and dynamism of system interrelationships. In consequence, they are often not useful. Further foundations for quality and rigour are needed, based on two sets of criteria: credibility and relevance. Credibility is the quality of being believable as a representation of a reality. Relevance refers to practical utility for learning and action.

The rigour of relevance requires continuous reflection on the potential utility of process and analysis. It is supported by a local focus and a participatory process. The modes of analysis accommodate and express complexity, diversity and change. People experience the process as creative, fulfilling and often fun. Social energy is released. The momentum of participation homes in on, and can be channelled towards, practical relevance in identifying options, expressing preferences, planning, and action. And this practical relevance in turn generates more social energy and commitment. So the rigour of relevance is sustained by virtuous circles of social energy. People do it, and do it well, because they see a point in it.

The values and preferences of poor local people typically contrast with those of the better off, outsiders and professionals. They need and want to be able to take a long view. They can manage greater complexity. Their values are typically numerous and detailed. Their preferences often differ from those supposed for them by professionals. Local people are themselves diverse, with sharp contrasts of preferences and priorities by age, gender, social and ethnic group, and wealth.

Participation, empowerment and mutual respect enable poor people to express and analyse their individual and shared realities. The principles and practices of participatory appraisal facilitate this analysis and expression. The realities which are expressed differ, as do the environments, resources, experiences, values, cultures, and livelihood strategies of individuals and groups. We can talk, then, empirically, as post-modernists do, of multiple realities; and we can talk normatively of privileging the multiple realities of lowers.

A person who is not poor who pronounces on what matters to those who are poor is in a trap. Self-critical analysis, sensitive rapport and participatory methods can contribute some valid insight into the lives, values, priorities and preferences of poor people. We can struggle to reconstruct our realities to reflect what poor people indicate to be theirs. But there will always be distortions. We can never fully escape our conditioning. But if the reality of poor people is to count more, we have to dare to try to know it better.

Paradigm of People as People

In an evolving paradigm of development there is a new high ground, a paradigm of people as people. Local, complex, diverse, dynamic and unpredictable, its conditions are difficult to measure and demand judgement. Good PRA aims to empower lowers. Its principles, precepts and practices resonate with parallel evolutions in the natural sciences, chaos and complexity theory, the social sciences and post-modernism, and business management.

On the new high ground, decentralisation, democracy, diversity and dynamism combine. Multiple local and individual realities are recognised, accepted, enhanced and celebrated. Truth, trust and diversity link. Doubt, critical self-awareness, and acknowledgement of error are valued. Reversals, positive-sums and 'both-and' thinking are mutual reinforcing.

To the new high ground the PRA experience adds empirical affirmations: that 'lowers can do it' , that social synergy and fun are a positive sum, and that uppers' behaviour, attitudes and personal responsibility are central. For the realities of lowers to count more, and for the new high ground to prevail, it is uppers who have to change.

In the natural sciences, conventional approaches, using hard systems and reductionist assumptions and methods, are in particular crisis when faced with many of our important problems (Mearns 1991; Appleyard 1992).

Scientific method is not competent to predict or prescribe for the complex open systems which matter most. Global environmental issues involve huge uncertainties and demand what Functowicz and Ravetz (1990) call a 'second order science' in which judgement plays a more recognised part. Precise understanding, prediction and prescription for local agro-eco-social systems can be similarly elusive. This is not a new discovery. Jeremy Swift wrote in 1981:

> *'A major World Bank livestock development project in Mali is based, for crucial calculations of sustainable grazing pressure, on the report of a highly competent ecologist in 1972; the calculations were redone in 1977/78 by a different, equally well-qualified ecologist, who halved the earlier*

carrying capacity. Nobody is to blame; the science is inexact.
But the consequences could be disastrous for the project, and
more so for the pastoralists involved'. (Swift 1981)

The evolving paradigm is permanently provisional. It differs from
Thomas Kuhn's presentation of scientific paradigms which is that
'probably the single most prevalent claim advanced by the proponents of a new paradigm is that they can solve the problems that
have led the old one to a crisis' (Kuhn 1962).

Kuhn's paradigms resemble structures which are built up and
built upon, with some of the solidity and ultimate fragility of a
fixed physical thing. When finally challenged, they crumble and
fall, to be replaced by a new structure. The new evolving paradigm
is more like a living thing which grows, changing form to fit its
changing environment, flexible, able to yield and able to expand.

PRA and the New High Ground

'If PRA as a longer-term process is to have a meaningful
influence on mainstream development practice, radical
institutional, personal and professional changes are neces-
sary'. (Cornwall and Fleming 1995)

'It is not that we should simply seek new and better ways
for managing society, the economy and the world. The
point is that we should fundamentally change how we
behave'. (Havel 1992)

The new high ground presents challenges. Empowerment is
through identifying the weak and enabling them to gain skills,
confidence and knowledge. They then analyse, monitor and evaluate; make their own videos; become consultants and trainers;
organise themselves; and negotiate resolution of conflicts.

The evolving paradigm implies and demands changes which
are institutional, professional and personal. Institutional change
needs a long-term perspective, with patient and painstaking
sequences of learning and reorientation. Professional change needs

new concepts, values, methods and behaviours, and new curricula and approaches to learning. Personal change and commitment to change have primacy, and can be sought experientially. Learning to change, and learning to enjoy change, are fundamental.

Two dimensions of responsible well-being for uppers stand out: the first, altruism or generosity to put the *last first*, is easier to accept, but the second, disempowerment, putting the *first last*, is new on the agenda and at first looks harder: uppers often see disempowerment as loss but, often, all can gain.

The PRA experience has shown that disempowerment can liberate not only lowers from subordination, but uppers from professional prisons and personal stress. The search now is for more ways for uppers to gain from exercising less power.

Personal belief, behaviour and being are then the crux. If whole systems are to shift and transform, it will be because of the sum and interaction of innumerable personal actions and changes in what sort of people we are. Personal change is a minefield, the subject of much evangelism, mythology, popular writing, and psychological and managerial lore. It is value-laden. It concerns what sort of people we are and become: closed or open, fearful or secure, callous or caring, hating or tolerant, violent or peacemaking. It raises the question: whose values count? Do we, the relatively powerful, have an obligation to enable lowers to express their values, to question and doubt our own, and to discuss them with others who differ? Do we also have a right or duty, with whatever reserve and caution, to present and act on our own values?

Participatory styles and management are liberating. Centralised control of more than the minimum is stressful as well as inefficient. Decentralisation decreases punitive management and fear. There are fewer errors of standardisation and control, and less of the deceptions of power. When responsibility is shared and dispersed, the strain of centralised work overload and of doing badly are diminished. The main responsibility for development is removed from overburdened shoulders, and conflict reduced by permitting and promoting local diversity.

The most seminal learning from the PRA experience is how fulfilling is it to facilitate participation. Gains to uppers take several forms. They overlap, but can be summarised:

- *Effectiveness:* Disempowerment offers new roles and new effectiveness. To facilitate participation is practical, and to use the ugly jargon, cost-effective. It works. Uppers can gain from the instrumental success of the approach.
- *Collegiality:* Power on a pinnacle is lonely. In a participatory mode, a boss is not isolated, but a team member. Relationships are more equal, with mutual learning and partnership.
- *Peace of mind:* Disempowerment spreads responsibility and diminishes stress. Openness, honesty and realism make for peace of mind.
- *Fun:* Until recently with PRA, I do not remember ever having read this word in any writing about development. Faced with the extremes of cruelty and deprivation, talk of fun seems frivolous. But fun – creativity, play, laughter, shared pleasures – are part of what most people value and wish for themselves and for others. Repeatedly, PRA experiences have been enjoyed by participants who conduct their own analysis and are creative, and are also a delight for facilitators who act as catalysts, and experience the pleasure of helping others learn, grow, achieve, and gain their own fulfilment.

All this comes together in responsible well-being. Richard Forsyth (1991) has suggested that well-being is doing good plus having fun. Some of 'doing good' would have its usual sense of altruism and generosity. But in the spirit of this essay, it goes further. It involves changes in dominant behaviour. These entail having respect, standing down, shutting up, and facilitating, enabling and empowering. It is then that effectiveness, collegiality, liberation, peace of mind and a fulfilment that goes far beyond generosity, can follow.

The frontier now is to develop and spread ways to help development professionals and other uppers to change. This frontier has always been there, though little recognised. The big shift for the development agenda now, and for the twenty-first century, is to focus priority on personal, professional and institutional change. PRA provides some leads, but is only one small part, one small beginning. Other inventions and actions are parallel, and more are needed on a vast scale.

The question is whether we, as development professionals, have the vision, will and guts to embrace and use these powerful and popular behaviours, methods and approaches, and:

- as economists and bureaucrats to decentralise, destandardise and support local diversity;
- as staff in NGOs to continue to evolve, apply, share and spread participatory approaches and methods;
- as teachers in universities, training institutes and colleges, to go ourselves and with our students to local people to learn, to revise our curricula, rewrite our textbooks, to lecture less and more to help others learn;
- as staff in government organisations, not to talk down but to listen, learn and facilitate, and to provide choices, and responsive services;
- as political leaders, to promote and sustain decentralisation, democratic values, tolerance, peace and the equitable rule of law;
- as people, to be self-critically aware, to respect others, and to value truth, trust and diversity;
- as uppers, to disempower ourselves, controlling only the minimum, devolving decisions, encouraging and rewarding local initiative, and finding fulfilment and fun in enabling others to express, analyse and act on their diverse realities.

For we can all think for ourselves and help others to do the same. We can all define responsible well-being in our own ways for ourselves. We can all celebrate local and personal diversity. In different ways, some small, some big, most of us can challenge centralised power, convention, and uniformity. And most of us can decide to empower others, lowers, the weak, poor and vulnerable, enabling them to express their different realities and make them count.

Development – good change – flows from innumerable personal decisions and action. It can be made to happen. There is no need to wait. There is a vanguard to join and new high ground to explore.

References

Absalom, E et al (1995) 'Participatory methods and approaches: sharing
  our concerns and looking to the future', *PLA Notes* no 22, pp 5–10
Appleyard, B (1992 *Understanding the Present: Science and the Soul of
  Modern Man* Pan Books (Picador), London,
Baumol, W J (1991) 'Toward a newer economics: the future lies ahead!',
  Economic Journal, no 101, pp 1–8
Burkey, S (1993) *People First: A Guide to Self-Reliant Participatory Rural
  Development* Zed Books, London and New Jersey
Cernea, M (ed) (1985) *Putting People First: Sociological Variables in
  Development Projects* John Hopkins University, Baltimore
Chambers, R (1983) *Rural Development. Putting the Last First* Longman,
  Harlow
Cornwall, A and Fleming, S (1995) 'Context and complexity: anthropo-
  logical reflections on PRA', *PLA Notes* no 24, pp 8–12
Euler, C (1995) 'Women prefer lunchtime', *PLA Notes* no 22, p 28
Forsyth, R (1991) 'Towards a grounded morality', *Changes*, vol 9, no 4,
  pp 264–78
Freire, P (1970) *Pedagogy of the Oppressed* The Seabury Press, New York
Freire, P (1974) *Education for Critical Consciousness* Sheed and Ward,
  London (original edition Editora Paz e Terra, Rio de Janeiro, 1967)
Funtowicz, S O and Ravetz J R (1990) *Global Environmental Issues and
  Emergence of Second Order Science* Commission of the European
  Communities, Luxembourg
Havel, V (1992) Condensation of a speech to the Davos Development
  Conference, reported in *New York Times*, 1 March 1992
Korten, D C (1980) 'Community organisation and rural development: a
  learning process approach', *Public Administration Review*, vol 40,
  pp 480–510
Korten, D C (1984) 'Rural development programming: the learning
  process approach', in Korten and Klauss (eds), *People-centred
  Development*, Kumarian Press, West Hartford
Korten, D (1995) 'Sustainability and the global economy: beyond Bretton
  Woods', *Forest, Trees and People Newsletter* no 29, pp 4–10
Kuhn, T (1962) *The Structure of Scientific Revolutions* University of Chicago
  Press, Illinois
Leach, M and Mearns, R (1996) *The Lie of the Land: Challenging Received
  Wisdom in African Environmental Change and Policy* International
  African Institute in association with James Curry, Oxford and
  Heinemann, Portsmouth NH
Mascarenhas, J and Hildalgo, R (1992) *Experience of a Participatory Rural
  Appraisal Exercise* Paper for International Course on Regenerative
  Agriculture, IIRR, Silang, Cavite, Philippines, 21–23 October

Mearns, R (1991) 'Environmental implications of structural adjustment: reflections on scientific methods', *Institute of Development Studies Discussion Paper* 284, IDS, University of Sussex, Brighton
Rowe, D (1989) Foreword, in Masson, J *Against Therapy* Collins, London
Swift, J (1981) 'Rapid appraisal and cost-effective research in West Africa', *Agricultural Administration*, vol 8, pp 485–92
Welbourn, A (1991) 'The analysis of difference', *RRA Notes* no 14, pp 14–23

8

Bottle Banks in Arcadia? Environmental Campaigning and Social Justice

Ken Worpole

Camberwell Green is probably one of the most resilient green open spaces in any city in the world. Located at the junction of three – frequently gridlocked – arterial roads in inner London, the noise and fumes from the cars, buses and lorries test the limits of human tolerance. On a hot summer's day you can almost cut the poisonous haze with a knife. There are high levels of social deprivation in this part of London and particularly high levels of alcohol abuse. The green itself is often used by small schools of drinkers, and the pubs in the immediate area are open all day, sometimes blaring out loud music. Fights and drunken sprawls are not uncommon.

In a harsh and difficult environment, Camberwell Green functions as a small oasis, still offering people somewhere to bring their children to play (which they do), a place to sit on a bench for a few minutes as a break from carrying the shopping (this is not an area of high car ownership), for couples to meet and talk, and for many to take a short-cut from one main road to the next that brings them briefly within the shade of a few trees. Such a site needs all the support it can get. However, it is also now the home of a row of bottle banks and recycling bins, which provide the final *coup de grace* to the original arcadian vision. The dream has most certainly fled. The bottle banks, sometimes filled to overflowing, with their surrounding pools of broken glass and bottles, their cardboard boxes and discarded plastic bags, only add to the degradation of the setting. One wonders precisely what social vision allowed environmentalist politics to add the final touch to the physical desolation of this unlucky neighbourhood.

The reason I became interested in Camberwell Green is that during the *Park Life* study (Greenhalgh and Worpole 1995) – the largest study of park use ever undertaken in Britain – one of the research methods used was traditional 'participant observation', and on three separate occasions I sat in, or walked around, Camberwell Green for half a day at a time, observing what was going on, the patterns of use (and abuse), and occasionally talking to people. I and others did this in many different parks and green spaces around the country. In the course of the study more than 100 parks were visited throughout the UK, 12 studied in detail, and more than 10,000 people surveyed in their use of these parks, and of those over a thousand were interviewed in person.

What became clear was that when most people talk about 'the environment', they are usually referring, when approving, to the cleanliness of the local streets, the lack of vandalism, the well-kept schools, shops and parks, a low crime rate and its sense of neighbourliness – a very different definition from that used by ecologists, environmental activists and academics interested in green issues. Research done by the Centre for the Study of Environmental Change (CSEC) at Lancaster University for Lancashire County Council (Macnaghten *et al* 1995) confirms this gap in meaning and understanding between the everyday use of the term – what we might term the vernacular environment – and the organic environment. It is also confirmed by a recent comment from Carolyn Harrison, who with Jacquie Burgess at University College London has done so much work on popular attitudes to environmental issues, noting that,

> *'People employ an inclusive definition of natural space which embraces un-named plots encountered on the way to work, the shops, pub and school and extends to include cemeteries, parks, gardens, woods and riverside'.* (Urban Environment Today, 1997)

The gap between popular and professional understandings of environmental issues also symbolises the gap between social and ecological concerns, or what Ebenezer Howard once despairingly described as the 'unholy, unnatural separation of society and nature' (in Hall, 1992), even if one generally believes, along with Ulrich Beck, that today we are living in a post-natural environment as a result of the global impacts of human activity (Beck, 1992).

One could go even further, and suggest that in some places on occasions, social justice politics are in direct conflict with environmental politics, and yet to date there has been a rather easy assumption that the two can be neatly aligned or reciprocated.

That this is not the case, as we have already seen in Camberwell, also emerges in a recent account of the 'Pure Genius' land occupation organised by 'The Land is Ours' movement in 1996 (Featherstone 1997). Dave Featherstone's sympathetic account of the occupation nevertheless criticises the naiveté of some of the organisers, whose quasi-ruralist belief-system failed almost completely in providing them with a way of understanding the complexities and indeed brutalities of urban politics and urban alternative lifestyles:

> 'The green movement's tendency to root itself in the values of an imagined idyllic countryside based in a rather rigid gaze to the past, which castigates the city as a virulent pathological excrescence, has led to a poverty of green perspectives on cities and a reticence to seriously engage in urban issues'. (Featherstone, 1997)

In the 'Pure Genius' occupation, two quite different objectives – to occupy a large piece of derelict land kept empty for its potential development value, at the same time as creating a new community for homeless and outcast Londoners – not only clashed with each other but almost destroyed each other, without the need for any external enemies or forces of oppression.

Social and Environmental Politics – A Great Divide?

There is a danger at present of finding ourselves quite unable to cross the divide between social politics and environmental politics, a divide which has its origins in the powerful faultline which fractures British (but especially English) culture, notably that between the city and the country, or between the urban idyll (cosmopolitan, collectivist, cerebral, intense and emotionally alienated) and the rural idyll (organic, self-sufficient, physically rewarding, intellectually alienated).

The danger represented by this divide is particularly acute at present, as linking social and environmental politics is fundamental to sustainable development. At the same time, green politics has reverted to rather understandable but essentially rural concerns with preserving the landscape, organic food production, and a concern for animal rights, rather than meeting the challenge of urban environmentalism which is much more to do with issues of social trust, combating poverty and homelessness, public health and employment issues, and greater equity and security for a growing proportion of families and individuals without meaningful work, adequate housing or any stake in civil society, let alone a relationship to the land or the natural heritage. As various writers note elsewhere in this book, poverty and sustainability are incompatible.

We therefore need to elaborate a different kind of urban environmental politics, especially in terms of methods, which starts from the social needs and understandings of communities, and their assumed desire to create better places in which to live (and raise families if they so wish), and which then works outwards to the wider understandings of environmental issues which currently make up the green agenda.

Greening the City?

One way of apparently overcoming this enormous gulf between town and country, which is often a matter of symbolic distance rather than spatial distance, is to green the city, and such policies have won widescale support and approval. The work of Groundwork in helping communities to reclaim derelict urban land for green space in its 'Changing Places' programme, the Countryside Commission's 'Urban Trees' and 'Millennium Greens' programmes, the Woodland Trust's 'Woods on your Doorstep' programme, together with the work of the Urban Wildlife Partnership and the National Urban Forestry Unit, the advocacy of energetic writers and campaigners such as David Nicholson-Lord, author of *The Greening of the Cities* (1987), and most recently the UK government's own report on *Greening the City* (DoE 1996), are all evidence of this turn to environmental reclamation as one of the principal forms of urban regeneration.

Some would argue, however, that these initiatives remain fairly marginal to the deep structural economic and social problems facing urban communities, and could even be counter-productive, given that many current urban problems are likely to be best solved by greater densities to support new amenities and jobs, rather than the further dilution of urban form by an emphasis on creating more open space. In fact, one can point to many examples of misapplied open space planning which have proved socially disastrous, leaving some housing estates even further isolated or cut off from the urban core.

A fuller critique of urban greening will have to be developed another time. However, it is currently one of the favoured policies in urban regeneration, even though it often repeats many of the same mistakes made in earlier urban regeneration strategies which concentrated on large-scale capital programmes for improving the built fabric and infrastructure, often ignoring local people's needs, interests, and indeed potential involvement, in favour of schemes that looked good on the drawing board and on the display stands at the town hall. In short, it concentrated on the physical environment rather than on supporting people-based initiatives and activities.

This was certainly the conclusion of the exhaustive analysis, *Assessing the Impact of Urban Policy* (Robson et al 1994), commissioned by the UK government to evaluate the 'overall impact of central government urban policy' in England in the 1980s. Among the principal findings were that money did not always get to those areas which needed it most; that disadvantage was continuing to be concentrated in many urban areas; that unemployment had become even more spatially concentrated over time; that residents of disadvantaged areas often maintained a high degree of place-loyalty and that this human and social dimension had been undervalued; that policies were often nullified by poor national and local government inter-departmental coordination and cooperation; and finally that economic and environmental goals had been prioritised over social and community interests – in retrospect seen to have been perhaps *the* major policy mistake.

What is at issue is finding the balance between people and things, between helping communities and social networks to strengthen their capacities to take on the long term business of maintaining (socially) sustainable communities and supporting physical improvements at the same time, a point which both Marilyn Taylor (Chapter 9) and Diane Warburton (Chapter 1) also emphasise. Physical and environmental regeneration without social regeneration is a road to nowhere, for as Anne Power and Rebecca Tunstall demonstrated in their study of British riots in 1991 to 1992, a number of these riots involved attacks and vandalism directed against expensive renewal projects, leading Power and Tunstall to argue that 'in some areas local activists suggested that these programmes were directly provocative, since most government resources went on buildings rather than on jobs, on large outside contractors rather than small local businesses...' (Power and Tunstall 1997).

Yet the vocabularies and practices of urban regeneration remain dominated by physical regeneration – now compounded by large scale lottery capital funding for new museums, art galleries, concert halls, town squares and large numbers of urban design projects, often invoking the mantra of urban renewal – as are the current debates about future house-building programmes and the need for new settlements. The anticipated need for 4.4 million new households by the year 2016 has produced a rather bad tempered and sectional debate dominated by land-use planning arguments, in which the views of influential bodies such as the Council for the Protection of Rural England, the Countryside Commission, the Royal Town Planning Institute, the Town and Country Planning Association, the Civic Trust and English

Partnerships are very strong on matters concerning locations, zoning policies and densities, but very weak on the changing patterns of social relations, household composition, let alone issues of gender and race.

Nor is there sufficient recognition of the fact that British culture is now clearly multicultural in its make-up, increasingly experimental and flexible in its familial and domestic relationships, and highly vulnerable to the massive economic restructuring processes which are changing the relationships between home, work and leisure, in quite fundamental ways. The social route to sustainability is rather more complex than the environmental route, but it is equally important.

A Question of Gender?

The gender issue is particularly germane to the debate about sustainable communities. Commentators such as Bea Campbell (Campbell 1993), and more recently Power and Tunstall (1997), have argued that the high levels of crime, vandalism and social disorder are almost exclusively caused by disaffected young men, and that it is often regarded as 'women's work' to clear up after them. The lost role and identity of the young working class male with poor levels of educational attainment, living in areas blighted by high levels of unemployment, and increasingly physically and symbolically separated from traditional mixed urban centres on far flung housing estates, is acknowledged to be one of the most pressing social issues of our time.

Yet most urban and environmental regeneration strategies are gender-blind. A recent discussion paper by Nicky May of Oxfam for the Joseph Rowntree Foundation has noted that 'almost all the mainstream literature (outside specialist feminist or equalities writing) is silent on the issue of gender, despite the fact that everyone agrees that it is women who are mostly involved in community regeneration' (May 1997). For what Oxfam has learned from its work in developing countries is that 'putting resources in the hands of women is more likely to benefit the entire family than if resources are controlled by men.'

As we know, it is frequently women who take on the care of children and the elderly, who do most domestic work, who become active in local amenity campaigns, who are more likely to use public transport because they are less likely to have access to a car, and therefore most fully engage with and are affected by the day to day environment in which they live. As we saw in the *Park Life* research, women and children are amongst the most consistent users of parks and other open space amenities, yet the parks profession remains dominated by men, who often display little real understanding of local needs, and who, for example, see play provision as a technical or engineering issue, or the banning of dogs from play areas an over-worrisome legal problem, rather than as urgent matters of real concern. It is worth noting that in the most well-known examples of successful urban park programmes in the US, most of them have been led by women.

Here, too, when we looked at best practice for the 1996 DoE study, *People, Parks & Cities*, (Greenhalgh and Worpole 1996) we found that most of the best examples of community involvement in restoring local parks to active use and management – in Stirling, Hartlepool, East Durham, Camden, and elsewhere, were all led by women. Women tend to start from the affective issues – safety, the education and well-being of children and other more vulnerable sections of the community, environmental health problems, whereas the men, who still dominate local government planning and amenity provision, are usually more instrumental, preoccupied with traffic control, violations of planning 'use-classes', waste-management, intrusive and dangerous industrial processes, the upkeep and staffing of buildings, and avoiding experiment and change wherever possible. The current crisis of legitimacy of local government in many towns and cities, and the flurry of concern with public consultation involving focus groups, citizens' juries, and neighbourhood committees, is a response to the breakdown of understanding and credibility between these two lifeworlds, which are often underscored by gendered forms of power and control.

Unless environmental movements acknowledge the central role that women play in local environmental and amenity activities – as opposed to the men who tend to be found leading the national campaigns – then it is unlikely that the utopian aim of reconciling the social with the environmental will come any closer to realisa-tion. Yet we must avoid the dangers of a crude kind of gender essentialism in the current concern for the best way forward for community development. There are often quite clear historical explanations for the 'lost role' of some men in some communities, in that the most difficult social conditions occur in conurbations most devastated by the loss of heavy industry or mass manufactur-ing – one thinks of Tyneside, Liverpool, Glasgow, Cardiff and Swansea, Oxford even – leaving communities with only very weak connections and networks with the wider society, and facing the prospect of moving from mass-production work and housing tradi-tions (and often large bleak wastes of derelict, polluted land) to more pluralistic, mixed economies and social patterns, including, one hopes, greater environmental diversity. This has been described as a general move from 'Fordist' to 'Post-Fordist' economies and cultures. Sustainability in my opinion is inextricably linked with the values of social and economic pluralism and diversity.

Interestingly among the organisations which have stepped into some of these areas most successfully with job creation schemes – or as they are now called in more sophisticated circles, intermedi-ate labour markets (ILMs) – have been environmental organisations such as Groundwork, housing associations working under the generic 'Housing Plus' programme, and physical environmental improvement programmes such as Glasgow's much-emulated WISE scheme. The welfare-to-work programmes of the new govern-ment will bring even more people into this sector.

Reframing Urban Environmental Policy

A recent study by the independent research network, Comedia, and the think-tank Demos, called *The Richness of Cities*, (Greenhalgh et al 1997) challenges traditional policy specialisms, with a view to re-framing urban policy. It was agreed at the outset that rather than commission working papers under headings such as housing, employment, social services, community development, environmental action, we have chosen to work – and hopefully to think – within the more flexible and comprehensive categories of *livelihood, habitat, connectedness* and *trust.* In this way it is intended to think and act beyond traditional binary oppositions – town/country, work/dole, women's work/men's work, public/ private, social/environmental – towards looser, foot-in-both-camps ways of formulating policy.

So far this has proved very productive, yet at present we are unable to find an answer to the crucial question as to whether the high density, compact city is more environmentally sustainable than the lower-density suburb or new town settlement. The British architect and master-planner, Terry Farrell, for example, says it is, as do other architects and urbanists such as Sir Richard Rogers, strongly supported by John Gummer and the rural lobby, who naturally have a vested interest in resisting any further develop- ment in rural areas.

However, a number of recent writers on the ecology of cities such as Michael Hough (1995), Tom Turner (1996), and the influ- ential Australian planner, Pat Troy (1997), as well as writers such as Martin Pawley (1997), reject this view entirely, believing that the energy costs of urban construction and maintenance, and the lack of responsiveness to topographical and natural processes, by far outweigh the energy costs of the increased car use occasioned by peripheral suburban or low-density development. At present it seems architects favour high-density cities (surprise, surprise), and planners favour dispersed settlements. The debate about urban policy somehow falls in between.

To complicate matters, many now believe that high-density living tends to be more socially mixed, and therefore more socially sustainable. So we may be in a position of having to choose between supporting greater social cohesion in high-density devel- opments, or greater environmental sustainability in low density settlements. Table 8.1 seeks to present the argument and counter- arguments about these issues in a more diagrammatic way:

This seems to me the crucial area where we really do need much more research, since at present, public and professional opinion is largely a matter of personal preferences and intellectual sympathies rather than a matter of sifting through hard evidence one way or the other. But the issue is critical and central to government policy across many boundaries. Certainly if riots tell us anything about

Table 8.1 *Arguments for and against high- and low-density living*

Higher Density	Lower Density
Ageing, energy-intensive infrastructure	Modern, energy-efficient infrastructure
More social mix	Greater social uniformity
Disorder as a virtue (Richard Sennett)	Order as a virtue (Alice Coleman)
Favoured by architects	Favoured by planners
Open-minded spaces	Single-minded spaces
Greater use of public transport	Greater use of private car
Disposal of rainwater & waste a problem	Disposal of rainwater & waste a solution
Safeway's mange-touts from Zimbabwe	Grow your own
Experimental lifestyles	The nuclear family
Mean streets where only men may go	A woman's realm
Fear of crime	Concern about animal welfare
24-hour city	9–5
Cosmopolitanism	Englishness
Albert Square	Brookside Close
Riots in 1980s	Riots in 1990s

where social relations are currently being tested to destruction – which I think they do – then the new areas of concern are to be found in sprawling low-density estates and suburbs with increasingly tenuous connections to the economic and cultural networks which characterise dynamic cities, and where there is little social and cultural differentiation, contiguity and exchange of the kind which supports tolerance and respect for difference.

In the current debate about what to do best to tackle the issues posed by the endemic processes of social exclusion, Perri 6 has argued that, 'policies to regenerate poor areas today would more sensibly start with learning rather than the state of the physical environment.' (6 1997). Note the use of the word *learning* rather than *education*, the active self-directing principle rather than the institutionally prescribed and delivered form of provision. If we do wish to support the development of sustainable communities we have to stress the active making and remaking of one's own local identity, place and culture, as exemplified in the work of organisations such as Common Ground and Groundwork, in the growth of community development trusts, and in more participative, deliberative forms of local democracy.

Responding to a Changing Environmental Agenda

The continuing growth of Groundwork in recent years is a case study in astute organisational responsiveness to a changing environmental agenda. Originally established by the Countryside Commission in 1982 as a single issue initiative to reclaim urban fringe derelict land, it has progressively moved away from its principle – and highly instrumental – role as an agency concerned with land reclamation to quite sophisticated and radical programmes of people-based community building. A lot of its work is done in ex-coalfield communities and other areas of high unemployment and low social morale, often focusing on tapping the energies and needs of young people. It was described to me recently by one of its senior staff as no longer being seen as a 'green' organisation but as a 'people-centred' social task force. It has also moved from being a 'countryside' initiative to an 'urban' regeneration movement. There are now, at the time of writing, some 41 separate Groundwork trusts, with more than 450 board members running them, employing 750 staff and involving between 60 – 100,000 volunteers.

Many of the local trust members and staff have moved across from the campaigning environmental movement – Friends of the Earth, Greenpeace, even no doubt the animal rights movement – to these very local and practical initiatives. Others have come from local government, from private sector landscape architecture practices, and elsewhere. The key to the success of Groundwork is its recognition of 'the local' as the salient value of environmental renewal. Each local trust is autonomous, once it has established itself on the basis of local self-management across public, private and voluntary sectors.

Groundwork in particular has tapped into new local networks which have emerged over the past decade in many parts of Britain, in which the same people who have been active campaigners around national and international issues have also supported local health food shops, have demonstrated a concern for food quality issues, have taken over allotments, supported 'box' schemes which deliver organic vegetables in urban areas, or Local Exchange Trading Schemes (LETS), and are likely to be active in more conventional parks and open space development issues. The health food shop now stands in relation to the new politics as the radical bookshop once stood in relation to earlier pre-occupations with class, race and gender. In the end all the great issues of the day eventually come home to where you live.

A recent national MORI poll commissioned by Barclays SiteSavers on behalf of Groundwork (Lewis 1997) revealed that fewer than half of all adults in Britain feel that they belong to their local area and less than a quarter of young people (aged 15 to 24) feel any sense of local belonging. Only one in eight young people believe that the area they live in is attractive. It is these affective relationships to place and a sense of self-worth that Groundwork now seems to be concentrating on, which is a long way to have travelled from site-clearance schemes and topsoil replacement. Unless other campaigning environmental organisations acknowledge that environmental awareness and the passion for environmental change starts at the end of the street, with the problems of fly-tipping, or blighted and neglected municipal playgrounds and parks, or the loss of a local orchard or copse, then the gap between rhetoric and reality will not be closed. This is particularly pressing at a time when some journalism and opinion moulding is seeking to challenge and undermine many of the larger global environmental claims, and in doing so attacking the very foundations of sustainable development altogether.

It is often argued that with the collapse of communism, environmentalism is the next great redemptive social philosophy, requiring a complete transformation in how we live, work, and make a home for ourselves in this world. It also offers a particular challenge to local government as it is presently constituted (Christie 1996).

At present the gap is still far too wide between most forms of environmental politics and the concerns of social justice, and if there is to be greater integration between the natural and the social, it will most certainly have to begin at the local level.

There will need to be some harder thinking than is presently evident about how environmental organisations and activists relate to people's everyday concerns, to the future role of local government (the principal carrier at present of Agenda 21 policies), and to more participatory forms of local community development. To recall a slogan from the local history movement of the 1960s, as well as campaigning around the big issues, it is also important to 'dig where you stand'.

References

Beck, U (1992) *Risk Society: Towards a New Modernity* Sage, London

Campbell, B (1993) *Goliath: Britain's Dangerous Places*, Methuen, London

Christie, I (1996) 'A Green light for local power' *Demos Quarterly* no 9, London

Department of the Environment (1996) *Greening the City* HMSO, London

Featherstone, D (1997) 'Reimagining the human city' *Soundings*, Issue 7, London

Greenhalgh, L and Worpole, K (1995) *Park Life: Urban Parks and Social Renewal* Comedia and Demos, London

Greenhalgh, L and Worpole, K (1996) *The Freedom of the City* Demos, London

Greenhalgh, L and Worpole, K (1996) *People, Parks and Cities* Department of Environment, London

Greenhalgh, L, Landry, C, Solesbury, W and Worpole, K (1997) *The Richness of Cities: Urban Policy in a New Landscape* Working Paper 1, Comedia/Demos, London

Hall, P (1992) *Cities of Tomorrow: An Intellectual History of Urban Planning and Design in the Twentieth Century* Blackwell, Oxford

Hough, M (1995) *Cities and Natural Process* Routledge, London

Lewis, D (1997) *Not Just a Pretty Place – Communities and the Local Environment* Barclays Sitesavers and Groundwork, London

May, N (1997) *Challenging Assumptions: Gender Consideration in Urban Regeneration in the United Kingdom* Discussion paper by Oxfam for the Joseph Rowntree Foundation, York

Macnaghten, P, Grove-White, R, Jacobs, M and Wynne, B (1995) *Public Perceptions and Sustainability in Lancashire* Lancashire County Council, Lancaster

Nicholson-Lord, D (1987) *The Greening of the Cities* Routledge and Kegan Paul, London

Pawley, M (1997) *The Architect's Journal*, 1 May 1997, London

Power, A and Tunstall, R (1997) *Dangerous Disorder: Riots and Violent Disturbances in Thirteen Areas of Britain 1991–92* Joseph Rowntree Foundation, York

Robson, B (ed) (1994) *Assessing the Impact of Urban Policy* HMSO, London

Troy, P (1997) This was the principal argument of a lecture given at Bartlett School of Architecture, London, 29 October

Turner, T (1996) *City as Landscape: A Post-Postmodern View of Design and Planning* E & F Spon, London

Worpole, K (1997) *Nothing to Fear? Trust and Respect in Urban Communities* Comedia/Demos, London

6, P (1997) *Social Exclusion: Time to be Optimistic* Demos Collection 12, London

9

Achieving Community Participation: the Experience of Resident Involvement in Urban Regeneration in the UK

Marilyn Taylor

'Poverty is not only an evil in itself, but sustainable development requires meeting the basic needs of all and extending to all the opportunity to fulfil their aspirations for a better life. A world in which poverty is endemic will always be prone to ecological and other catastrophes'. (WCED, 1987, p8)

'The world economy has as one of its main products marginal people – the unemployed, the underemployed, the disenfranchised – people who lack what traditional society provided, a sense of belonging and having a recognised role'. (Harman 1993, p1069)

In the past, the concerns of the environmental movement have been quite separate from those of the regeneration arena, except perhaps where regeneration has involved programmes to improve the physical environment. But there is a growing awareness in both movements of the connection between the physical, social, economic and political environments in which we function.

Quality of life is seen as an indicator of success for both environmentalists concerned with sustainable development and those
involved in regeneration. More importantly, community involvement has become an essential element in Local Agenda 21 and
here there may be useful lessons from the experience of housing
regeneration in the UK, where community involvement has been
a key strategy in tackling poverty and disadvantage, particularly
on public housing estates, for many years.

Poverty is incompatible with sustainability. In continental
Europe, the term 'social exclusion' is increasingly used to describe
those on the margins of the economy. It is an extremely apt
description of what is happening with public housing in the UK.
Public housing estates represent some of the bleakest environments
in the UK: poorly constructed and poorly maintained housing,
often on poor quality land and in desolate out-of-town environments. Damp and condensation are endemic and heating systems
wasteful and inadequate. On those estates fortunate enough to
have gardens, most are unkempt and the land is poor. Litter, noise,
graffiti, dog excreta, broken glass, boarded up properties and
vandalism are everywhere.

Power and Tunstall's 1995 study of 20 local authority housing
estates shows that:

- The number of economically inactive households has risen
  since 1971 and now forms a majority (63 per cent compared
  with 59 per cent for the local area as a whole).
- Only 41 per cent of heads of households had a job in 1991,
  compared with 59 per cent in 1971 – unemployment is three
  times the national average.
- One in three of the population is under 16. The national
  average is one in five.
- One in four children leave school with no educational
  qualifications compared with only 5 per cent in the local area
  as a whole.
- Reported crime on the estates is four times the national
  average (which means that people on the estate are four times
  as likely to be a victim).

This bleak environment is the product of poverty. Policies to encourage choice in housing have concentrated those with no choice in the least desirable housing: unemployed people, people who are outside the labour market altogether, low income households, what McIlvanney (1996) has called the 'adverse social by-products of economic policy'. Severe reductions in local government housing budgets have pared maintenance programmes to the bone, residents on low incomes cannot afford to maintain, insulate or heat their property properly, let alone look after the physical environment beyond their door.

For these people, the immediate priority is survival in the here and now. Conventional approaches to tackling poverty and achieving regeneration have failed, and the language of sustainability now has a considerable appeal to those involved in the regeneration field, who see the same areas featured over and over again in successive initiatives. Faced with localities whose social networks and economies are at breaking point, their concern is two fold: how to recreate communities and economies which are viable in the short term and sustainable in the long term.

The Disadvantaged Community

While the language of the market exalts the individual, those whom the market fails are prescribed 'community'. And yet poverty creates communities that are unsustainable. Informal caring networks are stretched to the limit by higher than average proportions of young people, of single parent families and of people on low incomes. Public housing is also where 'care in the community' for the most vulnerable groups in the population tends to be located – insofar as this is the only housing they can afford (Taylor, 1995). In our 'drawbridge society', it is the already stressed communities that are expected to support those in greatest need.

In many cases, marginalised social housing estates are less a 'community' than a concentration of isolated individuals. Most estates have many different 'communities' within them, groups who, living on the edge themselves, are suspicious and fearful of other groups around them, whether they are young or old, black or white. Poverty and stress are more likely to create division and territorialism than harmony, especially in a society which blames those in poverty not only for their own fate but for the breakdown of society as a whole. Fear of going out or leaving their homes to be broken into increases isolation, especially among those who are most vulnerable.

Most of us belong to many overlapping communities – the world of work, of a far-flung kinship network, friendship networks, communities of interest,and communities of place (Stewart and Taylor 1996). We have choice over where we live and which communities we want to identify with. Wellman (1979) argues that these dispersed networks are essential to modern life (see also Bulmer 1986 and Granovetter 1973). But people who are unemployed and on low incomes do not have these choices. Their community is likely to be dictated by the nearest bus stop or how far they can walk in safety – they may have no other community to fall back on, no other networks to rely on. They are reminded every day of their exclusion from the wider community, whether by the contrast between the negative media coverage of their own estate and the lives of other people as portrayed in television adverts, by the sound of arguments through poorly insulated walls, or by the angry graffiti outside the front door (such as 'Blacks Go Home'). Community for them is likely to be the problem rather than the solution.

If it is difficult to build socially sustainable communities in areas defined by lack of choice it is even more difficult to build or maintain a viable economy – at least at the formal and legal level – in areas that are defined by their economic exclusion. The level of income on estates is unlikely to attract commercial investment, shops are expensive, boarded up or empty and, for out-of-town estates, transport is expensive. Young people are second and third generation unemployed – small wonder their educational achievements are low and they turn to crime or drugs as a more attractive proposition. Public services are underfunded, demoralised and overstretched, increasingly seen as a mark of failure and dependency, a last resort for those who can't do any better. As such, they too are becoming 'unsustainable' – a target for spending cuts and political point scoring.

So far, this chapter has built a bleak picture. And yet, the very people, buildings, environment and services which are labelled as the problem are also the assets on which 'sustainability', in its broadest sense can and must be built. These are the people, after all, who will stay after all the experts and professionals have gone. It is not easy – regeneration starts from a very low base – and the statistics show that residents are 'swimming against the tide' (Power and Tunstall 1995). Nonetheless, despite the worsening statistics, residents – working with committed outsiders – have not only been able to stop further deterioration but have turned estates around and made them places people choose to live in.

A Strategy for Change

What is it that makes the difference between a viable community and breakdown? The Joseph Rowntree Foundation (JRF) Action on Estates Programme on which this chapter is based (Taylor 1995), began from the assumption that, if regeneration was to last, it had to be founded on the energies and vision of estate residents themselves. Drawing on the findings of 33 separate studies of regeneration initiatives, it concluded that there have to be four main building blocks to estate regeneration, if it is to last:

1) A tradition of local activity and organisation which builds confidence and capacity.
2) Transformed mainstream services, which engage local people and agencies together.
3) Strategic partnership between all stakeholders in the area.
4) Jobs, community-owned assets and income.

Together these ingredients can generate long-term regeneration , but none is enough on its own. The studies suggest that strong and resourceful communities are the 'social capital' (Putnam 1993) on which lasting regeneration rests. Physical improvements alone will not work, if local people have no investment in them or sense of ownership. As the experience of the 1980s showed, bringing in jobs and physical assets may simply leave local people feeling even more marginalised, as outsiders take the money they make elsewhere, or new owner-occupiers take up residence in conclaves which are symbolically and sometimes physically separated from the public housing. Without the jobs and assets that can create a viable local economy, community activity will only be a sticking plaster. Those who benefit will either leave or get demoralised and burn out.

Elsewhere, I have described the community development task in terms of Clegg's 'circuits of power' (Clegg 1989, Gilchrist and Taylor 1997). In building the foundation for regeneration, the task is to activate dormant 'circuits' or networks within communities which can power local action and create a momentum for change.

The Foundation: Building Community Capacity

'Capacity-building' is an overused term in British regeneration policy, but it does convey a sense of the potential to be realised at individual and organisational level. A local tradition of organising builds the capacity: experience, skills and networks from which further action can flow. It may be small-scale – play provision, environmental clear-ups, social get-togethers, self-help groups – but these, as Putnam (1993) has demonstrated, are the acorns from which more high profile initiatives grow. It is important that people have many different ways in. Young people are unlikely to want to go to meetings and events organised by adults; ethnic minority communities may feel most comfortable (and safer) in settings which reflect their own cultural traditions. Harman (1993) argues that diversity is essential to a healthy ecology – in communities, as in the natural environment. From these diverse activities, the confidence can grow to engage more widely, to find common ground with others.

Outside intervention often focuses on an individual organisation, but Milofsky (1987) warns against relying too much on the development of one organisation. He argues that 'a rich supply of neighbourhood-based organisations' is the most effective basis for sustainable community development. This builds organisational capacity, generates social 'entrepreneurs' and can respond to changing conditions as and when needed. Individual groups may come and go, but if people have been involved in a successful activity in the past, they are more likely to try again when the opportunity arises, or to have the confidence to join with others in order to realise more ambitious objectives. A network of overlapping groups holds the 'organisational intelligence' which can be drawn on for future activities. It can also act as a 'Greek chorus' commenting on and holding more formal organisations to account (Milofsky and Hunter 1994). In the light of this, it is counterproductive for outsiders to put all their eggs in one basket – unless that basket is woven from the variety of strands within any one community.

Where no tradition of activity exists, a number of techniques have been tried to ensure that new initiatives do reach a broad section of the community. Public meetings will always find it difficult to compete with more comfortable entertainments at home, especially if they are in the evening, when the children are home and people find it difficult (or unsafe) to get out. Different approaches may be more successful: Planning for Real exercises are fun, do not require that everyone is articulate and confident in stating their opinions, but have been extremely effective in developing a vision for the future of an estate and a programme of action that has widespread support. Community festivals have combined entertainment for adults and children with information gathering and giving. These reinforce informal networks as well as acting as recruiting grounds for a more formal commitment.

If activity is to last into the long term, it is particularly important that young people have a stake in it. On one estate, after a summer of riots, housing officers visited young people in prison and kept them in touch with activities on the estate. School projects have involved children and young people on many estates in environmental audits, estate design and local history projects.

Widespread involvement which will last into the long term requires imagination. It also requires time and resources. Too often, agencies and professionals who have spent months at meetings planning action for an estate will involve residents at the last minute and then get impatient if it takes time to organise a community response, especially if there is funding at stake. One Scottish estate in the JRF studies only knew it had been selected for a new Partnership initiative when people heard about it on the early evening news (Hastings et al 1996). The study from which this example is taken suggests that it takes five years to develop community networks to a stage where they can engage effectively in partnership.

The JRF studies also suggest that the most successful estate initiatives are those with access to resources. These may be relatively small – enough to pay a telephone bill, run a crèche or to organise a visit to see what is happening on another estate. But the more that is expected of community organisations, the more important resources will become. In Pembroke Street in Devonport, it was the residents who kick-started regeneration. That they were able to do so, and develop their own plans for the redevelopment of their estate, owed much to the full-time support they received from an independent community technical aid worker. The presence of a worker can also ensure that community capacity survives the ebb and flow of local energy, the loss of key activists and periods of inactivity.

There will be cycles of involvement. Plenty of people will want a say if they feel their quality of life is threatened or if concrete changes are being proposed – if there is an 'enemy' to organise against. But their time is precious and in a stressed community, they have many demands upon them – so they may be happy to leave the maintenance work to the few. It is important to be clear when widespread involvement is essential, when decisions need to be made or work progressed by a smaller group and how that group will be accountable to the wider constituency.

This section has referred to Milofsky's ideas (1987) about submerged networks which can be activated to meet community goals. These networks can be seen as the 'circuits' through which social capital is generated and power can begin to flow more effectively through communities (Clegg 1989). The task for change agents is to activate and extend the 'web of networks submerged in everyday life' (Melucci 1988). But a small local generator can only do so much. If power is to flow into marginalised communities, these local circuits have to be linked into the social, professional, political and economic circuits from which they have been cut off.

Building on the Foundation: Dependency to Partnership

Urban policy in the UK has introduced a succession of special initiatives in an attempt to kickstart regeneration. A one-off injection of capital resources can do wonders for resident involvement – if designers and planners are willing to listen to residents and take their expertise on board. But while special initiatives can inject much needed cash in the short term, it is the long term mainstream services which represent the major spending on estates. Transforming the way that this money is spent is crucial to lasting change.

Some of the most dramatic success stories over recent years have been in the design and rehabilitation of estates, where residents have worked closely with housing providers to create the kind of estate they want to live in. It is now commonplace to argue that giving residents this stake in the design of their environment ensures that they also have a stake in its maintenance and continuous improvement. The literature on regeneration is full of contrasts between top-down improvements which are neglected and quickly become another eyesore on the one hand, and tenant-led improvements on the other, which are a local source of pride and enjoyment.

Increasing emphasis is now being put on tenant management of housing and other services. Capital programmes like Estate Action and Housing Action Trusts have required this type of involvement and have been a spur to partnership in the management of housing and environmental resources. Tenant management can not only deliver more responsive services (Glennerster and Turner 1993, Clapham and Kintrea 1992), it challenges stereotypes of dependency as both insiders and outsiders see what can be done at local level. It can also provide local jobs and an institutional base for tenants from which other developments may grow.

But there are pitfalls. Firstly, not all residents want to manage their own services – few of the rest of us do. Dumping on estate residents the services others have found difficult to manage is not a recipe for lasting regeneration, especially if they are expected to do it on the cheap. Many residents have chosen to opt for a partnership with the local authority rather than outright control.

Secondly, there is an inevitable tension between taking on more responsibility and keeping the larger community involved. Groups who move from campaigning to service management have to develop a new relationship with others in the community. If they do take this responsibility they must be given the training and support that they need to do the job well, to be accountable to the community and encourage wider involvement. It is at this point that a strong and diverse tradition of community involvement – one that is not dependent on one activity or group of people – is most important.

Transformed local services will need to break away from traditional departmental boundaries which bear little relationship to residents' reality and find new ways of working across boundaries. Too often, residents are caught in turf wars between professionals or find themselves having to negotiate departmental or agency boundaries in an increasingly fragmented service environment. If networks between residents are the key to local capacity building, networks between agencies and departments are the key to effective institutional responses. Some commentators suggest that society has reached a point where relationships across boundaries are becoming more important than defining boundaries around organisations (Reed 1992, Clegg 1990). New 'circuits of power' have to be created at this level too. But multi-agency working still presents difficulties, despite the language of partnerships (Zipfel 1994).

Nowhere is this coordinated approach more important than at central government level. With the creation of regional offices, some barriers are beginning to be breached. But some of the most serious threats to local regeneration come from inconsistency between government policies. In one Partnership area on Tyneside, studies suggest that the amount of money that came into the area as a result of special initiatives was matched by the amount that had been cut from general public expenditure. Benefits policies which create poverty traps, education policies which leave many of the most hardpressed schools languishing at the bottom of league tables, care in the community policies which place further stress on already stressed communities, without the resources to

match all run counter to initiatives to regenerate the most marginalised areas. No wonder special initiatives find themselves going
back to the same areas time and time again.

Despite a series of new cross-departmental policies to tackle
poverty and exclusion, the old habits seem to persist. Agenda 21,
anti-poverty strategies, and regeneration policies clearly have
much in common, but often develop in isolation from each other
and involve different rounds of meetings and competing consor-
tia. For residents the promise of community involvement can turn
into a nightmare as they struggle to find the time to invest in all
these different initiatives.

From the Margins to the Mainstream: Strategic Partnership

If 'market' was the buzzword of the 1980s, 'partnership' and
'community involvement' are the mantras of urban policy in the
UK in the 1990s. Current urban policies, having attempted to
bypass local authorities in the 1980s, are now acknowledging the
importance of local government as a key actor, but access to special
funding is dependent on proof that they are working in partnership with other local actors, particularly business and the
community.

This is a welcome development. But years of experience have
demonstrated that the road from the rhetoric of partnership and
community involvement to reality is a long and difficult one.
Studies of the first round of Single Regeneration Budget partnerships[1] and its predecessor the City Challenge, suggest that,
although these funds have provided opportunities for residents to
define and run their own projects (MacFarlane 1993), the impact
of residents at strategic level so far has been limited (Clarke 1995;
Hastings et al 1996).

---

1 In the early 1990s, government amalgamated all its different urban regeneration
funds into a Single Regeneration Budget (SRB) which is administered through
regional offices of central government. Bids to the SRB Challenge Fund are invited
on an annual basis, and are required to show evidence of both partnership and
community involvement, although the latter is loosely defined.

Stephen Lukes (1974) distinguishes between three faces of power: where A has power over B; where A sets the agenda in which power relationships are played out; where B internalises A's version of how power works and accepts it as a 'given'.[2] Partnership initiatives are beginning to tackle the first but have a long way to go to tackle the second and third, before people in communities have any real say in how resources are distributed, how services and economies are run and who has power over what.

Residents are being asked to accommodate to local authority and central government structures – the language and 'rules of engagement' are those of traditional official decision-making processes. Reid and Iqbal (1996) distinguish between 'entrepreneurial' decision-making networks and 'collaborative' networks (see Table 9.1). The first are where the real decisions get taken; the second are essentially about legitimation. Much resident disenchantment with involvement comes from expectations that they will be involved in the first, when in reality they are involved in the second.

This dissatisfaction is reinforced, Hastings et al suggest (1996), by the drive to consensus within the partnership process. This can be very disempowering to residents, who are seen as obstructive if they disagree with official partners or do not feel able to present a united community view at the partnership table. But some of the most successful partnerships on the JRF research programme were plucked out of the jaws of conflict and entrenched positions. Residents come to partnership with years of experience of being marginalised. The urban unrest that we all fear and condemn is an understandable response to the despair on many estates and turning anger outwards is perhaps a healthier response than the apathy that turns it inwards. At a more formal level, conflict can be seen as a sign that partnership is working, that real issues are being put an the table. The challenge of finding new ways of working with diversity and difference is one which is beginning to be recognised as essential to democracy (see, for example, Gray 1996).

---

2 The analysis of the way in which powerholders structure our view of the world has been taken further in the work of Foucault and also has resonance with Gramsci's work on hegemony.

Table 9.1 *Inter-organisational cultures*

Competitive	Collaborative
'Can do'	Developmental
Flexible	Stable
Autonomous	Participative
Opportunistic	High control
Entrepreneurial	Trust-based
Power relationships not fixed	Power fixed
Selective	Inclusive
Output oriented	Process oriented

Adapted from Reid and Iqbal (1996)

Another common barrier to genuine partnership is the issue of representation. So often, the cry is heard from partners that community participants are 'not representative'. But the JRF studies suggest that representation can be something of a holy grail, an accusation which is thrown at partners when more powerful partners don't like what residents have to say (Taylor 1995). Furthermore, there is a sense in which residents are set up to be unrepresentative. The demands of partnership are immense and put great pressure on people from already stressed communities. Official structures incorporate local residents and distance them from their constituencies. Professionals and agencies prefer to call on the people who have learnt the ropes and with whom they have had dealings before. If partners complain that it's always the same people that turn up to meetings, they may have to accept that they have helped to create that situation. Partnership needs to be multi-faceted, so that there are opportunities for communities to work alongside partners at many different levels.

The metaphor of 'circuits of power', and the need to first reactivate circuits which have fallen into disrepair and then to link them into more powerful systems, has been discussed above. However, although these links into more powerful systems are now being made, they remain weak and liable to short-circuit. If the connections are to be strengthened there are two main challenges to be faced. First, partnership at strategic level requires fundamental changes in political culture on the part of partners. It requires that partners adapt to residents' priorities and ways of working rather than always expecting community participants to adapt to them. It requires that public authorities take risks and learn to accommodate diversity and difference. It requires that partners challenge their own assumptions about power and decision making. And it requires that there are many switches and relays between the community and the power-holders: as one respondent to our study remarked: 'It's as good as the weakest link' (Taylor 1995).

Secondly, if communities are to engage effectively with partners then they need to develop community structures which can reflect the diversity of interests and identities found in any community, and yet establish common ground from which to negotiate. This is not easy, especially in communities which are prey to conflict and division. The most successful partnerships in Hastings et al's research (1996) were those where residents had already developed a community umbrella which could negotiate the different interests on an estate in a way that most residents could sign up to. But even in these cases, residents had often tried two or three different structures before finding a structure that works for them. This is an area where there is still a lot to learn.

What is important is that outsiders do not impose blueprints. It is also important that professionals know when to take a back seat. In one Scottish estate, residents always act as spokespeople for the estate, even though there is a strong back-up team of workers. But there are several examples in our studies where this is not the case, of resident forums which are still dominated by professionals and of professionals who are unable to accept that residents should meet on their own (Hastings et al 1996).

Ultimately, residents are faced with tough decisions when invited to the partnership table. Are they just being used to give top-down approaches legitimacy or are they able to make a difference? Involvement in partnership is energy and time-consuming and Hastings et al (1996) question whether the gains justify the effort that is put into them. Can political cultures be shifted?

Sidney Tarrow, in his study of social movements, argues that modest reform is the most that can be expected. Despite the evidence of cooption in most of the movements he studied, however, he does suggest that changes in political culture have been achieved, albeit slow and incremental. Another social movement scholar (Zolberg 1972) argues that such movements can drastically shorten the distance between 'the present and the future' by putting issues on the agenda and acting as the focus for new alliances. This may be the way in which community involvement will achieve change – not by transforming the nature of political agendas overnight, but by gradually shifting the assumptions on which current structures and decisions are based and creating new alliances, new circuits through which power can begin to flow.

New Economies

As the principles of sustainable development recognise, economic development is essential in tackling poverty. And if partnership is difficult, the economic marginalisation of estates is an even tougher nut to crack. An immense amount of effort has been put into training, both to get people to the threshold of employment and to get them into mainstream jobs. Training inputs are impressive, but the numbers placed in employment less so. Postcode discrimination still applies – most employers are not interested. Current welfare benefits policy remains a barrier to employment for many who have a precarious employment record.

Capital investment programmes have created some jobs, but mostly in the construction industry, which is notoriously unstable and, although using local labour in construction schemes is growing in the housing association field, there are considerable legislative obstacles to their wider use. Some housing associations are moving further into training and economic development. Their assets provide a foundation for lasting economic development, but successful examples which go beyond training are still thin on the ground. Community enterprise still has its supporters, but critics argue that all they do is create low paid jobs on the edges of the labour market. Where the failure of small firms is already high, starting a business in communities which do not offer much of a market may be something of a doomed project.

Public housing estates are the product of economic marginalisation. To link them back into the mainstream economy is a
monumental task. However, the creation of a high-profile social
exclusion unit, along with current interest in social enterprise and
social entrepreneurs, suggests that the political will may now exist
to make some headway. If so, a new approach to economic development is needed. The Borrie Commission on Social Justice (1994)
argued for an 'intermediate labour market' which addresses market
failure, by putting the people who need jobs together with the
services that are needed but which are not attractive to the
commercial market. This requires social investment, which at
present comes mainly from the public sector. The *regies de quartiers*
in France (Saunders 1997) are one example. Some of the community regeneration organisations described by Stephen Thake
(1995), based on workspace provision, nursery provision, contracts
for training, childcare, and community care, community buildings, housing and so on, would also fall into this category. These
are still a fragile development in the UK and the majority are
heavily dependent on public investment, especially for start-up
money. Some of this has come from local authorities, who act as
'unofficial bankers'; some from short term government initiatives
such as City Challenge and Inner City Task Forces which, as they
come to the end of their term, have sometimes left behind an 'asset
endowment' in the shape of finance or buildings.

The development of these community regeneration organisations is an encouraging sign, but if they are to develop a critical
mass, they need a robust financial infrastructure to support them.
Such an infrastructure needs to recognise the particular risks (but
also benefits) of investment in communities where traditional
institutions will not lend and where returns may be low and long
term. Some answers to these dilemmas may be found in other
countries, community banks in developing countries, intermedi-
ary organisations such as the Local Initiatives Support Corporation
in the US. A Demos pamphlet has set out a number of ideas for
such social investment (Mulgan and Landry 1995). Legislation like
the Community Reinvestment Act in the US could also support
such investment (Falk 1993).

Research is currently underway to explore alternative
economies, based on LETS, volunteering, credit unions. This has a

particular resonance in the environmental movement and may offer new ways forward, but as yet it is too early to say. Care needs to be taken, however, that such alternatives do not simply create ghettos on the fringes of the rest of society.

Conclusion

Debates about sustainable development and about regeneration have, until recently, been pursued in isolation from each other. At first sight the language of regeneration bears little resemblance to the environmentalists' concern with the sustainability of the earth's resources. And yet, there is considerable overlap. Both require substantial changes in economic thinking: new ways of defining 'what counts' in economic development, which bring other values to bear beyond short-term financial gain. Both need to recognise that poverty and exclusion are unsustainable if we are to secure quality of life for future generations. Both are concerned with fundamentally changing the way in which citizens are engaged in the decisions that affect their lives.

This chapter has set out a strategy for change, based on the experience of regeneration. It engages people in communities in taking action to improve the quality of their lives, through developing networks of mutual support and collective action based on their own definitions of quality of life rather than those imposed from outside. On this foundation can be built new approaches to service provision, to decision making and to economic development. Building from the bottom up is not easy and requires time, patience and imagination. But only in this way will these areas begin to establish a sustainable future for themselves and their children, as full participants in society, rather than as 'marginal people'.

References

Borrie Commission on Social Justice (1994) *The Justice Gap* Institute for Public Policy Research, London
Bulmer, M (1986) *Neighbours: The Work of Philip Abrams* Cambridge University Press, Cambridge

Clapham, D and Kintrea, K (1992) *Housing Cooperatives in Britain: Achievements and Prospects* Longman, Harlow

Clarke, G (1995) *A Missed Opportunity: an Initial Assessment of the 1995 Single Regeneration Budget Approvals and their Impact on Voluntary and Community Organisations* NCVO, London

Clegg, S (1989) *Frameworks of Power* Sage, London

Clegg, S (1990) *Modern Organisations: Organisational Studies in the Post-Modern World* Sage, London

Falk, N (1993) 'Financing urban regeneration', in Hambleton, R and Taylor, M (eds) *People in Cities* SAUS Publications, Bristol

Gilchrist, A and Taylor, M (1997) 'Community networking: developing strength through diversity' in Hoggett, P (ed) *Contested Communities* The Policy Press, Bristol

Glennerster, H and Turner, T (1993) *Estate-Based Housing Management: An Evaluation* HMSO, London

Granovetter, M (1973) 'The strength of weak ties' *American Journal of Sociology* vol 78 no 6, pp 1360–80

Gray, J (1995) *Beyond Social Democracy* Demos, London

Harman, W W (1993) 'Rethinking the central institutions of modern society: science and business' *Futures* 1993, pp 1063–70

Hastings, A, McArthur, A and McGregor, A (1996) *Less than Equal: Community Organisations and Estate Regeneration Partnerships* The Policy Press, Bristol

Lukes, S (1974) *Power: A Radical View* Macmillan, London

MacFarlane, R (1993) *Community Involvement in City Challenge: A Good Practice Report* NCVO Publications, London

McIlvanney, W (1996), 'The amoeba strikes' *Community Care*, p 11 July 1996 issue

Melucci, A (1988) 'Social movements and the democratisation of every-day life', in Keane, J and Meir, P (eds), Hutchinson, London

Milofsky, C (1987) 'Neighbourhood-based organisations: a market analogy', in Powell, W W (ed) *The Nonprofit Sector: A Research Handbook* Yale University Press, New Haven

Milofsky, C and Hunter, A (1994) 'Where non-profits come from: a theory of organisational emergence', paper presented to the Association for Research on Nonprofit Organisations and Voluntary Action, San Francisco, October

Mulgan, G and Landry, C (1995) *The Other Invisible Hand: Remaking Charity for the 21st Century* Demos, London

Power, A and Tunstall, R (1995) *Swimming Against the Tide* Joseph Rowntree Foundation, York

Putnam, R (1993) *Making Democracy Work: Civic Traditions in Modern Italy* Princeton University Press, Princeton, NJ

Reed, M (1992) *The Sociology of Organisations* Harvester Wheatsheaf, Hemel Hempstead

Reid, B and Iqbal, B (1996) 'Redefining housing practice: interorganisa-
    tional relationships and local housing networks' in Malpass, P (ed) *The
    New Governance of Housing* Longman, Harlow
Saunders, R (1997) *Resident Services Organisations: A New Tool for
    Regeneration* Priority Estates Project, London
Stewart, M and Taylor, M (1996) *Empowerment and Estate Regeneration: A
    Critical Review* The Policy Press, Bristol
Taylor, M (1995) *Unleashing the Potential: Bringing Residents to the Centre of
    Estate Regeneration* Joseph Rowntree Foundation, York
Taylor, M (1996) 'The canary in the coalmine: issues facing the voluntary
    sector', in May, M, Blunsden, E and Craig, G (eds) *Social Policy Review
    8* Social Policy Association, London
Thake, S (1995) *Staying the Course: The Role and Structures of Community
    Regeneration Organisations* York Publishing Services, York
WCED (1987) *Our Common Future* Oxford University Press, Oxford
Wellman, B (1979) 'The community question: the intimate networks of
    East Yorkers' *American Journal of Sociology*, vol 84, no 5, pp 1201–31
Zipfel, T (1994) *On Target: Extending Partnership to Tackle Problems on
    Estates* PEP, London

10

Developing Community Local Agenda 21s

Ken G Webster

Past UK governments have attempted to attach a community glow to education, health, local taxes, with community governors in schools, care in the community and the community charge. Before the May 1997 General Election, New Labour visited the US and returned with a new mantra: 'the individual, society, and state'. Community in its many guises has become a popular notion and has gained political credibility. Though a difficult concept to define, community has become an apparatus, a vehicle and a mechanism for righting all wrongs. Will this be matched by a new commitment to support communities and those working in them? Or will communities be rejected yet again if they fail to produce the politicians' dreams.

Local Agenda 21 (LA21), one of the main outcomes of the 1992 Earth Summit, presents a rare opportunity for communities and their local authorities to develop new working relationships together. It places great store on the community's ability to take a leading role in bringing about the changes needed if the world is to achieve sustainability. Governments have delegated the task of responding to Local Agenda 21 largely to local authorities and their communities. But can they work together, what are the implications of working together, and do the skills and networks exist that will make it a successful relationship?

WWF-UK's work on LA21 has not been intended to produce a finished, off-the-shelf model. The observer will find traces of effective practice drawn from many quarters. However, the work is underpinned by firm principles, such as:

- The issues being addressed have real local relevance.
- Making real the links between environmental sustainability and lifestyle decisions and expectations.
- The process of community engagement seeks to improve the relationship between 'top and bottom' in order to find new directions together.
- Increasing meaningful dialogue between communities and local government, leading to more informed policies.
- Identifying and removing the blocks and barriers that inhibit community participation in local government.
- Enabling all participants to develop and practice new skills.
- Local people prepare a local plan which identifies their own role, as well as that of other organisations.
- There is no single right answer.

These principles underpin a process that addresses the environmental, social and economic dimensions of sustainability. WWF's mission to protect and enhance the natural environment can only be achieved by addressing the challenges placed on the environment by people. Because people live within a range of social, economic and political paradigms, it is essential that our presently unsustainable lifestyle is addressed through these paradigms.

This paper sets out to illustrate some of the opportunities that are created by LA21, and the blocks and barriers facing communities and local authorities in their work for sustainability. It provides a rationale for a strategy for community action that is informed by the work between local authorities, the voluntary sector and community groups in the UK and elsewhere.

WWF has taken a strong position on the potential role of communities in achieving a more sustainable future. WWF's goal is to 'stop, and eventually reverse, the accelerating degradation of our planet's natural environment, and to help build a future in which humans live in harmony with nature' (WWF-UK Mission Statement). But if this goal is to be achieved it is essential that the links are established (or re-established) between the natural environment and people: a link which recognises social, economic, political and cultural systems, and a shared notion of quality of life.

The dominant political and economic imperatives have pushed social and cultural traditions into the background with the result that we are increasingly losing sight of natural systems and the human scale. So the challenge is to grow a new vested interest in the natural environment by relating it to the human needs of everyday life. Not easy when 'quality of life' and 'standard of living' are often mistakenly used to mean the same thing, and when standard of living is measured in terms of consumption per capita and jobs. Solutions for sustainability must also take account of the disparity between lifestyle expectations in the so-called developed world and the rights to a reasonable quality of life for our 600 million neighbours elsewhere on the planet who are living below even the most basic standards. For them, quality of life means simply having a reliable source of clean drinking water, adequate food and safe shelter.

With this in mind, the WWF response to Local Agenda 21 has been to reach communities through their local authorities. The local authority is an important influence on most people's lives and its approach to sustainable development will indirectly and directly impact on the lives of people living in local communities. WWF's approach is to work with key people in local authorities and the community and to explore new ways of working, developing new skills, and building new confidences between each other. The objective of the process is to provide the opportunity to jointly explore a range of themes, all of which include community participation in local decision-making. After only a short time, communities have developed neighbourhood or parish Local Agenda 21 action plans which describe what needs to be done to improve their local environment but, as importantly, what they can do and what others can do to achieve their plan. The active participation of communities raises questions about the ability of the local authority to hear and act on community action plans.

Communities rightly ask if their views are valued and welcomed; if their community voice is likely to be heard and acted upon; if the local authority is prepared to remove the barriers and increase community accessibility to their policy development processes; if elected members are prepared to train in order to be better equipped to work alongside a proactive community, and if the local authority officers are prepared to learn new 'people skills' that will improve their ability to relate to the community. Without accepting the implications and challenges raised in these questions, any benefits are likely to be short-lived.

Both Ends of the Telescope

Local Agenda 21 represents something which is both big and small, and it brings meaning to the slogan 'Think Global Act Local' because it is about 'me' the individual and 'we' the group. Through one end of an imaginary telescope we should be able to see the big picture – macro politics and economics; through the other end, the local and personal picture – micro actions and expectations. LA21 requires us to think of our impact on our neighbours, both those next door and those on the other side of the world. The New York Earth Summit II conference was described as a failure because it failed to produce a finished convention. Even if it had produced such an elusive document, the content would have been at the macro scale.

Although LA21 is not about hedgerows, recycling, and cycle paths per se, all may properly feature in local plans. LA21 is about our quality of life, our expectations, and our effect on other people's quality of life elsewhere in the world. It is an educational process through which we can all learn to make informed lifestyle decisions. There are many exciting community projects that exemplify the values promoted in LA21 (see Box 10.1).

Many of these schemes predate LA21, but the issues are the same and they demonstrate that the skills needed for community participation already exist. LA21 is about rehearsing our rights and responsibilities within a system that has a social, economic, political and cultural context, and a local and global perspective. It is about basic human rights and dignity. It has been forecast that more than half the world's population will be living an urban life within only a few years. The move from rural to urban is not always a matter of choice nor is it an alternative idyll. For many

Box 10.1 Community projects

In Salford a project called 'Urban Oasis', which is based in a 1960s high-rise estate, takes as its starting point the alienation caused by the lack of personal safety, and the dehumanising compound mentality imposed by the need for six foot railings and electronically operated entrance gates. After only a few months, residents have begun to reclaim their basic human rights by taking control of the grounds surrounding their tower block. Now they have an orchard, an organic vegetable garden, a duck pond, raised gardens made from reused stone sets that had been previously used as a defence against Peeping Toms. The community barbecue is well used and the verdict is: 'the Chinese do the best barbecues, their food is great'. There is a plan (and lottery funding) for an orangery in which they are going to open a community cafe and sell organic produce to the elderly in the neighbouring blocks.

In Peshawar, Pakistan, a community waste collection and composting project which started with nine and ten year-old boys grew into a numeracy scheme because the boys had to be able to read house numbers to know which houses were in the scheme. Whilst they were learning their numbers it was a good time to teach them to read, and also something about health and hygiene. Then of course the girls wanted to learn. The children's standards of basic health and learning is raised, farmers are learning the benefits of composting, and the community are actively engaged in domestic cleanliness and hygiene.

people, especially in the developing world, it is a result of losing an unequal struggle between powerful external economic forces and their own relative powerlessness. LA21 alone will not solve these problems, but through the creative application of the principles promoted within it, it can become a mechanism for generating consciousness and action for change.

The Shrinking World

No one can escape the consequences of a world economic model that is fundamentally unsustainable. We can pretend to ignore it if we choose to – this is not a defence of wilful disregard but a consequence of our freedom of choice. In pursuit of sustainability, freedom of choice is put to the test and its consequences examined and known. But knowing has to be accompanied by the ability to

Box 10.2 Cameroon

In Cameroon, the increasing incidence of rural poverty and government reluctance to implement new forest law has led to an increase in unsustainable logging for export as either pulp, construction timber or veneers. This type of environmental degradation has been intensified by the rapid rise in rural poverty. Between 1983 and 1994 the number of households below the poverty line rose from 49 per cent to 71 per cent, cash crop farming incomes fell by 60 per cent and food producer prices by 40 per cent. It is no wonder that jobs in the logging industry are seen as an opportunity for survival and traditional living as an unaffordable

understand and the willingness to act. For instance, do individuals or communities have a right and a responsibility to know and understand the disruption caused in developing countries as a result of Western consumerism? In some countries freedom of choice is an unaffordable luxury, especially in the face of a combination of internal political and economic instability (see Box 10.2).

LA21 presents challenges to communities all over the developed world, especially by encouraging the ability to see the world through the eyes of other people. There is a tendency in the West, which has been reinforced over many hundreds of years, to see the world through Eurocentric eyes, and expect the world to do the same. It is time we developed the capacity to learn from elsewhere where perceptions have a different genesis. In a speech full of vivid imagery, Paul Wangoola illustrates many examples of perceptions of the world through African eyes (Wangoola 1994). Of the devil he says:

> 'The Africans have no concept of the heathen, infidel, and believer. If allowed, this becomes the basis of cultural arrogance, religious bigotry, oppression and dispossession. You cannot destroy the devil – the devil will always be with us, the point is to manage it not annihilate it. The African's life is therefore one of perpetual negotiation and compromise; important in dealing with our enemies who we do not seek to destroy but instead with whom we seek to create space and coexist'.

Of the relationship between environment and community he says:

> *'Men and women only have the right of access to nature*
> *for their community subsistence needs and no more. The*
> *collective good, the community welfare, has primacy over*
> *individual rights'.*

If we are to achieve sustainability or even a reduction in unsustainability we have to accept the challenge of seeing and doing differently and learning from others. There is no single right way, no magic formula, and no quick fix. It is important that individuals and communities have a capacity for global awareness, the momentum for personal and local activity and an ability to recognise and deal with their own impact on the world.

From Education to Consultation

Agenda 21 identifies local authorities as one of several key groups. Local authorities in the UK, for instance, are strategically important because their wide ranging powers and responsibilities impact on everyone sooner or later. In identifying local authorities, Agenda 21 says,

> *'As the level of governance closest to the people, they (local*
> *authorities) play a vital role in educating, mobilising and*
> *responding to the public to promote sustainable develop-*
> *ment'.* (Agenda 21, Chapter 28)

In those few words there is the mandate for something quite exceptional. It is about process and action, about top and bottom working together. It sets sustainable development as its goal, and identifies a mechanism for achieving it through education and public action.

The first objective set for local authorities is that:

> *'By 1996, most local authorities in each country should*
> *have undertaken a consultative process with their popula-*

tions and achieved a consensus on 'a local agenda 21' for the community'. (Agenda 21, Chapter 28)

This objective uses three key words: consultative, consensus, and community, each of which is loaded, if not burdened, with historic precedent. Today, in our compartmentalised post-modern world we have learned to overcome our inability to find an adequate definition of community by embracing its fragmentation in the label we give it. Hence we might describe communities of interest, communities of faith, communities of location, the business community and so on. But what does 'consultative' mean, and in its juxtaposition to 'consensus', care is needed to resist fascist inclinations to railroad people towards a single 'right way' forward.

Consultation and consensus-building must allow for differences, especially when the audience for consensus is so fragmented. If consultation means 'effective communication' then the traditional model of consultation leaves much to be desired. It is not enough to simply present the work of 'experts' to the community and ask them to comment. This is not communication, it is a fait accompli, because the community are excluded from the development of the ideas. No surprise therefore that the community either fails to turn up to consultative meetings, or if they do the occasion degenerates into a free for all. The community are too often then dismissed as apathetic and the status quo remains effectively unchallenged.

In a participative model the process is proactive with all parties included and their voices heard from the outset. Apathy is the last word to be used to describe participants' reactions to this process when its effectiveness is so demonstrable. Charges of apathy are more an indictment of the accuser than the accused. Experience of working with local authorities is teaching us that those who can embrace a participatory rather than purely representative form of democracy are less likely to feel threatened by engaging the community from the outset.

There are many examples of communities that have developed the skills and confidence to create sophisticated plans for local action. There are also good examples of local authorities that are gradually improving their accessibility as a result of the opportunities presented by community participation. The City of Bradford Metropolitan Council has already trained more than 300 of their officers in sustainability, and is building a neighbourhood networking scheme. Reading Borough Council is supporting seven neighbourhood LA21 schemes – with the next three already in the pipeline, and they are promoting a process that will bring the groups together to share their thinking. The council is introducing sustainability reporting into committee papers and end of year accounting of progress towards sustainability; there is a recognition that the process is ongoing and organisation-wide.

The way forward for communities and local authorities is far from clear because in most cases the journey towards sustainable development is unfamiliar. There are those who criticise LA21 as yet another 'talking shop', but it will only become that if people allow it to happen. There are others who allow themselves to become obfuscated by the jargon which, if indulged, could entice us into inactivity. But rather than analysing and defining ourselves to a standstill in pursuit of the holy grail of THE right answer, it is much more important that communities and local authorities have the courage to look for any number of likely right answers. Thus the community that identifies dog mess as its most pressing local concern will not have created a sustainability nirvana, but they will have begun a journey that has relevance and direction for them. WWF's role in these circumstances has been to work alongside the local authority and communities to reflect back what people are learning and to then disseminate it widely. It is an educational process that is sometimes painful and often risky for the officers, politicians, and community members who are sharing an unknown journey with its personal and professional challenges.

WWF does not escape the challenge of a process that demands increasing cross linking between different parts of the same organisation that have their own traditions. The lessons include keeping focused on long term goals, creating new opportunities, increasing people's capacity to make better informed life decisions: to expect and manage the tensions created by a rapidly changing scene, and create the space for reflection, evaluation and reporting. The all important outcome in educational terms is to continuously project the process of lifelong learning for sustainability to as wide an audience as possible.

There is a role for every one: from the 'thinkers', 'thinking doers' to the 'doers', for all ages and all sectors of the community. Among the many challenges is the need to develop an educated and reflective society that has the capacity to take a leaf out of Paul Wangoola's book by managing its own devils.

How To Do It?

If we were asked to design a table from which four adults could eat a meal it would be necessary to identify the problem we are trying to solve and then its parameters. We can start by asking a series of basic questions: about the area it is to occupy, about the frequency of use, about its means of support, about the size of the users, whether it should be heat resistant, and so on. But without care it would be too easy to produce something that conforms to our preconceived notions of a table: four/three/two/one legs, square/round/rectangular top. All we would be doing is tinkering with the accepted and comfortable norm, our minds too easily slipping towards familiar and safe territory. Instead, we should challenge the question by asking if the use of the word 'table' actually fixes our thinking from the outset, rather than liberating it. Given modern lifestyles which might be either on the move, or perhaps in front of the TV, a question which is more open-ended might be more appropriate: such as 'Design an arrangement by which four adults can share a meal'. Then of course we would need to establish the problems and parameters of a meal ....

In LA21 we are set the task of achieving sustainable development and at one level the problem can be described quite simply: our present way of life in the developed world is environmentally unsustainable therefore it has to change. From a design point of view we have an advantage in that we have no preconceived notion of what large scale sustainability looks like, let alone how it can be achieved: we are not asked to design a 'table'. Our solutions therefore have to be innovative.

We can start with the parameters. Jonathon Porritt describes three 'mega symptoms' of modern world dysfunctionality which we might use as out design parameters: the first is that 'we like to think that good science will help us to overcome some of the vicissitudes of subjectivity and emotionality', the second refers to the economic models which 'have ceased to deliver the goods', and the third is 'social decline and collapse' (Porritt 1996).

We should perhaps add the increasing dysfunctionality and alienation of the political tradition. William Sullivan discusses the need to 'increase social trust needed for working together towards common ends by enlisting rather than crushing individual initiative or stifling dissent. The difficulties appear once the issue is posed as to how to address this task, which is nothing less than revitalising democratic life' (Sullivan 1995).

So, four parameters of our design for environmental sustainability might include:

1) the need for good and appropriate science;
2) major changes to the dominant economic model;
3) the rebuilding of social structures;
4) the restoration of trust in the political system.

There is, of course, a close interrelationship between each and they can be closely referenced to the social, economic, political and cultural context described earlier. There is a distinct macro feel to these parameters and it is necessary at this point to turn round the telescope and look for their conversion to the micro and their meaningfulness for the individual and communities. Failure to address these parameters will simply result in a five legged table; that is, something different though strangely familiar. An essential part of the eventual solution is the involvement of those who have a stake in the outcome. Therefore before anything can happen at a local community level it will be necessary to create a new tradition of participation between local authorities and communities as the two major players. A local process is needed through which people can identify their personal equivalents of our four parameters.

The four-legged table approach is to convene a public meeting, perhaps on a weekday when most people who are working cannot attend, invite a keynote speaker, break up into workshops and publish the outcomes of the group discussions as the product of community consultation. There are advantages to this approach; it is quick, neat, recognisable and safe. However, in terms of bringing about long term change it lacks involvement and engagement in the issues, ownership of the solutions designed and personal commitment to ongoing implementation.

The answer is, of course, that there is no single guaranteed answer. In returning to the table analogy, a solution drawn from the 'suspended platter' end of the continuum might equate to a design that achieves commitment and trust and the knowledge that people are not being exploited and that their voice will be listened to; where the politicians give their support and leadership, and the executive recognises that working towards shared interests is in the interest of good local services and also sustainability. In this model, it is safe to take risks and be innovative, to hold a long term and holistic view, and to push back the boundaries. It is a process that involves all sectors within society, from individuals and their families, schools and colleges, youth clubs, and business, to resident associations, voluntary groups and of course local government. It also has an international perspective. Everyone involved is participating in sub-conscious and conscious learning experiences that are reflected upon and evaluated, at one extreme by at least asking 'how are we doing', and at the other by establishing appropriate indicators of success, systematic evaluation and regular reviews.

LA21 is not about community education or community development per se, but it cannot succeed unless people of all backgrounds and interests are involved in a learning and development experience. There is no single right way forward and much can be learned from people whose perspective differs from the mainstream. This includes those who are working at the extremes of society, such as 'travellers', who can be seen as the experimenters and the innovators that have largely disinvested in the mainstream. Much of the underpinning philosophy of the traveller is a radical alternative vision for achieving a lifestyle that has much to offer sustainability. It seems alien to most people mainly because it bucks convention.

LA21 is not utopian but it is an invitation to explore and share personal and group visions for the future, and then express them in terms of changed personal and collective behaviour, attitudes and values. A vicar in one of the WWF pilot projects commented that, 'I for one have no problem with this vision thing'! Perhaps the traveller and the vicar remind us there are other values than those such as profit and competition which have so dominated recent years.

The intention may not be to reinvent local government, but without largely changing the way local authorities relate to their local communities and involving them in the process of policy development and implementation, LA21 will remain a four-legged table. There are physical, cultural, psychological and historical blocks and barriers to greater community participation in local democracy. These have to be confronted in learning and confidence building experiences that are aimed at those at the top and at the bottom. LA21 is about the top and bottom together moving in a new direction.

This type of solution to the 'table' problem set out earlier not only begins to solve the problem but in so doing has also found space for more than the original four adults we thought we were catering for! The process did not begin with the answer already tucked up someone's sleeve. Instead, because the process starts by involving all stakeholders in activities through which they identify their own concerns and vision (parameters) before looking for solutions, their ownership of the eventual outcomes is much stronger. Often, people who have experienced this process also discover other benefits which strengthen them. Just look at the residents of Salford's Urban Oasis for evidence (see Box 10.1).

What's Stopping Us?

Communities and their local authorities are strategically important within LA21. If sustainability is to be achieved, both must develop the capacity to work together more closely on their shared agenda than is the custom in most places. Unless both are able to listen to and work with the other it is too easy for the traditional 'consult/confront' relationship to continue.

In the democratic model, the community elects its representatives at periodic intervals. The track record of effective communication between these intervals depends more on the assertiveness and confidence of the individuals concerned than any tradition of systematic participation. With varying degrees of effectiveness, elected members are in touch with their community/electorate through open door policies and regular surgeries, and officers of local authorities might have mechanisms for communication and public relations.

Far less often are the community and representatives of the local authority involved in a proactive and participative process with the intention of developing new policy. There are good examples of participation, such as the Easterhouse Estate in Glasgow where residents and architects have shared the design process of replacing inadequate highrise housing. Also, a number of local authorities have been adventurous in their involvement of communities in LA21: Reading Borough Council, Bradford Metropolitan Council and Gloucestershire County Council are three such examples.

LA21 invites a fundamental revaluation of all the functions and operations of the local authority and of its relationship with those it represents. Achieving this new state has to be an evolutionary process, which is not to say that it lacks rigour or determination. There are many sensitive balances and community dynamics which if ignored, can result in imposed changes which traditionally cause either a community backlash or disinterest. For local authorities where there might be a recent history of confrontation with parts of the local communities (for example over a planning decision), a sudden change towards genuine participative approaches might well be regarded with suspicion and open hostility. Some local authorities that have approached this way of working have initially been met with charges that they are 'simply attempting to renege on their responsibilities'. If the local authority wishes to take its communities with it, any change of direction has to be carefully signposted and its objectives made transparent.

Evolution implies moving from the present position by building on existing strengths and overcoming weaknesses. It means building on what already exists. But who knows what already exists? Is there sufficient local data? Is there knowledge of local people with specific skills? All local communities and local authorities are different, so there is no single identifiable starting point.

In its piloting work with both rural and urban communities, WWF, with the Community Education Development Centre, has been adapting existing community education and community development methods to engage communities in the development of neighbourhood or parish Local Agenda 21 Action Plans. Following an external evaluation of this work with Reading Borough Council, WWF has produced a set of Key Issues and Process Guides that can be used by other local authorities to establish a process of community participation in LA21. The Key Issues divide into seven areas: staffing, communication/publicity/marketing, participation, monitoring and evaluation, resources, commitment, and education and training. The Process Guides include: in-house and external setting up, developing neighbourhood identity and strategy, formation of action plans, maintaining and spreading the initiative, and group autonomy.

A criticism that will be made of this approach is the time needed to establish the process. Some will say that more conventional consultation, where a draft plan is presented to communities, will be quicker and cheaper to produce. Others will prefer to establish expert panels or thematic forums. But in all cases it is necessary to consider which approach is more likely to generate trust, participation, on-going commitment and input from communities. Will all approaches lead to empowerment, improved democracy and a reflective, questioning, learning community? How likely is it that all approaches will be sustainable entities in their own right?

Only time will tell, but the early indications from the first community groups that are engaged in this process suggests a growing awareness of their potential role in addressing local issues. The first Action Plans coming out of the work are predictably parochial in their content: dog fouling, traffic, open spaces, health and so on. But this is where people are now.

The conventional route of policy development is through experts, with little or no emphasis on promoting – let alone enabling – open community participation. There might be historic reasons for this, but if the demand is for policies that promote sustainability it is essential that local authorities, as a major player, support a model that is capable of hearing both community and expert voices. Both have expertise in their own subjects: the community in the issues that affect them most directly, and the 'expert' in a specific thematic area. Both have a role in achieving sustainability but both need to learn new skills. For this reason development programmes are beginning to appear that address the training needs of elected members and officials of local authorities, and also those members of the community wishing to develop a local facilitation role.

In a process led approach there are two main 'popular curriculum' areas. The first relates to the process through which community participation is achieved, the 'people skills' such as facilitation, assertiveness, group work, confidence building, and so on. The second is for the content that supports community participation, such as visioning, planning, information, and technical and scientific input.

It is necessary to integrate the process and content into the community agenda. A sustainable community, one on which a sustainable future is dependent, is a learning and reflective community. It is a community that is able to transfer and assimilate information, that is reflective, analytical, and solutions orientated. If this is what the politicians mean when they talk about community approaches, then they deserve all the support we can give them.

References

de Bono, E (1994) *Parallel Thinking. From Socratic Thinking to de Bono Thinking* Viking, Middlesex

Hollins, M and Percy, S (1996) *World Wide to Street Wise. Lessons from the WWF/Reading Borough Council GLOBE Project* WWF Publications, Godalming

Jacobs, M (ed) (1996) *The Politics of the Real World* Earthscan, London

Jones, C (1995) *Working in Neighbourhoods* WWF Publications, Godalming

Jones C (1996) *Working in Parishes* WWF Publications, Godalming

Porritt J (1996) Unpublished speech WWF-UK Reaching Out Conference, 10.5.96

Sullivan, W M (1995) 'Institutions as the infrastructure of democracy' in Etzioni, A (ed) *New Communitarian Thinking: Persons, Virtues, Institutions, and Communities* University of Virginia Press, Virginia

Wangoola P (1994) 'On the African World Outlook' Unpublished conference paper; CEA Occasional Paper

11

Education and Engagement for Sustainability: the CADISPA Approach

Geoff Fagan

CADISPA 1988 to 1996

CADISPA (Conservation and Development in Sparsely Populated Areas) was initiated in Scotland at the Jordanhill College of Education in 1988. It was designed as a partnership between WWF-UK and the College which arose out of concern that the conflict model of engagement between conservationists, development agencies and local people was dysfunctional. A way had to be found where local people:

- living in areas of sparse population in Scotland could initiate local development which was environmentally sensitive and sustainable;
- could meet their own needs and aspirations for development without compromising environmental credibility;
- through educational processes, materials and initiatives, could develop skills and understandings which addressed the often conflicting interests of conservation and development.

The route to allow these principles to be realised was through education, both formal and informal. However, the kind of education process and assumptions behind curriculum design departed from the conventional in that the learning came from and relied upon the reality of local people. This reality meant their living experiences, their structures, stories and successes.

This chapter describes CADISPA operations as the framework on which a trans-European partnership is structured; and a process of engagement which seeks to place at the heart of all discussion and decision making the very local people who will be most affected by any change to their locality. It outlines the thinking and assumptions underpinning the CADISPA approach, and its relevance to the issues which lie at the heart of the sustainability debate. It illustrates the problems faced by local people and match these to preferred local solutions. It also illustrates how the CADISPA methodology allows local people to own the solution and call it theirs. Three case studies are included, two from Scotland and one from CADISPA Prespa in Greece, which illustrate the CADISPA approach. The chapter concludes by posing and attempting to address the central assumption of the CADISPA process: that education can deliver.

By 1992 CADISPA had researched and published two books which illustrated how this popular education could be effected in a primary and community education context (Dunlop et al 1993, Fagan 1993). In 1993, as a direct result of the Earth Summit, the European Union asked that CADISPA (now a family of four with the original Scottish initiative joined by partner developments in Italy, Spain and Portugal), refocus and begin to develop the thinking and practice behind Education for Sustainability. Most importantly perhaps, CADISPA was also asked to show how local people could be brought to the centre of a community development process which gathered together opposing positions and which led to an outcome which would prove sustainable for their communities. Local people, with the help of an education facilitator were to:-

- find their own way forward;
- become powerful enough to enable the choice of local people to be the final outcome;
- be able to take what information they needed from opposing factions and, within that, make sensitive development decisions.

This process was seen as essentially different from the environmental education programmes which had gone before it. By 1995, CADISPA had refocused. It had negotiated and published its operational plan and had piloted and designed its community led education processes and targeted 30 locations in Scotland's most remote areas with which to work over the next five years. In the December of that year, WWF-UK withdrew from CADISPA, following an internal review of its LA21 activity in Scotland. However, in January 1996 the University of Strathclyde, by now the host of CADISPA as Jordanhill College had become its Faculty of Education, agreed to sponsor the Project as an integral university activity until new funding partners could be found.

The Debate which CADISPA Informs

The environment debate is debilitated by fundamentalism. On one side of this debate are those people who recognise with missionary clarity the appalling cost of human activity to the biodiversity and fabric of the globe. This is hard to deny. On the other side, there is a belief that the eradication of poverty, quality of life, and economic security come first. On any analysis of past behaviour, this, too, is hard to deny.

The CADISPA position is a midway point between these two which recognises the limitations of both. For CADISPA, and many local, ordinary people, the absolute dark green position of the environmentalists, although understandable, is on the eccentric fringe. Local people have a dislike and distrust of zealots, whether right or wrong, and protect themselves by covering their ears.

CADISPA recognises the legitimacy of local people to use their environment for self-support and economic sustainability. It also recognises the importance of an educational process which will help local people develop a deep understanding of the need to be prudent and sensitive in the use of the environment, and recognise self-support and self-sufficiency as being different to selfishness or self-interest.

The central question in sustainability, that of community, ownership and individualism, is rocked on either side by powerful academic forces. Is the apparent move towards post-modern individualism, individuated opportunity and self as centre, at odds with a 'corporate' vision of the future? This is a profound and important debate for everyone concerned with sustainability for it will inform the shape and aspirations of our children's world, and must be tackled with as much enthusiasm as other more traditional concerns in the environmental debate.

CADISPA: New Communitarianism and Individuation

The CADISPA project recognised very early that many people living in sparsely populated areas had neither the networks, the market potentiality or the finance to support isolated self sufficiency. They had to work together out of necessity. They were forced to view opportunity collectively and spread the risk, spread the load and share the benefits. Out of necessity would come a new community fortified by strength and common direction. Is this a legitimate position? Is it possible that new economic and engagement models may be emerging? The debate over sustainability may begin to offer the emergence of activity which departs from the traditional responsibility for new economic development as being by individual, isolated and personal effort. This is an important issue for CADISPA, for it accepts as legitimate that economic engagement risk and development must become the responsibility of collections of local people.

However, perhaps all this talk of post-modernism and individuation is redundant. Is it not also possible to circumnavigate these difficulties by suggesting that the environment is essentially the product of a personal construct process? If correct, this notion may allow access to the value base of a person's constructs and thereby access to a change in behaviour. Allow people to reassess their constructions of environment and they will begin to see a different picture emerge. These are intellectually difficult areas for they relish the debate about beliefs, truth and values and see them as the legitimate forum for the discussion of environmental and/or development futures.

As all sensitive educators know, it is access to the hearts and minds of learners which is both the key to change and the hardest lock to open.

CADISPA and Local People

CADISPA is more than a technique. It represents a paradigm of thinking which embraces technique, values, power-sharing, action and education. It is a democratic process and one which accepts as its starting point that local people are key actors in making life more sustainable for themselves. CADISPA represents a departure from the more normal prescriptive notion of rural development where, in Scotland, local authorities and Local Enterprise Companies may develop a view of what is needed, seek minimal endorsement of their plans and progress them with, or without, significant local engagement.

CADISPA believes that it is local people who are the main actors in any sustainability context. It senses that both power and authority are beginning to move away from elected and non-elected institutions and towards congregations of local people. This raises important questions of competence. However, CADISPA has always engaged on the basis that local people have 'capacity' to spare.

> '... the communitarian individual is very much an individual. She is an individual who does not stand as an isolate but as a being existing out of a dense social ground'. (Elshtain, 1995)

CADISPA operationalises its processes based upon that position. Give local people the freedom and responsibility to develop their own patch. Make the decisions theirs. Start from where they are and support them whilst they make sense of the information and formulate decisions. Trust local people to make their own sustainable decisions. Given accurate information in a way which can be quickly understood, they will make sensible, sensitive choices within sustainable parameters. They, like the professionals and paraprofessionals who criticise this approach so quickly, are 'formatted' by the same cultural value base. They know the 'correct' answer and are as concerned as anyone else to protect their environment and mitigate the effect of any local development which might destroy or change forever the quality of their locality for themselves or their children.

For small communities to survive local people must put in place the concrete symbols of achievement and engagement. To these must be added other less concrete but equally tangible factors of belonging: the celebration of culture – being and place. The community must see in itself the future – it must also see itself as being an active part of an economic process. This sense of 'belonging', 'being' and 'contributing' is central to all sustainability issues.

This formula dictates that local people be confronted with the balance between aspiration and degradation; opportunity and responsibility and individual vision against the common good. They need help in doing this. This is at the heart of the educational process.

CADISPA recognises the galvanising effect of corporate learning and action. It believes the very strength of 'sustainability' comes from collective communitarian values where duties and responsibilities are enmeshed in a collective vision of the future. A local community's concern for the future of their children can not be matched in quality or quantity by any professional of any kind in local or central government. They cannot match the territorial understanding, cultural nuances and social understandings of local people. Professionals must recognise this and see the depth of this understanding as opportunity not threat.

Capacity-Building and CADISPA: The Heart of the Debate

There are dilemmas associated with capacity-building which need to be addressed. Capacity-building, with its emphasis on individual learned outcome and expression, may be the fan which drives the tempest, an individualised storm of selfishness and opportunity which destroys all sense of community or communitarianism in its path.

Box 11.1 Case study: Traffic and the slow lane

In one of Scotland's most isolated and painfully beautiful places 37 tourist cars an hour plough over the mountain pass and decant their passengers in the tiny hamlet at the road end. There are a small fishing pier and four car parking spaces. They take photos of the loch, walk up and down, perhaps relieve themselves where they can and then get back in their cars – meeting the other 37 cars on their journey back: blocking the passing places, taking their photos, over heating their engines, spreading their picnics, fighting the midges. The next hour it is the same ... and the next and the next.

Local people have asked the Council (100 miles away) to solve their summer time problem. Stop the traffic, build more spaces for parking, toilets, a cafe ... anything but please help. Although sympathetic, little or nothing has happened. Ever.

The problem this hamlet faces is connected in a cyclic way with its resolution. All the ingredients are here: plenty of tourists, environmental degredation and a need for increased economic activity.

This situation needs a framework which, cooperatively:

* welcomes the tourists and encourages them to stay;
* encourages them to contribute;
* manages the exposure and minimises the damage;
* controls the impact;
* employs local people.

No professional knows the intense feelings associated with living in this hamlet. Local people do. They understand – they experience, the intense frustration of kerb-crawling, photo-happy trippers every day of their collective working lives during the summer months. Then for the whole of the winter – nothing. This situation exists in every one of 1000 communities in every part of rural Scotland. The agency professionals cannot hope to address and understand each. It follows therefore that in large part the only solution for these communities is self help.

Is capacity-building therefore the Reaper or the resolution to local sustainability?

The thread which runs through this chapter is the engagement of local people in their own affairs and locality. It has tried to identify the frustrations, and fortitude of local people and has suggested that the only salvation for local communities is for local authorities and local development agencies to find ways of sharing power and bringing local people to the heart of the decision making. This necessarily means that local people must be able to wear comfortably the mantle of local responsibility.

Capacity-building, the mid-1990s catch-phrase of the intellectual and political elite, needs careful handling for it may well be the very process by which communities will be destroyed. This is the hub of an important debate between individualism and collectivity; between communitarianism and a self located post-modernism which must be addressed by environmentalists and educators alike.

Enabling local people to become more informed and powerful will mean that individuals within those communities become more powerful. A group of very powerful, well informed, opinionated and self-interested people may have all the necessary components for fracture and disarray. This is the dilemma for capacity-builders.

Mix this capacity-building process with individuated selfishness and ambition and it might become a truly volatile and destructive mixture. However, local people are also demanding more say and involvement. To achieve that, and a position of equality in any negotiation, they need information, understanding and process skills. To achieve this means they will need a process of capacity-building. This potential for community fragmentation must be weighed against the risk of non-engagement, alienation, isolation or anomie which might arise as a result of non-intervention. It would seem, therefore, that capacity-building is here to stay.

CADISPA and Education

How do local people know what environmental cost and economic benefit might be associated with a development if they are not being taught or told?

> 'There are choices but these people are never really shown
> these choices ... they are not given space to think ... [this]
> entails a simple premise: that if people are to learn that
> they have, and can make, choices, it is important that they
> are in conversations by choice'. (Smith, 1994)

CADISPA neither tells not teaches. In the CADISPA experience, education is viewed as essentially democratic: a process of dialogue, reflection, action and information and an exploration of values. It fully recognises that to help local people build their competence to the point where they feel confident in pressing for a developmental agenda, without understanding fully the implications for the environment, is only half the job.

However, it also recognises the reality which ordinary people experience. They, generally have little time for environmental preaching and there is an undisputed gap between what they know deep down they should do and what they will do. This yawning gap exists in all of us. Competence means confidence to act. It also means intellectual competence to understand and make decisions based on that understanding.

Throughout its engagement with local people CADISPA uses dialogue as the basis of its educational practice. It helps local people seek the information they need, it supplies expert advice about impact and cost, it helps each group understand the information they have collected, and facilitates, if required, the designing of an action agenda. This agenda would then belong to local people; it will be from within their understandings and perceptions of the world. It will also be based upon their analysis of the cost to the environment and to their quality of life of a particular action.

So, CADISPA would never preach a particular environmental line. However, it would enable local people to become environmentally literate from within the agenda they themselves have designed. Rarely will local people see this as environmental education – and this is essential, as, for many people the very hint of 'education' is sufficient to place them on the defensive. However, education it is; and of a most profound kind.

CADISPA therefore has a different, radical interpretation of the education process. It has a view of environmental education which stems from inside the heads of local people. It recognises that the most secure way of protecting the environment is to help local people develop it for their economic and cultural stability – and it recognises sustainability as a holistic concept which embraces culture, values and behaviour as well as economics and environment. In short CADISPA starts from where people really are – not where a professional would wish them to be. Local people start there too: always.

Can Education Deliver?

The prescriptive, service model of local authority provision may not be the only institution under threat of collapse. There is also an accelerating movement away from a prescriptive, superimposed and suspended view of knowledge. A new paradigm of thinking which recognises that local people and their view of their circumstances and their locality, however seemingly unsophisticated, is the world view which really matters to them. The understanding this gives them, however parochial, is the only one that matters.

There is an obvious dilemma here for educationalists. If education is to deliver sustainable behaviour it must be process and reality led. It must be recognised as the process which brings understanding, awareness and competence from within the context of peoples' lives. If educators define education as being only school-based, tangential and stratified learning, divorced from real life and underpinned by an external authority, it will not deliver what is needed.

In all the experience CADISPA has built over time one overwhelming cry is heard time and time again: 'We want no more of education and training. This time is our time. School is out and left far behind'. For many people schooling was at best a non-entity, and at worst a humiliating, divorced and unsuccessful experience. A repetition of this would be a disaster.

The educational process necessary to deliver sustainable behaviour must seek to re-engage local people in learning and internalising sustainability. It must be a 'popular' process, helping local people identify what they need to know, engaging in research to find what is needed; and to talk critically and collectively about the information gathered. It must help build action strategies and rebuild the construction of what is understood. It must reflect on action taken and help in the design of future plans. This is the education of the future.

This education is not divorced from real life. It is democratic, action led, endorsed only by local people and lasts only as long as it is needed. It involves local people justifying and designing their preferred action, and understanding the complexities of real problems whilst risking themselves in the process of resolution. A democratic experience where power in the learning process is shared and output, knowledge and programme are negotiated.

From within this position education can and will deliver. It is a fundamental challenge to the notion of worthwhile knowledge; to the teacher as priest and to fossilised learning. It is also fundamentally challenging to local people and, thereby, lies at the very heart of useful, worthwhile learning. Don't call this 'education' for people will run away – simply help people do it and they will fly. Local people need a professional's help to do this; they don't need their endorsement to kill it.

CADISPA and Local Agenda 21: Letting the Land Live

CADISPA does not plant trees. It does not dig ditches or protest at the building of roads and bridges deemed necessary by local people for their long term survival. It operates on the principle that the environment is best conserved by local people being engaged within it. The environment is protected by being used. Whether this is by crofting, sheep farming, mountain guiding or eco-trekking, it is best protected by the economic engagement of local people who thereby need to protect it in order that it, the environment, can support them.

The environment is a part of a cultural, aesthetic and economic asset of the locality. This position is at the heart of LA21 and the sustainability circle comprising local people, environment, culture and economics.

If sense is to be made of the commitment to alleviate poverty in this and the developing world, and protect the environment, two objectives must be achieved:

1) Local people must be allowed and encouraged to use their

local environment in a way which is sustainable both for the environment and for themselves.

2) The environment must be made central to daily living.

Most people in the North would recognise the need to halt the stripping of natural resources to feed the debt repayments and the market demands of the developed world. The quest for maximum return on invested capital and the fluidity of multinational companies lies at the root of much environmental damage and unsustainable behaviours. However, until the people of the developed world are willing to face a different future for themselves, the force for change will not be sufficient to redirect the energy necessary to promote change. 'There is no consensus, no public meeting of minds, on the nature of the good life, hence the triumph of private caprice ...' (Walzer 1995).

This is not a crisis made by industry. It is a crisis sustained by the unwillingness of local people to lend the guidance to industry that it needs. However, change there must be. This highly competitive voyage to environmental oblivion cannot be allowed to run like some demented machine from a science fiction horror movie. Industry will always respond to the parameters placed around them. It is local people who need to agree the boundaries within which industry is asked to operate.

The Process of Social, Economic and Environmental Regeneration

Many, many people living in the most sparsely populated areas of the UK have pluri-jobs. They work at different times, in different places doing different things. No single activity is sufficient to give a secure income, but a collective income is sufficient (just) to make ends meet. In a strange way the spread of risk this offers also contributes to security. If one activity fails, the effect on the entire income stream, although serious, is not devastating. So for some urban-based professionals who might be unnerved by the uncertainty of pluri-job existence, to local people in the remotest regions this feature probably makes life more, not less, secure. This,

Box 11.2 Case study: Isle of Tiree

The Isle of Tiree lies off the Argyll coast in the south west of Scotland. It is an island of 800 people. It has a ferry and airport, a secondary school and two hotels. Its shape, rather like a scallop, ensures that the windsurfing is excellent from which ever direction the wind should choose to blow. Because of this it is fast becoming the wind surfing capital of the UK.

This small island has an infrastructure which dates back to the times when it functioned as a World War II aircraft carrier – a huge RAF Air Base defending the north Atlantic approaches and the Clyde from hostile attack. Old ex-Ministry of Defence buildings litter the countryside, some of which have been converted for community use.

CADISPA was asked to become involved in the island activity by a small group of residents representing these community groups. They had tried for some years to get a wet weather facility built on the island to make better use of the tourist trade and to enable local people improve their own quality of life.

These three groups (the Community Council, the Swimming Pool Committee and the Local Hall Committee) had made representations over three years to all the authorities and had singularly failed to move their agenda forward. CADISPA brought with it a neutral, non-sectoral agency (the university), the best technical assistance on offer in Scotland, experts in groupwork process and an inside knowledge of European Union funding.

At the first meeting (December 1995) the local group representatives each talked of their frustrations and aspirations. They questioned each other about what each wanted and listened to the stories of success and failures from each other. By the second meeting there were six community groups represented and by the fourth group meeting 11 community groups. Over that time CADISPA helped people explore the reasons for the difficulty, gave information about EU Objective 1 finance and new legislation recently put in place by the Scottish Office, and helped the group define a collective agenda to which all could feel committed. At each session issues of sustainability were discussed.

CADISPA supported the group as it applied to the Scottish Office for funding to give them a part-time development worker and supported them again when the local authority and Local Enterprise Company (LEC) greeted their proposals with little enthusiasm.

In August 1996 the Tiree development group placed before the local people at a public meeting the proposals and timescale for the development. They asked for a public mandate to endorse the proposal that the Tiree Development Group apply for funding which would allow the development over five years of:

- a multi-functional sports and community centre;
- an indoor swimming pool
- a dance and drama studio;
- a Gaelic arts and language centre;
- a new cattle auction mart;
- a sheep scanner.

In total the bid to a variety of funding agencies totalled £1.9 million. Applications were to be completed and submitted by December 1996 with a start date expected in September 1997. Local councillors and representatives of the LEC had been invited to all the development meetings and notes of progress at each meeting were sent to representatives at the EU Objective 1 Partnership, local authorities, the LEC and the Scottish Office. CADISPA has helped in the preparation and submission of documents, information processing, research and groupwork processes. The local people are committed to making the development as eco-friendly as possible. They also see the project as a significant step towards sustainability which will create jobs, improve the quality of life, make best sense of the tourist economic opportunity and celebrate and record the history of the Gaelic language on Tiree.

£1.9 million is a lot of money – and will take some finding. However, with persistence and support there is simply no reason why the people on Tiree should not get what others have already got. In the early days it was difficult for local people to grasp the meaning of a £1.9 million development; this is now accepted and understood.

This opportunity is there for the taking. Local people on Tiree have simply organised, collectivised and acted. The signs are that they will be successful.

however, should not be used to hide their acute anxiety over income stability.

There is a strong feeling that living at the very margin of Europe, in the most fragile and isolated villages, has left them adrift: their voice unheard with the resources spent elsewhere. Time and time again the magnificent scenery is used in argument against them as some sort of recompense for being lonely, non-involved and underemployed.

Taken together, the pluri-job economy, the isolation, the way things have always been, the feeling of being abandoned and the immediate recognition that self help may be the only way, is a powerful driving force for change. It is into this perception which CADISPA locks. CADISPA seeks only to help local people help themselves. It recognises that economic security and quality of life motivates and sustains people and, only when a position of semi-security is reached, allows them the freedom to focus on wider issues.

Sustainability is therefore as much about poverty relief as environmental protection. So, we argue, help must be offered to local people to build the capacity to gain the security and quality of life they feel they need. Secure this from within their culture, their systems and their view of the world, and explore with them the information, their view of their future and the impact of their preferred change. Help them in making decisions, gathering resources, refocusing and reflecting. This is the CADISPA method. It has not a hint of education anywhere except everywhere.

Localness as Globalness

CADISPA has placed all its resources and staked its credibility to the principle that it is local people who will do what is needed to protect and maintain the environment whilst preserving and developing their communities and economic opportunities. Make the land work, encourage particular activities and seek local engagement: this must be the way.

However, many people only recognise this as romantic nonsense. For them the salvation of the planet lies in the hands of politicians, educational institutions, multinational companies and local authorities. Local people are minor actors in the game. This is fundamentally wrong. Local people, far from being the simple recipients of products and positions sent down by these institutions, are, in effect, the controllers and negotiators in that process. They are at the hub of change not the periphery. Their behaviour, the way they engage, the demands that they make and the products they are willing to accept or buy, make them central and very powerful in the business of sustainability. Of course, they too are subject to the same powerful marketing messages as everyone else and this is where education and choice are so important.

CADISPA has been criticised for spending all its resources in helping local people make these choices and in gathering resources to effect change. It has purposefully chosen not to expend its resources in an academic debate with multinationals, governments and institutions in the belief that these will, in time, do what the multitudes of local people require of them.

Educate and emancipate: take people from where they are to where they would wish to be. This is the recipe for local engagement. Enable local people to understand the information about production and real costs, and trust them to make the necessary choices. Informed choice above all is the key to change.

From Local to Me and Mine

Local people build their understandings of the global issues by reference to their intricate relationship with their local place. In effect the world is their world. This is the core existence of most people: it is the local world which really matters to them. It follows then that in getting this right in every local case the global 'revolution' will have happened without pain or pattern. Localness is therefore Globalness.

This position recognises localness as something much bigger. It recognises localness as part of a much larger framework. Not from local to global but local to personal and from personal to global. The concern local people may have for developing countries and the unfairness with which they must cope is recognised, but at a distance. Their real world surrounds them. The society within which they live most of their life and which gives place to their behaviour is the only world for most people. This world is known intimately by them.

Contrast this with the view of the world from an economic development agency and local authority perspective. There is, quite literally, a universe of difference. The central question raised by CADISPA with its commitment to popular action is about the relationship of local people to these representative structures. There are two separate issues here which, when taken together, represent a substantial challenge to local authority politics and superimposed decision making.

Firstly, there is an apathy eating at the heart of local representative democracy and, secondly, on single issues, people are beginning to see the almost immediate results of direct action.

Box 11.3 Case study: CADISPA Greece – Psarades Prespa

Traditional houses in Greece's Prespa region are square stone buildings in a range of brown and rust colours. Topped by red-tile roofs, they cluster together in 12 villages and almost seem part of the earth they sit on. Now, however, the terracotta towns are punctuated with modern concrete blocks. Since the 1950s, when young people started leaving villages such as Agios Germanos and Psarades for cities, local customs and know-how, including repairing homes the traditional way, have been disappearing.

Repairing stone houses has always cost more than residents could afford to pay, and when they did attempt to fix them, without knowledge of specialised traditional techniques, they usually ended up damaging the crumbling buildings further. So they tore down their traditional homes to build new cement structures – which they actually prefer because they come with all the modern amenities old houses lack, or else they simply abandoned houses and barns. Psarades has many empty stone buildings with caved in roofs.

CADISPA Prespa has been active in reskilling local people enabling them to rebuild their homes within conservation guidelines and with financial backing from the national Greek and local Prespa government. Traditional architecture is purest in Psarades village. Built on the shore of Megali Prespa lake, the village has been designated a traditional settlement by the government.

It is also the last stronghold of a local breed of dwarf draught cattle, named after the village. Once found throughout the region, only 100 head of these small, black or brown animals remain. They were a source of good beef, but supplied no milk, and worked hard in the fields. They have been improved and replaced by bigger breeds and dairy cows. Psarades cattle also had an important role in Prespa's ecological balance: they grazed in wet meadows and kept fast-growing reeds at bay, creating fish and bird breeding grounds. Even today, the 100 animals graze along the lake's shores. But that's not enough, and these fertile meadows are disappearing. It's a perfect example of how human activities can sometimes increase biodiversity. The shrinking gene pool of European domestic stock is a growing problem and the EU has a programme to encourage breeding of obscure bona fide domestic races. CADISPA is currently seeking EU support for Psarades cattle raising, which will help re-establish an animal on the brink of extinction. So far, the entire stock has been tagged, counted and logged on a database.

'In every society, people who do things differently are always labelled crazy', says Haris Nikolau. He is one of the four brave small-scale farmers in Prespa who have gone organic. For the last 15 years, 97 per cent of

Prespa's farmers have intensively cultivated large white beans, recognised world-wide for their quality, in the fields adjacent to the area's two lakes. The result: less fertile soil, and pesticides and fertilisers seeping into the lakes. Haris had already turned to organic cultivation techniques on his own small holding in 1990. By the time CADISPA launched its organic farming project in 1993, he, like the other two, had trained as park guides and was ready to get serious about cultivating their fields the natural way. Another farmer has since joined the project.

The first field was infested with insects in 1993, which he overcame using a mild pesticide that met organic farming standards. Since then, pests have not been a problem. Fellow Prespa farmers may not look upon the handful of small organically cultivated fields with scepticism for long. They can see that the crops are as healthy as those in their own pesticide-sprayed fields. They are becoming curious and talk with the four farmers, who happily explain how and why they are switching farming techniques. It's an education process that does not involve classrooms.

Perhaps more tangible incentives are cost and health: not only is organic farming cheaper – no money is spent on chemical fertilisers and pesticides – but organically grown beans and other produce command a higher market price.

Source: CADISPA Greece (1995)

Local authorities disregard both at their peril for direct action is fast becoming recognised as a legitimate and appropriate route for 'community of interest' action.

Does it really matter that local people may not fully understand, in a way acceptable to a local authority, the implications of their preferred development? Does it matter that the development may not fit the long-term regional development plan?

For most people the world is their world.

It is becoming increasingly clear that unless local authorities and agencies can find a way to accommodate the wishes of local people in being part of the action, the authority structure itself will be under severe strain. New partnerships with shared power structures and engagement processes need to be designed and adopted. The writing seems truly on the wall for the traditional service model of local authorities and development agencies. This is a serious concern for local authorities because it challenges the power base built over many years. Not a tentative challenge easily resolved: but a challenge which strikes at the very heart of local service provision and democracy.

Ideally, local people should make all the decisions in their locality which might affect their present or future. This is not a romantic or ideological fantasy. Sustainability, in part, is enabling people to feel safe in their locality. They must 'own' and thereby protect the territory which affects their quality of life. This ownership is of critical importance and local authorities must recognise and embrace structures which draw local people to the centre. Like a sustainability jigsaw: tiny piece by tiny obscure piece the picture emerges. Not one of them precocious enough to think that they are sustaining the globe, yet each of them contributing, without fully knowing, to that outcome. Sustainability is localness: and localness is globalness.

Conclusion

This chapter has tried to cover much ground: from the simple description of an earth breaking project to tentative philosophical debate on emerging paradigms of thinking around sustainability. It has raised, as a serious issue, the potential for the demise of small communities, and local authorities and agencies, unless ways can be found of accommodating local people in a power sharing process. It has also tried to raise issues of individuation and self-centredness which will destroy those collectives of people we call communities. This, it has argued, has serious implications for the implementation of sustainable practice.

A case has been made for putting the environment back into a frame whose parameters include economic behaviour and cultural celebration as the main elements of sustainability. It has said quite clearly 'let the land live'. It has argued for a definition of education as a process which draws its programme and power from local people. It challenges the role of the professional as expert and decision maker, and pushes them into a more sensitive and helpful role as true 'civil servants'. It has recognised that this will be very difficult.

Illustration has been offered of how the environment might be best 'protected' by active inclusion in people's lives, and a case made for supporting economic and cultural reliance on the local environment as the only way in which it can be truly sustained for the children of our children. It has also tried to suggest that local-ness might be the only expression of globalness which has any meaning for ordinary people: localness is globalness.

Since 1988, CADISPA has tried in small ways to tackle community disintegration, environmental degradation and feelings of hopelessness, marginality and the perception of unimportance in rural Scotland and the remote areas throughout Europe. These feelings are neither specific to CADISPA projects nor the rural community. This is important, for the popular educational approach developed by CADISPA and the University of Strathclyde may hold seminal lessons for all community development processes, both rural and urban, and in the developing relationship of local people to the local authority and economic development agencies which serve them.

CADISPA has never set out to confront powerful agencies with the necessity of change – but it has singularly forced these institutions into that position. This was not the plan. It has been an unintended outcome of practice and a very welcome one too. Local people are at the heart of sustainability: it is only a matter of debate as to how they may be best enabled to secure for their children the essential elements of security and quality of life. CADISPA is but one way. There will be many, many others.

References

Bell, S, Dunlop, J and Weston, R (1993) *CADISPA Primary* WWF-UK, Godalming

CADISPA Greece (1995) Case study from *The CADISPA Portfolio* 2nd edition WWF International, Gland, Switzerland

Elshtain, J B (1995) 'The Comunitarian Individual' in Etzioni, A (ed) *New Communitarian Thinking: Persons, Virtues, Institutions and Communities*, pp 99–109 University Press of Virginia, Virginia

Fagan, G R (1993) *CADISPA Community* WWF-UK, Godalming

Smith, M (1994) *Local Education: Community, Conversation and Praxis* Open University Press, Milton Keynes

Walzer, M (1995) 'The Communitarian Critique of Liberalism in Etzioni, A (ed) *New Communitarian Thinking: Persons, Virtues, Institutions and Communities*, pp 52–70 University Press of Virginia, Virginia

12

Ethnic Community Environmental Participation

Judy Ling Wong

Although the total number of people belonging to ethnic communities is calculated as 5.8 per cent of the UK population, they are not evenly distributed across the UK. The local reality often finds the ethnic communities making up a significant proportion, or even the majority, of the population as we experience it.

Ethnic communities in the London Borough of Brent, numbering 109,000, makes up 44.9 per cent of the local population. Eight London authorities have between them 19.66 per cent of all ethnic people within the UK. As one moves across these huge boroughs, one will encounter entire streets and small local areas with up to 100 per cent people from ethnic communities of different origins. Birmingham has a population of ethnic communities of 206,000 which exceeds the entire population of Blackburn; the population of Blackburn itself stands at 136,400, with an ethnic community population of 21,000 (Runnymede Trust, 1994).

Within this picture, logically, one can ask how it can be possible that such large numbers of people can be neglected in the traditional outreach programmes of so many organisations whose remit implies the engagement of everyone in environmental awareness and participation. The fact that working with ethnic communities is not on the agenda of those working in environmental action points to the powerful consequences of how we see the world, and of how we respond emotionally to it. The coming together of thinking and feeling dictates whether or not we involve ourselves with a particular area of work or life. It shapes how we go about it and contributes to the success or failure of a venture.

Lessons from a True Story

When I was working as an interpreter for the National Health Service, I once took a Chinese-speaking Vietnamese little boy to the hospital. On arrival, we were informed that there was to be a delay of three hours for the appointment, so I suggested to the little boy Kin and his mother Fung (the names have been changed) that we should go and walk along the river, and go and see the hundreds of ducks in St James' Park. We bought a loaf of bread from the hospital shop and we were off. Kin was filled with ecstatic expectation and his mother with disbelief. As we progressed along the river, Fung said, 'You know, these English people are really peculiar about animals. You see all these birds flying about? We would have eaten them all.' We went onto Charing Cross bridge, so that Kin could experience the trains thundering past him. A pigeon landed and started to walk along the handrail. Fung looked at me, pointed to the bird, and said, 'And pigeon soup!'

When Kin, Fung and I finally arrived at St James Park, there was the familiar sight of the ducks scuttering about on the bank and in the water. Adults and children were feeding them with bread, cake, seed, and their own lunch. Fung shook her head and remarked with astonishment, 'All these ducks – just to look at !' Kin took the bread and fed the ducks wildly. Fung and I settled down on a bench. After a while, she said to me, ' They really are beautiful, aren't they?' Fung had lived through the terrors of a long war. Still, given the opportunity, she sat and enjoyed the simple pleasure of watching some very funny and some very beautiful ducks.

Fung's ability to encompass two starkly different alternative interpretations of nature highlights the twin principles of sustainable development – our survival within nature as the supporting nurturing environment, and the distinct human ability for the appreciation of qualities of nature beyond the ruthless drive for the survival of the fittest.

Fung and Kin, perhaps typical of first generation Vietnamese refugees, live in an area which must count as one of the worst living environments in the UK. They live on income support in a tiny council flat, in a concrete jungle in a heavily polluted area of the inner city.

The Environment as a Setting for All Life

In this country, most of the time, when we mention the word environment, it is dominated by a peacetime vision of the protection of wildlife in a world of plenty, heavily coloured by the wish for the preservation of a mythical nature untouched by humans. The preservation and conservation of wildlife and of the significant natural areas which are left are of course of paramount importance, but the context for environmental participation is much wider. It is the environment in general, urban and rural, as a setting for all life – plant life, animal life and human life.

Additionally, beyond basic survival, it is a specifically human quality to have the capacity for the attribution of values and meaning to experience. Everyone is therefore connected intrinsically to the pillars of sustainable development – to fulfil human spiritual, social and physical needs, and to preserve the diversity and quality of the environment.

World Peace and the Survival of the Environment

The survival of the environment is dependent on the relationship between different ethnic groups. Both the peacetime management of the environment, and the conscious nurturing of intercultural understanding, in order to prevent mass genocide and large-scale devastation of the environment through human conflict, are essential to the survival of people and the environment.

In the UK, black and white ethnic communities are often seen merely as local minority cultures. In fact, they are communities whose origins connect us with world majority cultures. Within the UK, they place within our society a unique and vital opportunity for cultural interaction. They enable us to be in touch with the relationship between people and nature within scenarios across the world. They are the 'world within the UK' which enables us to gain facets of awareness and inter-cultural skills which in turn enable us to forge relevant local and global environmental policies.

Contact with Nature

Many new arrivals from different countries of origin, who we have notionally accepted as full members of our communities, are given so little support that they remain lost within the new culture of the country which is now their home. They are often urban-bound and have little or no opportunity to be in touch with nature at large. Many have never seen the British countryside. Contact with nature at large plays no part in Fung and her husband's lives. They do not know where to go, and their children will remain city-bound.

Traumatised by years of war, and reduced to a position in which the concern for anything which does not contribute to her mere survival is a privilege, Fung has shown that people can still retain the capacity for the appreciation and enjoyment of natural beauty. We should remember the vast numbers of people whose lives find a continuity with this desperate scenario. Many groups here and across the world feel that the privilege of concern is 'not for the likes of us', from those who live on land strewn with landmines to those living in poverty in appalling deprivation in wealthy countries, or simply, many of those who work for a basic living within a perceived framework of personal powerlessness and disconnectedness to issues which deeply affect the quality of their lives.

Fung and Kin are now safe as refugees in this country. Access to the countryside, visits to nature reserves and areas of natural beauty can certainly contribute significantly to their healing as persons, and to the quality of their lives in general. Given the opportunity, such contact can lay down the basis for the motivation to engage in environmental participation. There are vast potential energies yet to be released from our ethnic communities, which will form a significant contribution to environmental care.

A VAST MISSING CONTRIBUTION

Fung and Kin have never been in touch with an environmental organisation. They are typical of hundreds of thousands of people who are unlikely to contribute to the care of nature, whether it is working for the survival of plants and animals, or for the quality of the air they breathe. They have no access to the enjoyment of the wider environment. They have no information or resources for action. They have no influence over the qualities of the immediate environment in which they live. As a consequence of living in some of the worst local environments, we should note that many of our ethnic communities retain an untapped drive to improve the quality of the environment.

The remaining natural areas exist only under the protection of our social system. Their continued existence depend on the support of public opinion. At the moment, Fung and Kin are unlikely to lend their weight here.

The non-inclusion of first generation arrivals in environmental participation creates an 'instant family tradition' of exclusion from contact with nature and environmental participation. As it is not part of his mother's life to be environmentally aware and involved, Kin is unlikely to experience family life as a normal entry point to environmental participation.

What Can We Do?

FACILITATING ENVIRONMENTAL PARTICIPATION BY NEWCOMERS BELONGING TO ETHNIC COMMUNITIES

I would like to return to the proposal that the coming together of thinking and feeling forms an important part of the basis for action. In common with many other non-participating groups in society, black and white ethnic community groups need facilitation to go through the same process of engagement with environmental participation.

The three major categories for environmental engagement for ethnic communities are:

1) The facilitation of access to the enjoyment and the use of elements of the natural environment. This puts them in touch with nature at large and takes them through an experience which enables them to take up their rightful ownership of the environment, and creates the entry point for their engagement with the conservation, preservation and development of the natural environment.

    This includes facilitating the use and enjoyment of nature reserves, activities within an outdoor setting, parkland, inner city nature reserves, canals, and an introduction to the small but vital elements which keep urban communities symbolically linked to nature, such as window boxes, pocket parks, school nature areas, community gardens and allotments.

    It takes them through the following process:

    - Facilitation of contact with nature leading to the love of nature
    - Facilitation of environmental awareness of the elements of nature
    - The coming together of the love of nature with the awareness of the threat to the environment brings about the motivation to protect and care for the environment, as it is normal and human to protect what we love.

    Significant community partnership by the committed can be furthered through partnership with environmental agencies.

2) The facilitation of ethnic communities to the contribution to the conservation, preservation and development of elements of the natural environment. This includes contribution to the care of nature at large and involvement in the policy and management of natural areas. It includes the creation, management and development of elements and areas within the urban setting symbolically and practically engaging people with nature at large.

    This involves facilitating access to information, expertise and resources with regard to the elements of the natural environment.

3) The improvement and development of the immediate environment in which ethnic communities live, and the contribution to sustainability through action within the personal lives of individuals. This addresses issues such as litter, the awareness and understanding of energy issues, practical action such as insulation and recycling, the understanding and management of environmental risk such as air pollution.

This involves:

- Facilitation of access to information, expertise and resources
- Enabling the acquisition of the skills needed, such as the interpretation of technical data, about the management of aspects of their immediate environment.

In addition to the above, the approach taken to involve ethnic communities needs to be socially and culturally relevant. Issues of empowerment, community development, and the potential for economic engagement and community enterprise need to be integrated with environmental participation.

A Working Definition of 'Community'

Many different definitions for 'community' have been proposed which attempt to address different scenarios, adapted to the agendas and the perceived client groups of environmental organisations. I would like to propose a working definition which actually diagnoses the various scenarios which are encountered:

> *A community is a web of relationships defined by a significant level of mutual care and commitment.*

Coming back yet again to the proposal that the coming together of thinking and feeling can lead to action or non-action, proactive environmental organisations will take action to involve ethnic communities in environmental participation only if they think and feel that:

- Ethnic communities are an integral part of the community in a multi-cultural Britain.
- There is an essential and significant missing contribution yet to be made by ethnic communities, especially in the context of globally and locally relevant actions.
- As British citizens, the members of ethnic communities have a right to the access and enjoyment of the environment.
- Ethnic communities have the right to be empowered to influence the quality of their environments, which are often of poor environmental quality.
- They care about ethnic communities and are therefore committed to their wellbeing.
- Environmental action has social and cultural meanings which are significant to ethnic communities.

Within the proposed definition of 'community', the proactive organisations would need to see themselves as being within the community, working as part of it, rather than as an organisation working with a community outside itself.

Through the impact of the work of the Black Environment Network (BEN), many organisations have begun to:

- instigate the beginnings of an organisational culture change in relation to working with ethnic communities;
- acquire awareness and skills to work effectively and meaningfully with ethnic communities;
- create new ways of working with ethnic communities, especially in the area of interpretation.

This is done with a view to:

- undoing some of the harm that has been done in the non-recognition and isolation of the presence within society of communities stemming from different countries of origin;
- building up a relationship of mutual care and commitment, with a focus on engendering partnerships for environmental care and sustainable development.

Some of the significant themes which arise in working with ethnic communities are:

- The creation of a sense of belonging and ownership of this country by ethnic communities.
- The recognition of the relevance, importance and richness of different cultural interpretations of life, and in particular of nature, in a multicultural world.
- Sustainable development means working towards an integrated society and subsequently an integrated world. The outlook we undertake and the behaviour of each of us affects the future of the world and therefore changes all our lives.
- The promotion of multiculturalism as a challenge to racism, and as a contribution to national civil harmony and world peace.

Into the Future

Sustainability and an Integrated Approach to Environmental Participation

Much of British culture is still dominated by a puritanical attitude, in which work and play have exclusive dividing lines. Work is seen to be what we should and must do.

It is still early days for many organisations to shift away from recruiting people to their limited agenda through converting people to causes rather than by inspiring them. The manner in which their agendas are framed are, in the main, restrictive and strait-jacketed, making it difficult for the necessary multi-faceted, innovative and dynamic approaches to community participation to be possible.

The normal unpredictability of the progress of community involvement, with its ebbs and flows of levels of interest and target oriented achievements, alongside the fulfilment of enjoyment, and social and cultural meaning, within a vast range of activities, has seen many organisations flounder in their commitment to this approach.

This state of affairs is the result of the failure to appreciate that everything we do with people can only survive and develop as part of people's lives. There is a lack of faith in the cumulative effect of the varying levels of contribution of the years of people's lives, stretching into the future, carried by their inspired wish to remain environmentally engaged. A commercialised organisational culture of instant target ticking does not key well into the need for invest-ment in an process which unfolds at its own specific pace.

With Local Agenda 21 there is a slow dawning of conscious-ness that, with the enveloping and overwhelming themes we need to deal with, there can be no solution through the target ticking efforts of formal organisations. The solution lies with mass involve-ment through the power intrinsic in the way people live their personal lives, with the turning on of each light switch, with each step to the local shop. There is no power through control, but there is the subtle power of being related and in touch. A sea change in organisational culture needs to happen – they need to care and therefore act, and others will respond and care and act.

Within the concept of sustainable development, we can only take an integrated approach to environmental participation in which everything has a niche for environmental care and every environmental action is a social and cultural action.

Working with ethnic communities has shown us that we cannot work with these groups of people unless we recognise who they are, unless we make the effort to understand their concerns and make our work relevant to each others' lives. Those who have become environmentally involved have done so only because they wish to be involved, because we demonstrated that we care about them and created opportunities through which they have become engaged with the environment. This field of work has highlighted an area of knowledge which we can use to involve any non-partic-ipating group in sustainable development. The key to successful involvement is to build up a web of relationships in which there is a significant level of mutual care and commitment, with a focus on environmental themes.

Freud, drawing from the experience of the rigid society of his time, concluded that there are two great areas in our lives – love and work. A major theme for the more fluid searching society of our century is to reunite these divided themes – to consciously make love and work the same thing. Work needs to be the expression of our care for each other, locally and globally.

Sustainable development means the laying down of a way of assuring the future of this entire planet. It is about global harmony and cooperation within the commitment to human needs and to our planetary setting for all life. The rectification of the isolation of ethnic communities in this country is symptomatic of the road we are to take. Let's start on this road at home, drawing together the multi-faceted fabric of our society. We will then be well on our way, because through our ethnic communities, home is also the world.

References

Runnymede Trust (1994) *Multi-Ethnic Britain: Facts and Trends* Runnymede Trust, London

13

Halcyon Days

Sue Clifford

Halcyon Days
– times of calm, peace and happiness –
nature benign, culture at ease with itself
the obverse of nature tempestuous and culture rampant.

Halcyon Days – the words come from a rich collision of myth, legend and fable which recall the sailor's story of the kingfisher (halcyon in Greek) incubating its eggs at sea for the seven days before and the seven after the winter solstice, when the sea was always calm.

Kingfishers actually make their nests in holes in river banks in the spring, and their eggs take 21 days to hatch. But it would be wrong to construe that the ancients did not know much about the bird, better to appreciate that they knew a good deal, and about poetry too. Certainly the words have had the power of persistence, and carry with them a rattlebag of possible explanations, provoking all kinds of questions and musings.

Knowledge – Values – Wisdom

All manner of things change if you take as your starting point that people know things, that they care about nature, value their surroundings, want quality in their lives and are willing to put in effort if they feel they can influence things.

Thousands of years of 'empirical research' in almost every corner of the earth, has provided us with an extraordinary bank of knowledge about nature; cultural evolution in parallel has borne diverse value systems.

Scientific knowledge, in a handful of centuries, has added vast amounts to our understanding and capabilities; it has focused on facts, replicable states, leaving aside anything difficult to count, cost, exchange or substitute. Intangible benefits, subjective perceptions, emotional attachments and expressions of value need other languages and other champions.

We contend that the quest for living for the mutual benefit of nature and ourselves can only be achieved if everyone wants to join in and can become involved. In creating or reinventing a benign rapport with nature we must all give of our manifold 'expertise'.

We perceive that compartmentalisation of disciplines, and leaving decisions to politicians and their professional acolytes has solved some problems and created others. We believe that encouraging people at large into more mixed debate about change, from their own strongest starting points, builds courage and enables them to give of their best.

Parish Maps

Making a Parish Map is about creating a community expression of values and about beginning to assert ideas for involvement; it is about taking the place into your own hands. The Parish Map's power is in its seeming simplicity and inclusiveness. Propelled by the question 'What do you value in your place?' makes everyone the expert; no one else can tell you what is important to you. It embodies the reasons why you should want to respond: the implication is that 'your' place belongs to you, and through this recognition comes responsibility for it.

So much surveying, measuring, fact gathering, analysis and policy-making leaves out the very things which make a place important to the people who know it. Parish Maps are socially created, lots of people reading their neighbourhoods, discussing, exploring and demonstrating how rich their everyday landscape is, and how much seemingly ordinary things mean to them. Having begun to share their ideas, people often begin to cherish their locality and each other more. They begin to show developers, local authorities and others the importance of the locality they have defined, and their willingness to act in its defence or think imaginatively about enhancing it.

In making a Parish Map people negotiate with others to make choices and compromises. The map hangs on public display and provokes continued discussion and action. Social intervention in creating and recreating the particularity of a place is not easy. It reminds us that communities are driven as much by tension as concord, that the fluidity of insiders and outsiders needs constant bridge building, that it is hard work to sustain enthusiasm and effort.

But we are exploring just one gentle weaving of a more responsive democracy, a first step from decision-'taking' to decision-making. Most decisions about our surroundings are 'taken' by other people, sometimes on our behalf, sometimes despite our needs – they are removed from us. Our politicians are often ill at ease with pluralism: 'you have voted', they say, 'we have the mandate, you should leave us to get on with things'. But we envisage a more pliable, more plural and more permeable democracy than this voting-plus-five-year-passivity system we currently have in the UK.

We are more interested in real participation for a common purpose. This implies people coming together to have ideas and make them work. It is about sharing responsibility and educating each other. It is not about top-down decisions or bottom-up empowerment. It should entail a genuine lateral search for some kind of foothold for all to influence decisions and to grow together in commitment to nature.

The knowledge kept safe in books, on compact discs and hard discs, is not the same as practised knowledge kept alert on the ground. The tension between being really involved in processes which bring about change and creatively working on the locality together, means we have more depth of responsibility, more knowledge, more understanding of each others needs and those of the place, it helps to build sensitive value systems. It helps us to extend wisdom.

Nature – Culture – Place

Common Ground was founded on the belief that our relations with nature and the land are fundamental to our short and long term wellbeing. We are convinced of the ecological imperative and that humanity and imagination are needed to help us all create a new ethos of wanting to care. To this end we have worked through poetry, in its deepest sense, to help people stand up for the things they value. Our argument is a plain one – we all need to take responsibility for the ordinary and commonplace things to make our everyday lives better. We need to be involved, so that nature and history are close to us, so that we can have some influence and feel part of a pattern of our own creation.

We have located our activities where nature and culture come together – in *place* – and we have spread our interest over everyday nature, ordinary histories, commonplace buildings, vernacular landscapes, popular stories, particular legends, great and subtle variegation in cultures. Places have meaning to people. This declaration of value and significance must be part of the definition of place, setting it apart from the abstract notions of 'site', or 'resources' or 'environment'.

Common Ground has tried to offer ideas about linking people and place, partly by encouraging people to stand up for what they value in their own place, offering our own thoughts on the importance of the ordinary, demonstrating that professionals can be interested in values as well as facts, by supporting communication between the fragmented and institutionalised, and by adding culture to the discussion.

The focus is on the small-scale, the parish, the neighbourhood, the locality, the arena in which people feel at home, which they feel they own through familiarity. It is non-exclusive, it does not elevate the rare, the spectacular, the wild, the beautiful or the endangered, but helps people raise their own questions about meaning and particularity – about local distinctiveness.

Local Distinctiveness

So much twentieth century farming, industry, tourism and development, has reduced biodiversity, ironed out variegation and suppressed the personality of places.

Common Ground has coined the concept of local distinctiveness and offered it as an open work for others to explore. Local distinctiveness is about anywhere, it is about what makes your place different. But diversity is only the beginning, it must also be about meaning, identity, patina and detail. Importantly it focuses on locality, not the region or county or city. It is about assemblages and accumulations not about compartmentalisation or one moment in history (including ours), it must be about accommodation and constant dynamism not preservation. It includes the invisible as well as the physical – symbolisms, festivals, legends may be as important as hedgerows, hills and houses.

Unless a place has meaning to the people who inhabit it and use it, it is unlikely to be well cared for. Little things (detail) and clues to previous landscapes and memories of former lives (patina) may be the very things which breathe significance into the streets or fields. Try to define these things for others or at a grand scale and the point is lost. The connectedness of things makes the richness: we could be talking of habitats and history, buildings and breeds of sheep, musicians and mounds, landmarks and legends, but one example must suffice.

Orchards and Community Orchards

Centuries of careful work has seen us grow, in Britain, 6,000 varieties of eating and cooking apples, hundreds more of cider apples, as well as hundreds of pears, plums, cherries, damsons, nuts ... this is biodiversity extended and maintained by culture. Some, like the many different perry pears of Gloucestershire, adhere so strongly to place they will only grow within a few miles radius of where they originated – this is where local distinctiveness begins.

When you lose an orchard of tall trees you sacrifice not simply a few old trees (bad enough, some would say) but you might lose fruit varieties particular to that locality, the wildlife, the songs, the recipes, the cider/perry/cherry brandy, the hard but social work, the festive gatherings, the look of the landscape, the wisdom gathered over generations about pruning and grafting, dabbling and discerning about aspect and slope, soil and season, variety and use. In short, the cultural landscape with its many layered local distinctiveness is comprehensively diminished through a seemingly simple act.

Relying on gene banks or 'museums' of fruit tree varieties may keep the variety in existence, though it leaves us vulnerable to disease or tempest, but importantly it also severs the knowledge from everyday use and the wisdom built in that particular place. We must learn more from local knowledge, we must value it and create the conditions for its continuity. Science and technology have made huge advances, but the depth of understanding about growing things with nature has been accruing over generations all around us. How can we rebuild an interest in this richness?

Consider celebration: Apple Day, October 21st, is about celebrating diversity at the local level, linking the apple we eat with the landscape, implicating us all. We began it in Covent Garden, central London's old market, with one event in 1990; by 1997 over 200 events of all kinds were being run by and for local people across the country. Apple Day has the potential to become a popular symbolic moment for checking on biodiversity and sustainability, locally, nationally and beyond, drawing in people who have no apparent interest in the fashion and jargon of the environmentalist.

From being a commonplace feature in most landscapes across Britain, the orchard has dwindled. Post-war losses include 90 per cent from Devon, 95 per cent from Kent, 95 per cent from Wiltshire, 75 per cent from Gloucestershire. The ordinary has become special in a generation. These figures have their echoes in loss of plants, animals and birds. British Trust for Ornithology figures for 1969 to 1994 suggest terrible losses amongst the birds which love fruit: song thrush –73 per cent, mistle thrush –39 per cent, bullfinch (commercial fruit growers can still gain licences to trap and kill) –76 per cent, even the blackbird –42 per cent. Commonplace in one decade can become rare in the next. The notion of focusing only expert effort and solely on the special, denies everything we should have learned about ecology. Common Ground believes that a benign relationship with nature and the land can only be reinvented and achieved with popular effort over all the land.

Consider the Community Orchard: a place run by and for local people, in city, in suburb or in village. The focus is trees, blossom, harvest – a place for festive gatherings, communal food growing, quiet contemplation, playing, wildlife watching, animal grazing, skill sharing, extending education, building responsibility, tree growing, nurturing biodiversity, keeping and extending local varieties. Here community action can play host to biodiversity and sustainability, the foundations for local Agenda 21. Community orchards provide an enjoyable focus for steps towards sustainability by local communities themselves.

To produce eatable fruit, in the country and the city, demands confidence in the clarity of the air and the sweetness of the soil. Working towards eating the apple straight from the tree in a city orchard could be a wonderful affirmation (indicator) that things are getting better.

In Colnebrook, once Middlesex, recently Surrey, now Berkshire (though the county council has now disappeared), struggling to maintain its identity, the community had quite forgotten Richard Cox, the man who dabbled the Cox's Orange Pippin into existence in the last century. This apple is now worth about £90 million pounds to the national economy, and is the most popular apple in Britain. Common Ground brought together the Colne Valley Groundwork Trust, Surrey County Council, Spelthorne (now Slough) Borough Council, local schools and people, with the artist/blacksmith Richard Farrington to create three seats which tell the story of Richard Cox. In and around the seats, Cox's Orange Pippin and other apple trees provide a small community orchard. Only a few hundred feet above and half a mile away jets arrive and leave Heathrow Airport. The project has raised a half-acre plot from boring grass where no one goes, to a sweet orchard filled with wild flowers and creatures, a place to remind one to tell the stories of the place, and to learn more than scrumping.

Power – Influence

Within the last decade there has been a growing interest in empowerment in the environmental movement: the city housing, community action and advocacy planning activities in the US, the UK and elsewhere in the 1960s has shifted its shape and its protagonists. But what is power? In many ways it is an unattractive idea, especially where the assumption persists, though it changes hands, that the point of having power is to exert it over someone, or something, or some place.

Common Ground has worked rather to help people to aspire to influence, to believe in their own values, to seek to augment and share their knowledge. We have challenged professionals and colleagues as much as local people, to refresh thinking and practice. People need to negotiate with each other in order to understand, to learn and to tolerate their differences, this means social endeavour, working together.

Community involvement presupposes community. We need to create the circumstances for people to come together and make relationships, build responsibilities, take care of each other and their place. Much of what we do is to create the conditions for congregation and for celebration.

Walking and Talking

Walking slows the pace, focuses towards detail, concentrates the senses, allows musing, gives time and room for talking. Walking is a way in to locality, to ourselves, to our past and future. Ritual walking can help people remember and share their understanding of their place – it can help young curiosity interweave with vestiges of old knowledge. It can encourage abstract expertise, coming in from the outside looking for a circumstance to practice on, to make links with indigenous wisdom often diffident, severed, unpractised.

One intention for Common Ground, as yet unrealised, is to bring together a performance group with people of the community to gather memories, stories, legends, work, recipes, customs of the locality and to use these in various ways to create an annual walk for everyone in the place. The walk is intended to reinvest places with meaning, and build bridges between different factions in the community as a basis for celebrating and caring for locality.

Walking and drama, performance, live art, story-telling, can offer daring, strange ways of telling to help us see things differently. Bringing places alive along a track with local people involved in the making of a repeated drama will not create passive observers but increasingly will enfold people, creating a feeling of excitement yet safety, so that they can talk of what they care about, tell what they know. Someone for example, may take the role of keeper of the walls or the bluebells, a local tale may be played out in the high street, light may be used to draw attention to the trees by the canal. Revisiting the walk on an annual basis would create constant need for planning, preparing, sharing ideas, drawing new people in with thoughts of creative collective activities from performance to organisation to cooking for the returning throng.

We have worked experimentally with The Common Players (a performance group) and people of Dulverton in Somerset. Working together for a few months they attracted 250 people on an extraordinary walk which began in the car park with carrots in trees and a woman railing from her bed in the centre of the river; just one of many memories now etched on the minds of those who had not experienced the flood which, undermining houses and pitching at least one bed into the torrent, had left vegetables high and dry at the whim of nature.

May Day May Day

So much of the environmental message has been apocalyptic, beyond our control, we have tried to offer a positive posture, an optimistic sense that things can be challenged, and that small local actions can add towards a rhythm which changes the world.

May Day is a traditional moment of regeneration and of turning things upside down. More than once Common Ground has taken a page in a national newspaper on May Day to offer direct ideas for direct action. The first – *May Day May Day, Nature's Call for Help* – listed 101 ways for anyone to get started. The second

– *Common Ground Rules for Local Distinctiveness* – offered a broadsheet, an A-Z from apple varieties to walling techniques, dialect words, legends, recipes, customs, creatures, geology: each one demonstrating locality. Mixed with these are assertions ('Our imagination needs diversity and variegation. We need standards not standardisation') to provoke convergent thinking about what makes nature, culture and places rich.

Far from the old style compartmentalised and abstract thinking, the twenty-first century must be about building connections, integrating, giving and taking responsibility, building a progressive and plural parochialism.

For example, we could think in terms of 'ecologies of scale', bringing things back to the local could be part of the building of responsibility as well as local distinctiveness. It might be decided to reopen small quarries close to town. Local materials would be visible in the making of buildings reinforcing the identity of place, giving local lichens and mosses an easier purchase. Local people would be more aware of what it means to build anew, the impact being on *their* view, roads and jobs, perhaps choosing more careful reuse of old buildings, and designing with in-built flexibility in new buildings. Energy would be saved in the global equation and neighbourhood pollution cut with smaller lorries on shorter journeys. Jobs would be local, ways of using the indigenous materials would be passed on, daily knowledge of the place being riveted back into local culture.

Paradox – Poetry

So much argument is offered as linear, rational, theory-based. We are pounded by the idea that economics is the foundation upon which all decisions should stand, that objectivity leads to better decision making. But the reduction of values to costs or counting, marginalises most of the things we have 'higher feelings' about. One result is that most people are unable to join the debate, except in cynical post mortems and satire.

Our lives are filled with paradox, bounded by emotions, riven with subjectivity. Our culture is about values. Our relationship with nature is about values.

Common Ground tries to embolden people to do things themselves, to stand up for what they care about, and to do it socially and publicly. Our focus has been the real bit of the world in which people do things everyday. Our scale has been the local, the land, nature, history and place to which people feel affinity and ownership through their ordinary experience. We are convinced that places have meaning to people, and must continue to do so if they are to be relaxed in them and sustain an interest in their care.

We are also aware of the play of paradox in the everyday, of both caring and taking for granted. Our aspirations are to arouse curiosity, feed the imagination, nurture creativity, applaud quality, subjectivity and emotional engagement, and to link culture with nature in overt ways.

We have sought to encourage people to start from where they are and to explore the relevance and power of reaching towards other interests and ways of looking. We set out in the belief that local people together know more and care more than they are ever credited with; that they can make brave decisions, guide change and keep the strands of history and richness of nature healthy and vibrant.

What we are after is a more pliable, more local democracy, one which allows access to all, takes a long time to come to decisions if necessary, which acknowledges representation and direct action, that seeks to talk and talk, before committing to even small scale change, and in the understanding of the impacts that change may have.

Discussion about values is much harder than arguing about numbers, monetary costs, economic indicators. It is so difficult that it has been pushed to the edges of much professional endeavour. This does not mean it is not important. Much of the best in our lives is intangible, unquantifiable, difficult to express.

Poetry, in its widest sense, can help us to appreciate the richness of nature and culture as they interweave around us. Poetry can help us to deal with paradox, see the detail and richness in the everyday, express our subjectivity, locate ourselves in the world of emotions. Poetry can help us to see the simple together with the complex, enable us to catch sight of many layers of meaning.

Poetry can slow us down, make us move at the level of our deeper understanding.

We want to raise people's aspirations and confidence to get the kingfisher back, that neon flash, down every stream in city and country, and through its presence to feel uplifted: to know that the fields are benign, that our work is safe, that our food is wholesome, that the city has quiet social places and sparkling clear water, full of little fish and children playing. The kingfisher as a symbol of the startling in the everyday, a utilitarian indicator of health in our relations with nature and each other, something that we can help persist, something which gives us pleasure, poetry we can partici- pate in – halcyon days.

References

From Place to Place: maps and Parish Maps Common Ground 1996

Local Distinctiveness: place, particularity and identity Common Ground 1993

Celebrating Local Distinctiveness Common Ground for Rural Action 1994

Places: the city and the invisible, by Sue Clifford, Public Art Development Trust 1993

The Apple Broadcast Common Ground 1994

May Day May Day. Nature's Call for Help A2 broadsheet 1988

Common Ground Rules for Local Distinctiveness A2 broadsheet 1992

Holding Your Ground: an action guide to local conservation, by Angela King and Sue Clifford Temple Smith 1985, Wildwood House 1987

Second Nature, Richard Mabey, Sue Clifford and Angela King (eds) Jonathan Cape 1984

Index

Page references in **bold** refer to boxes, figures and tables